GCSE AQA
English Language

AQA's Grade 9-1 GCSE English Language course is tougher than ever
— but this brilliant CGP book has everything you need for success.

It's packed with clear explanations, exam-style texts and plenty of indispensable
practice questions... there's even a full practice exam at the end of the book.

What's more, we've included in-depth advice for the final exams, including graded
sample answers that show you exactly how to score the top marks!

How to access your free Online Edition

This book includes a free Online Edition to read on your PC, Mac or tablet.
You'll just need to go to **cgpbooks.co.uk/extras** and enter this code:

2094 7918 3113 3742

By the way, this code only works for one person. If somebody else has used
this book before you, they might have already claimed the Online Edition.

Complete
Revision & Practice
Everything you need to pass the exams!

Contents

Section Four — Writing — Creative and Non-Fiction

Section Five — Paper 1 — Sample Exam and Graded Answers

Section Six — Paper 2 — Sample Exam and Graded Answers

Section Seven — Practice Exams

Published by CGP

Editors:
Joe Brazier
Emma Bonney
Emma Crighton
Jennifer Underwood

With thanks to Catherine Heygate and Holly Poynton for the proofreading
and Laura Jakubowski for the copyright research.

Acknowledgements:
AQA material is reproduced by permission of AQA.

With thanks to iStockphoto.com for permission to use the images on pages 93 and 121

Letter on page 37 to Princess (later Queen) Victoria from King Leopold I of Belgium,
August 1832, from The Letters of Queen Victoria, Volume 1 (of 3), 1837-1843.

Extract from The Snow Child by Eowyn Ivey on page 94 © 2012 Eowyn Ivey. Reproduced by
permission of Headline Publishing Group & Reagan Arthur Books/Little Brown and Company

First interview on page 107 adapted from "Of the life of an orphan girl, a street-seller",
London Labour and the London Poor, volume 1 by Henry Mayhew, published in the 1840s.

Second interview on page 107 adapted from "Of children sent out as street-sellers by their parents",
London Labour and the London Poor, volume 1 by Henry Mayhew, published in the 1840s.

Article entitled 'Confessions of a Nanny' on page 123 © Guardian News & Media Ltd 2013.

Letter written by Charlotte Brontë on page 124 from "Charlotte Brontë and
Her Circle", by Clement K. Shorter, 1896 (pages 80-82).

Every effort has been made to locate copyright holders and obtain permission to reproduce sources.
For those sources where it has been difficult to trace the copyright holder of the work, we would be grateful
for information. If any copyright holder would like us to make an amendment to the acknowledgements,
please notify us and we will gladly update the book at the next reprint. Thank you.

ISBN: 978 1 78294 414 0

Clipart from Corel®
Printed by Elanders Ltd, Newcastle upon Tyne.

Based on the classic CGP style created by Richard Parsons.

Exam Structure

Understanding the structure of your exams is really important. You need to know what to expect on the day.

You will sit **Two** different papers

1) Paper 1 is called 'Explorations in Creative Reading and Writing' — it focuses on fiction.

2) Paper 2 is called 'Writers' Viewpoints and Perspectives' — it focuses on non-fiction.

3) You will have 1 hour 45 minutes for each paper.

4) Both papers are split into two sections — Section A covers reading, and Section B covers writing.

5) Each paper is worth 50% of the GCSE.

Both papers have **Five** questions...

Have a look at pages 3-8 for more detail on the individual questions on each paper.

For paper 1, there will be a question paper and a separate insert containing one extract from a work of literary fiction — it will be from either the twentieth or twenty-first century.

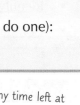

You should spend the first 15 minutes reading through the source and the questions.

Section A: Reading is worth 40 marks. It has four questions:

- Question 1 is worth 4 marks. You should spend about 5 minutes on this.

- Questions 2 and 3 are worth 8 marks each. You should spend about 10 minutes on each of these.

- Question 4 is worth 20 marks. You should spend about 20 minutes on this.

Section B: Writing only has one question (there'll be a choice of tasks, but you only need to do one):

- Question 5 is worth 40 marks. You should spend 45 minutes on this.

For paper 2, there will be a question paper and a separate insert containing two non-fiction sources — one from the nineteenth century and one from either the twentieth or twenty-first century (whichever wasn't used in paper 1).

If you have any time left at the end of the exam, use it to check through your work.

You should spend the first 15 minutes reading through the sources and the questions.

Section A: Reading is worth 40 marks. It has four questions:

- Question 1 is worth 4 marks. You should spend about 5 minutes on this.

- Question 2 is worth 8 marks. You should spend about 8 minutes on this.

- Question 3 is worth 12 marks. You should spend about 12 minutes on this.

- Question 4 is worth 16 marks. You should spend about 20 minutes on this.

Section B: Writing only has one question:

- Question 5 is worth 40 marks. You should spend 45 minutes on this.

You need to know what each paper is going to look like...

Make sure you've really understood this page, especially the number of marks available for each question — if you allow just over one minute per mark, you'll be on track to get everything finished in time.

The Assessment Objectives

If you've understood the basic structure of the exams, now's a good time to look at each of the questions in more detail. First, here's the background to what the questions are about — the assessment objectives.

Each Assessment Objective refers to a different Skill

1) The <u>assessment objectives</u> are the things that <u>AQA</u> say you need to <u>do</u> to get good marks in the exam.

2) They'll come in handy when you're working out what you need to do for each of the <u>questions</u> — there's more on how each of the <u>assessment objectives</u> apply to the <u>individual questions</u> on pages 3-8.

3) These exams test <u>assessment objectives 1 to 6</u>. Here's a brief description of each of them:

Assessment Objective 1

- <u>Pick out</u> and <u>understand</u> pieces of <u>explicit</u> and <u>implicit</u> information from the texts.
- <u>Collect</u> and <u>put together</u> information from different texts.

Assessment Objective 2

- <u>Explain</u> how writers use <u>language</u> and <u>structure</u> to achieve their <u>purpose</u> and <u>influence</u> readers.
- Use <u>technical terms</u> to support your analysis of language and structure.

Assessment Objective 3

- <u>Identify</u> different writers' <u>ideas</u> and <u>perspectives</u>.
- <u>Compare</u> the <u>methods</u> used by different writers to convey their ideas.

Assessment Objective 4

- <u>Critically evaluate</u> texts, giving a <u>personal opinion</u> about how successful the writing is.
- Provide detailed <u>evidence</u> from the text to <u>support</u> your opinion.

Assessment Objective 5

- Write <u>clearly</u> and <u>imaginatively</u>, adapting your tone and style for various <u>purposes</u> and <u>audiences</u>.
- <u>Organise</u> your writing into a clear <u>structure</u>.

Assessment Objective 6

- Use a wide variety of <u>sentence structures</u> and <u>vocabulary</u>, so that your writing is <u>clear</u> and <u>purposeful</u>.
- Write <u>accurately</u>, paying particular attention to spelling, punctuation and grammar.

Remember what the examiner is looking for...

These assessment objectives are the basis for the exams (and their mark schemes), so try to keep them in mind as you're revising. The next six pages will show you how to apply them to each of the questions.

Paper 1 — Questions 1 and 2

The first question on paper 1 is just a bit of fact-finding. Question 2 requires a bit more analysis.

You need to find **Four Facts** for **Question 1**

1) Question 1 will test the first part of <u>assessment objective 1</u> — it will test your ability to <u>find</u> information or ideas in the text.

2) The information might be <u>explicit</u> (it will be obviously written out in the extract), or it might be <u>implicit</u> (you will need to work it out from what is said in the text).

3) The <u>question</u> will usually look something like this:

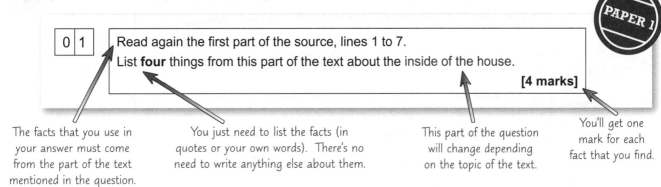

| 0 | 1 |

Read again the first part of the source, lines 1 to 7.
List **four** things from this part of the text about the inside of the house.

[4 marks]

PAPER 1

The facts that you use in your answer must come from the part of the text mentioned in the question.

You just need to list the facts (in quotes or your own words). There's no need to write anything else about them.

This part of the question will change depending on the topic of the text.

You'll get one mark for each fact that you find.

Question 2 is about the **Effects** of **Language** on the **Reader**

1) This question will test the <u>language</u> part of <u>assessment objective 2</u> — you'll need to write about how the writer uses <u>language</u> to achieve <u>effects</u> and <u>influence</u> the reader.

2) The <u>question</u> will usually look something like this:

Make sure you only analyse this part of the text.

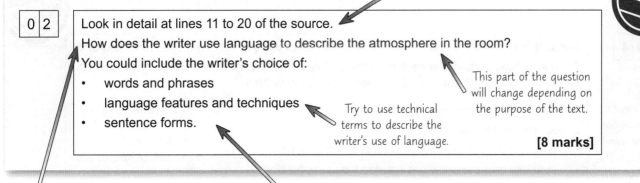

| 0 | 2 |

Look in detail at lines 11 to 20 of the source.
How does the writer use language to describe the atmosphere in the room?
You could include the writer's choice of:
*   words and phrases
*   language features and techniques
*   sentence forms.

PAPER 1

Try to use technical terms to describe the writer's use of language.

This part of the question will change depending on the purpose of the text.

[8 marks]

For questions that ask 'how' the writer has done something, you need to write about the methods the writer has used and their effect on the reader. In this case you need to focus on the effects of the writer's language on the reader.

Make sure your answer includes quotes that demonstrate each of the things mentioned in the bullet points.

The structure part of assessment objective 2 will be covered in paper 1, question 3 (see page 4).

Question 1 is only worth four marks, but it's still important...

Writing a good answer to question 1 is a good way to gain some easy marks before you have to tackle the more complex analysis questions. For question 2, remember to cover all three bullet points in your answer.

Paper 1 — Questions 3 and 4

Question 3 is similar to question 2, except it's about structure rather than language. After that, you have to answer question 4, which is worth 20 marks. You'll need to write more for this.

Question 3 asks about the writer's use of **Structure**

1) This question will test the <u>structure</u> part of <u>assessment objective 2</u> — you'll need to write about how the writer uses <u>structure</u> to achieve <u>effects</u> and <u>influence</u> the reader.

2) The <u>question</u> will usually look something like this:

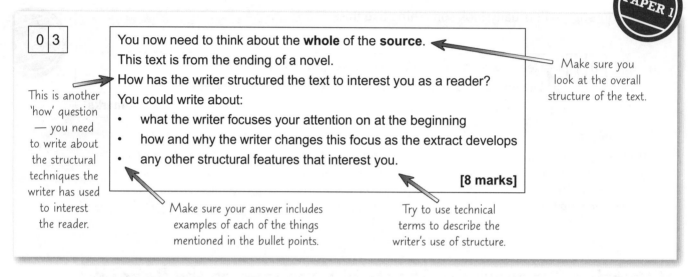

This is another 'how' question — you need to write about the structural techniques the writer has used to interest the reader.

Make sure you look at the overall structure of the text.

Make sure your answer includes examples of each of the things mentioned in the bullet points.

Try to use technical terms to describe the writer's use of structure.

You need to give a **Personal Judgement** for **Question 4**

1) This question will test <u>assessment objective 4</u> — you'll need to <u>evaluate</u> the text <u>critically</u> and give a <u>personal response</u>.

2) The <u>question</u> will usually look something like this:

Make sure you only analyse this part of the text.

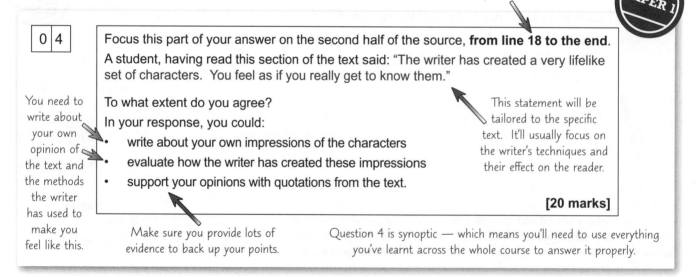

You need to write about your own opinion of the text and the methods the writer has used to make you feel like this.

This statement will be tailored to the specific text. It'll usually focus on the writer's techniques and their effect on the reader.

Make sure you provide lots of evidence to back up your points.

Question 4 is synoptic — which means you'll need to use everything you've learnt across the whole course to answer it properly.

Don't forget to give your opinion in question 4...

To get all the marks for question 4, you need to provide a personal evaluation of the text and back it up with detailed evidence — use a range of short examples from the text to show what you've based your opinion on.

Paper 1 — Question 5

Question 5 is the writing question in paper 1, and it's worth 40 marks.

You only need to do **One** of the tasks for **Question 5**

1) Question 5 is a creative writing task that will test assessment objectives 5 and 6 — examiners will be looking for you to produce an interesting, well-organised and accurately written piece.

2) There will be a choice of tasks, but you only need to do one.

3) The tasks will usually be on a similar theme to the text from the reading section.

4) The question might look something like this:

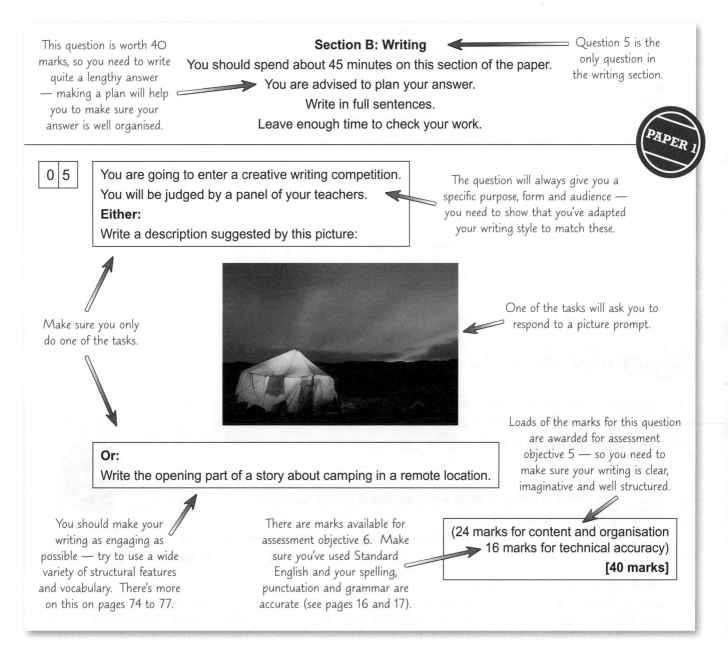

This question is worth 40 marks, so you need to write quite a lengthy answer — making a plan will help you to make sure your answer is well organised.

Section B: Writing
You should spend about 45 minutes on this section of the paper.
You are advised to plan your answer.
Write in full sentences.
Leave enough time to check your work.

Question 5 is the only question in the writing section.

PAPER 1

0 5 You are going to enter a creative writing competition.
You will be judged by a panel of your teachers.
Either:
Write a description suggested by this picture:

The question will always give you a specific purpose, form and audience — you need to show that you've adapted your writing style to match these.

Make sure you only do one of the tasks.

One of the tasks will ask you to respond to a picture prompt.

Or:
Write the opening part of a story about camping in a remote location.

You should make your writing as engaging as possible — try to use a wide variety of structural features and vocabulary. There's more on this on pages 74 to 77.

There are marks available for assessment objective 6. Make sure you've used Standard English and your spelling, punctuation and grammar are accurate (see pages 16 and 17).

Loads of the marks for this question are awarded for assessment objective 5 — so you need to make sure your writing is clear, imaginative and well structured.

(24 marks for content and organisation 16 marks for technical accuracy)
[40 marks]

Question 5 is focused on your creative writing skills...

In this part of the paper, the examiners want you to show that you can write imaginatively. Make sure you use plenty of descriptive language and try to produce as interesting a piece of writing as you possibly can.

Paper 2 — Questions 1 and 2

Paper 2 starts with two questions that test your ability to find information and ideas in the sources.

You need to find **Four Facts** in **Question 1**

1) This question will test the first part of <u>assessment objective 1</u> — you will need to show that you can <u>find</u> information or ideas in the text.

2) The <u>question</u> will usually look something like this:

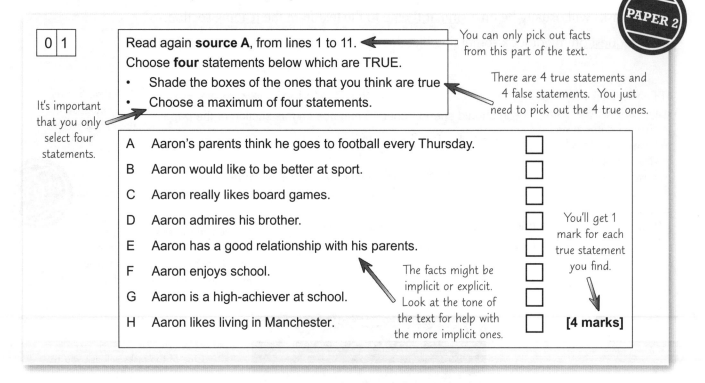

It's important that you only select four statements.

0 1

Read again **source A**, from lines 1 to 11.
Choose **four** statements below which are TRUE.
*   Shade the boxes of the ones that you think are true
*   Choose a maximum of four statements.

You can only pick out facts from this part of the text.

There are 4 true statements and 4 false statements. You just need to pick out the 4 true ones.

A   Aaron's parents think he goes to football every Thursday.

B   Aaron would like to be better at sport.

C   Aaron really likes board games.

D   Aaron admires his brother.

E   Aaron has a good relationship with his parents.

F   Aaron enjoys school.

G   Aaron is a high-achiever at school.

H   Aaron likes living in Manchester.

The facts might be implicit or explicit. Look at the tone of the text for help with the more implicit ones.

You'll get 1 mark for each true statement you find.

[4 marks]

Question 2 asks for facts from **Both** sources

1) Question 2 will test both parts of <u>assessment objective 1</u> — it will test your ability to <u>find</u> information and ideas in <u>two sources</u> and <u>summarise</u> what you find.

2) The <u>question</u> will usually look something like this:

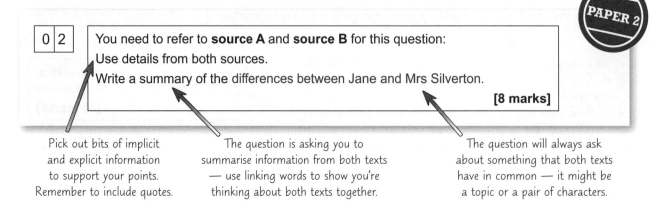

0 2

You need to refer to **source A** and **source B** for this question:
Use details from both sources.
Write a summary of the differences between Jane and Mrs Silverton.

[8 marks]

Pick out bits of implicit and explicit information to support your points. Remember to include quotes.

The question is asking you to summarise information from both texts — use linking words to show you're thinking about both texts together.

The question will always ask about something that both texts have in common — it might be a topic or a pair of characters.

Prove that you know what's going on in the two source texts...

For these two questions, you need to show that you've really understood the texts. In question 1, shade in the statements you're sure about first. In question 2, try to make perceptive links between the sources.

Paper 2 — Questions 3 and 4

Question 3 on paper 2 is pretty similar to question 2 on paper 1 (see page 3) — it's all about how the writer has used language. Question 4 is about two writers' attitudes and how they have conveyed them.

Question 3 covers the Effects of the writer's use of Language

1) This question will test the <u>language</u> part of <u>assessment objective 2</u> — you'll need to write about how the writer uses <u>language</u> to achieve <u>effects</u> and <u>influence</u> the reader.

2) The <u>question</u> will usually look something like this:

| 0 3 | You now need to refer **only** to **source B**, the entry from Jenny's diary. How does Jenny use language to express her frustration? **[12 marks]** |

This is another 'how' question, so you need to write about the techniques the writer has used to achieve their purpose. Have a look at paper 1, questions 2 and 3 for other examples of 'how' questions.

Your answer should include lots of quotes and technical terms to back up your points. Try to refer specifically to particular words, phrases, language features and techniques.

This part of the question will change depending on the purpose of the text.

Question 4 asks you to Compare Perspectives

Question 4 is synoptic — which means you'll need to use everything you've learnt across the whole course to answer it properly.

1) This question will test <u>assessment objective 3</u> — you'll need to <u>identify</u> and <u>compare</u> different writers' <u>attitudes</u> and <u>perspectives</u>, and <u>how</u> they're conveyed.

2) The <u>question</u> will usually look something like this:

| 0 4 | For this question, you need to refer to the **whole of source A** together with **source B**. Compare how the two writers convey their different attitudes to dieting and healthy eating. In your answer, you should:
• compare their different attitudes
• compare the methods they use to convey their attitudes
• support your ideas with quotations from both texts. **[16 marks]** |

Make sure you cover everything mentioned in the bullet points — you need to write about what the writers' attitudes are and how they are similar or different.

Make sure you give quotes and examples from both sources.

Try to identify how the writers have used language and structure to show subtle differences in their attitudes. This will show the examiner that you've really understood the text.

This part of the question will change depending on the topics covered in the texts.

Pay attention to how many marks each question is worth...

Question 3 is very similar to question 2 on paper 1, but don't forget — it's worth quite a few more marks. Question 4 is your chance to bring all your skills together and really show that you've understood the texts.

Paper 2 — Question 5

Paper 2, question 5 is another 40 mark writing task. This time, you need to give your own perspective on a theme. The theme will be similar to the one that was covered by the two sources in the reading section.

The last question is a **Writing** task

1) Question 5 is a writing task that will test assessment objectives 5 and 6 — examiners will be looking for you to produce an interesting, well-organised and accurately written piece.

2) You'll need to write in the form of a non-fiction text, such as a newspaper article.

3) The question will ask you to give your own perspective on a similar theme to the one covered in the reading section of the paper.

4) The question will usually look something like this:

Question 5 is the only question in the writing section.

Section B: Writing
You should spend about 45 minutes on this section of the paper.
You are advised to plan your answer.
Write in full sentences.
Leave enough time to check your work.

This question is worth 40 marks, so you need to write quite a lengthy answer — making a plan will help you to make sure your answer is well organised.

0 5 'School uniforms are a pointless expense. They are never worn correctly, they are uncomfortable and they restrict pupils' creativity.'

Write a letter to your headmaster in which you persuade him to agree with your point of view on this statement.

The task will usually ask you to respond to a prompt. It might be an opinion, a scenario or a statement.

The question will always give you a specific purpose, form and audience — you need to show that you've adapted your writing style to match these.

Loads of the marks for this question are awarded for assessment objective 5 — so you need to make sure your writing is clear, imaginative and well structured.

(24 marks for content and organisation
16 marks for technical accuracy)
[40 marks]

There are marks available for assessment objective 6. Make sure you've used Standard English and your spelling, punctuation and grammar are accurate (see pages 16 and 17).

You will need to adapt your tone, style and register...

Your answer to question 5 needs to be well-suited to the purpose, form and audience given in the question, so think carefully about which tone, style and register (see pages 42-43) would be the most appropriate.

Planning Answers

Now you know what to expect from the questions, the next few pages will help you to answer them.

Read the questions Carefully and Calmly

1) You should give yourself 15 minutes to read through the questions and the texts at the start of the exam.

2) Always read the questions before the exam texts — that way, you'll know what to look out for.

3) Make sure you're clear about what the questions are asking you to do by underlining the key words.

| 0 | 2 | Write a summary of the differences between the two main characters. |

4) Once you've read the questions, carefully read through the texts. It's a good idea to highlight key words or phrases that will help you to answer the questions — but don't spend ages doing this.

Remember, it's your exam paper and you can write on it if it helps you.

Jot down your Main Ideas before you start writing

1) Don't spend too much time planning. You don't need to do a plan for the simple fact-finding questions, but you might want to jot down some points and highlight the texts for some of the reading questions, particularly Q4. You should do a plan for the writing questions on both papers.

2) Don't go into too much detail — just get your main ideas down, and outline the structure of your answer.

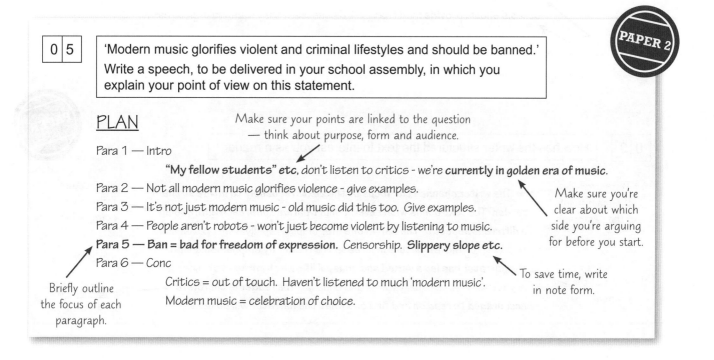

You don't need to plan every answer in these exams...

You won't need a plan for every question, but make a brief plan to help you with some of the longer questions. It'll help you to organise your ideas. Leave time to check your work at the end, too.

P.E.E.D.

To get good marks, you need to explain and develop your ideas properly. That's why P.E.E.D. is useful.

P.E.E.D. stands for **Point, Example, Explain, Develop**

To write good answers for the longer reading questions (2-4 on both papers), you must do <u>four</u> things:

1) Make a <u>point</u> to answer the question you've been given.

2) Then give an <u>example</u> from the text (see page 11 for more on this).

3) After that, <u>explain</u> how your example backs up your point.

4) Finally, <u>develop</u> your point — this might involve saying what the <u>effect on the reader</u> is, saying what the <u>writer's intention</u> is, <u>linking</u> your point to another part of the text or giving your <u>own opinion</u>.

The <u>explanation</u> and <u>development</u> parts are very important. They're your chance to show that you <u>really understand</u> and have <u>thought about</u> the text. Here are a couple of <u>examples</u>:

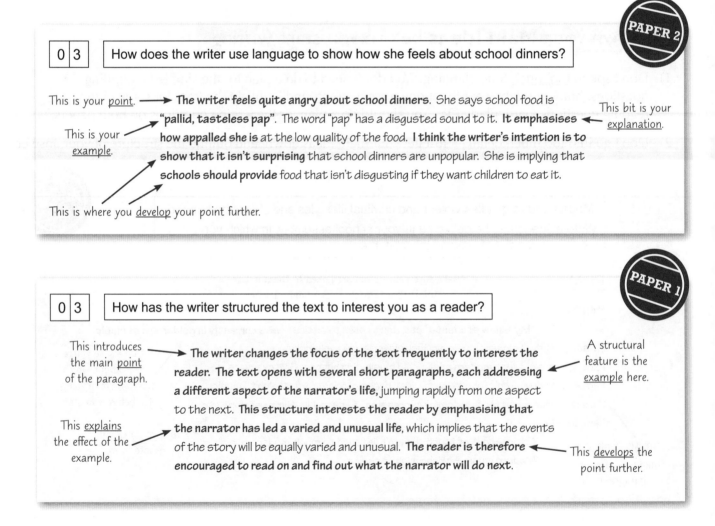

PAPER 2

| 0 | 3 | How does the writer use language to show how she feels about school dinners? |

This is your <u>point</u>. → **The writer feels quite angry about school dinners.** She says school food is "**pallid, tasteless pap**". The word "pap" has a disgusted sound to it. **It emphasises** ← This bit is your <u>explanation</u>.

This is your <u>example</u>. **how appalled she is** at the low quality of the food. **I think the writer's intention is to show that it isn't surprising** that school dinners are unpopular. She is implying that **schools should provide** food that isn't disgusting if they want children to eat it.

This is where you <u>develop</u> your point further.

PAPER 1

| 0 | 3 | How has the writer structured the text to interest you as a reader? |

This introduces the main <u>point</u> of the paragraph. → **The writer changes the focus of the text frequently to interest the reader.** The text opens with several short paragraphs, each addressing a different aspect of the narrator's life, jumping rapidly from one aspect to the next. **This structure interests the reader by emphasising that** ← A structural feature is the <u>example</u> here.

This <u>explains</u> the effect of the example. → **the narrator has led a varied and unusual life**, which implies that the events of the story will be equally varied and unusual. **The reader is therefore** ← This <u>develops</u> the point further. **encouraged to read on and find out what the narrator will do next**.

P.E.E.D. should help you to explain and develop your points...

Other versions of P.E.E.D. also focus on explaining and developing — P.E.E.R. (Point, Example, Explain, Relate), P.E.E.C.E. (Point, Example, Explain, Compare, Explore) and so on. Use the one you've been taught.

Using Examples

This page has some tips about the first 'E' in P.E.E.D. — giving examples to back up your points.

Use Details from the text to Back Up your points

1) Whenever you make a new <u>point</u>, you need to use short pieces of <u>evidence</u> from the text to <u>back it up</u>.

2) You should try to use a <u>mix</u> of different sorts of <u>evidence</u>.

3) If you're using <u>quotes</u>, try to keep them <u>short</u>. It'll really impress the examiner if you <u>embed</u> them in a sentence, like this:

> The writer refers to the situation as "indefensible", suggesting that he is extremely critical of the way it has been handled.

Using short embedded quotes like this lets you combine the 'example' and 'explain' parts of P.E.E.D. in one sentence.

4) <u>Paraphrased details</u> from the text also work well as examples. You just need to describe one of the <u>writer's techniques</u>, or one of the <u>text's features</u>, in your own words, like this:

> The writer begins the paragraph with a rhetorical question that emphasises her feelings of disgust.

5) Here are a couple of <u>examples</u> to show you how to work your evidence into your answer:

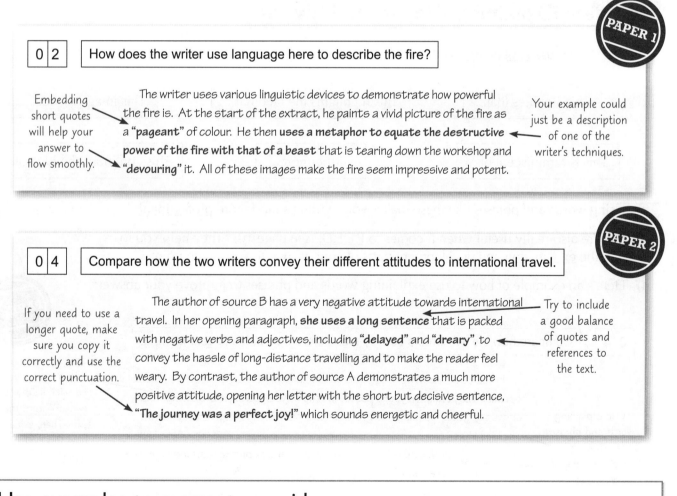

PAPER 1

0 2 | How does the writer use language here to describe the fire?

Embedding short quotes will help your answer to flow smoothly.

The writer uses various linguistic devices to demonstrate how powerful the fire is. At the start of the extract, he paints a vivid picture of the fire as a **"pageant"** of colour. He then **uses a metaphor to equate the destructive power of the fire with that of a beast** that is tearing down the workshop and **"devouring"** it. All of these images make the fire seem impressive and potent.

Your example could just be a description of one of the writer's techniques.

PAPER 2

0 4 | Compare how the two writers convey their different attitudes to international travel.

If you need to use a longer quote, make sure you copy it correctly and use the correct punctuation.

The author of source B has a very negative attitude towards international travel. In her opening paragraph, **she uses a long sentence** that is packed with negative verbs and adjectives, including **"delayed"** and **"dreary"**, to convey the hassle of long-distance travelling and to make the reader feel weary. By contrast, the author of source A demonstrates a much more positive attitude, opening her letter with the short but decisive sentence, **"The journey was a perfect joy!"** which sounds energetic and cheerful.

Try to include a good balance of quotes and references to the text.

Use examples to support your ideas...

Backing up your points with evidence from the text is also crucial for questions like paper 1, question 4 and paper 2, question 3. Make sure that you go on to explain how the evidence supports your point, though.

Writing Well

In these exams, it's not just what you write that's important — it's how you write as well.

Keep your writing Formal but Interesting

1) For these exams, it's important that you write in <u>Standard English</u>.

2) Standard English is the version of English that most people think is '<u>correct</u>'. There are a few <u>simple rules</u> that you can follow to make sure you're writing in Standard English:

- Avoid using <u>informal</u> words and phrases (e.g. putting 'like' after sentences).
- Avoid using <u>slang</u> or local <u>dialect</u> words that some people might not understand.
- Avoid using <u>clichés</u> (words and phrases that are so commonly used that they've lost their effect) like 'at the end of the day'.
- Use correct <u>spelling, punctuation and grammar</u> (have a look at pages 16-17).

3) You should also try to make your writing as <u>engaging</u> as possible by using things like varied <u>sentence lengths</u> and interesting <u>vocabulary</u>. For example, don't overuse the word 'nice' — try to use other adjectives like 'admirable' or 'charming' instead.

Use clear Explaining Words and Phrases

1) You should use <u>explaining</u> words and phrases to make your answers easy to <u>follow</u>.

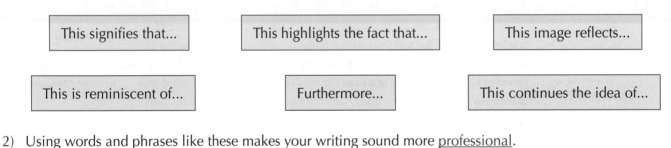

| This signifies that... | This highlights the fact that... | This image reflects... |
| This is reminiscent of... | Furthermore... | This continues the idea of... |

2) Using words and phrases like these makes your writing sound more <u>professional</u>.

3) They're also really useful when it comes to <u>P.E.E.D.</u> (see page 10). They help you to <u>link</u> the <u>explanation</u> and <u>development</u> parts of your answer to your main point.

4) Here's an example of how to use explaining words and phrases to <u>improve</u> your answer:

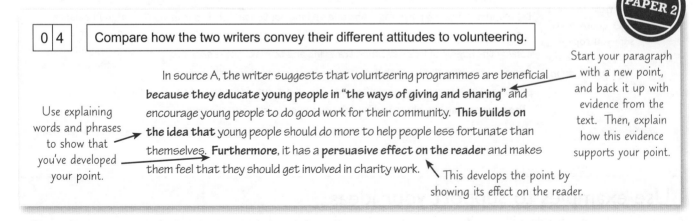

PAPER 2

| 0 4 | Compare how the two writers convey their different attitudes to volunteering. |

Start your paragraph with a new point, and back it up with evidence from the text. Then, explain how this evidence supports your point.

In source A, the writer suggests that volunteering programmes are beneficial **because they educate young people in "the ways of giving and sharing"** and encourage young people to do good work for their community. **This builds on the idea that** young people should do more to help people less fortunate than themselves. **Furthermore**, it has a **persuasive effect on the reader** and makes them feel that they should get involved in charity work.

Use explaining words and phrases to show that you've developed your point.

This develops the point by showing its effect on the reader.

Writing Well

Use **Paragraphs** to structure your answer

1) You need to <u>organise</u> your points <u>clearly</u> and <u>link</u> them together
— to do that you need to write in <u>paragraphs</u>.

2) You can use different paragraph <u>structures</u> to organise your points in different ways. For example:

- You could write a paragraph for every <u>point</u> you want to make, and each paragraph could have a <u>P.E.E.D.</u> structure (see page 10).
- You could make two points that <u>contrast</u> or <u>agree</u> with each other within a paragraph — this can be useful when <u>comparing</u> two texts.
- You could make one point and <u>link</u> together lots of <u>examples</u> with <u>different</u> explanations within a paragraph.

However you structure your paragraphs, make sure you include all the parts of P.E.E.D. in your answer.

3) <u>Linking</u> your paragraphs together <u>smoothly</u> makes your writing sound <u>confident</u> and <u>considered</u>. You could use linking words like these to help you do this:

| However... | In contrast... | On the other hand... | Equally... |

| In the same way... | In addition... | Alternatively... | Conversely... |

4) Take a look at the answer below for an <u>example</u> of how to use <u>paragraphs</u> effectively:

PAPER 1

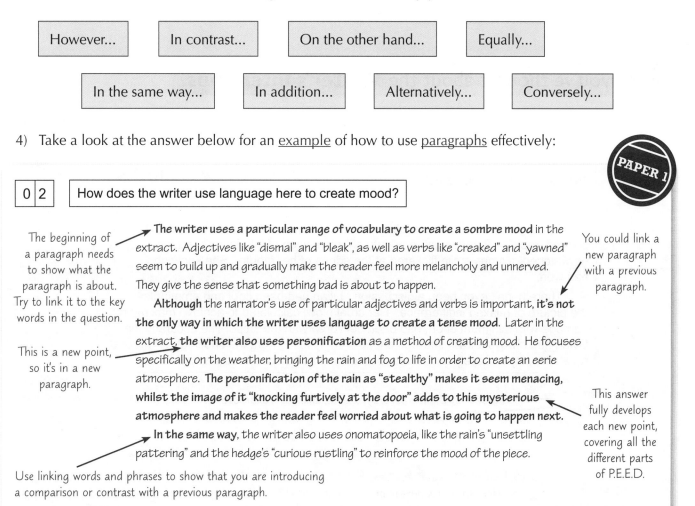

| 0 | 2 | How does the writer use language here to create mood? |

The beginning of a paragraph needs to show what the paragraph is about. Try to link it to the key words in the question.

The writer uses a particular range of vocabulary to create a sombre mood in the extract. Adjectives like "dismal" and "bleak", as well as verbs like "creaked" and "yawned" seem to build up and gradually make the reader feel more melancholy and unnerved. They give the sense that something bad is about to happen.

You could link a new paragraph with a previous paragraph.

This is a new point, so it's in a new paragraph.

Although the narrator's use of particular adjectives and verbs is important, **it's not the only way in which the writer uses language to create a tense mood**. Later in the extract, **the writer also uses personification** as a method of creating mood. He focuses specifically on the weather, bringing the rain and fog to life in order to create an eerie atmosphere. **The personification of the rain as "stealthy" makes it seem menacing, whilst the image of it "knocking furtively at the door" adds to this mysterious atmosphere and makes the reader feel worried about what is going to happen next.**

This answer fully develops each new point, covering all the different parts of P.E.E.D.

In the same way, the writer also uses onomatopoeia, like the rain's "unsettling pattering" and the hedge's "curious rustling" to reinforce the mood of the piece.

Use linking words and phrases to show that you are introducing a comparison or contrast with a previous paragraph.

Your answer needs to have a clear structure...

Organise your ideas into paragraphs, and use the phrases on this page to link them together smoothly. A clear structure will show the examiner that you've thought about your answer, and make it easier to read.

Reading with Insight

To get the top grades, you need to show that you can 'read with insight' — you've got to make it clear that you understand more than just the obvious things. You can think of it as 'reading between the lines'.

You need to look Beyond what's Obvious

Looking beyond what's obvious will help you to make sure you've done the 'D' part of P.E.E.D. — look back at p.10 for more on this.

1) You may understand the facts a writer gives you, but you'll need to write about more than just those facts in your answers.

2) You can show insight if you work out what the writer's intentions are and how they want the reader to feel.

3) Here are a couple of examples of the kinds of things you could write:

> *The rhetorical questions make the reader doubt whether homework is a good thing. The writer seems to want to make readers feel guilty.*

⟸ Think about the reasons why the writer has included certain features — show you've understood their intended effect on the reader.

> *There is a strong sense that the writer is suffering after the loss of his friend. Perhaps the writer felt he needed to make sure the memory of his friend was kept alive.*

⟸ You could comment on the writer's attitude and why you think they chose to write the piece.

Show you've thought about the Writer's Intentions

PAPER 1

0 4 A student, having read this section of the text said: "Lilian is essentially an unlikeable character".
To what extent do you agree?

> Dylan glowered across the table at Lilian. She was composed and collected, her pointed, reptilian features gathered into an expression of infuriating complacency; as he watched, a smug smile flickered at the edges of her mouth. She knew she had won.
>
> There hadn't even been a discussion. Lilian had been cool and emotionless, the picture of relaxed indifference. Her cruel blow, calculated to achieve maximum damage with minimum effort, had been delivered with the sniper-like accuracy that Dylan had always known she was capable of. Reeling from the shock of her abrupt revelation, Dylan barely had time to collect himself before the others had arrived.

Always show how your interpretation is based on the text.

I agree that Lilian is portrayed as an unlikeable character in this extract. She is depicted as **"smug"** and she appears to be gloating. However, even though the writer is using the third-person, **he is still showing us Lilian from Dylan's perspective.** He has clearly been offended by her and so is biased against her. **Some readers might side with Dylan against Lilian**, finding her arrogant and malicious. **Having said that, other readers might** suspect that Dylan's pride has been wounded, and he is being overly harsh on Lilian as a result. **Personally, I think the writer is using this description of Lilian to influence** the reader's opinion of both her and Dylan by demonstrating that they both have flaws.

Try to pick out how the writer has made you feel like this.

Try to offer an alternative interpretation that goes beyond what is obvious in the text.

Show you've thought about what the writer is trying to achieve beyond the obvious.

Reading with Insight

Inference means working things out from Clues

Making inferences is especially important for paper 2, which is all about writers' viewpoints and perspectives.

1) Writers don't usually make things obvious — but you can use <u>evidence</u> from the text to make an <u>inference</u> about what the writer <u>really</u> wants us to think.

2) You need to analyse <u>details</u> from the text to show what they <u>reveal</u> about the writer's intentions:

> *The writer uses words like "endless" and "unoriginal", which imply that he did not enjoy the film.* ⬅ The writer's <u>language</u> indicates their <u>emotions</u> and <u>attitude</u>.

> *The writer sounds sarcastic when she calls the contestants "the finest brains the country could scrape together".* ⬅ The writer will often use <u>tone</u> (see page 42) to <u>imply</u> what they really mean — look out for <u>sarcasm</u> or <u>bias</u>.

3) You could use <u>phrases</u> like these to show that you've made an <u>inference</u>:

| The writer gives a sense of... | The writer appears to be... | This suggests that... |

Try to Read Between the Lines

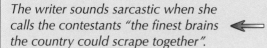

PAPER 2

`0 3`   How does the writer use language to show how she feels about the Internet?

> In today's world we are plagued by information. Gone are the days of blissful ignorance; instead we inhabit an era of awareness, where the invention of the Internet has brought the sum total of the world's knowledge to our fingertips. It has reduced us to a collection of walking, talking encyclopaedias. We are gluttons for information, and yet the immediate availability of this information has irrevocably extinguished the dying embers of our curiosity. No longer do we wonder about anything, we simply look it up. I am willing to concede that the Internet might be one of man's greatest inventions, but hey, so was the atomic bomb.

Analyse the writer's individual word choices for clues about their attitude (see pages 44-45).

Think about how the tone changes over the course of the text.

The writer makes quite a lot of **seemingly positive claims** about the Internet: she grandly asserts that it has created "an era of awareness" that has brought all the world's knowledge "to our fingertips". **However, the tone of the text suggests** that she has a negative attitude towards the Internet. She uses words like "**plagued**" and "**gluttons**" to describe the availability of information and **seems nostalgic** about the "'blissful ignorance" that existed before its invention. **She sounds reluctant to admit** that the Internet is "one of man's greatest inventions" and her **sarcasm** is made plain when she says, "but hey, so was the atomic bomb."

Writers will often use sarcasm to imply what they really mean (see page 53).

Use words like 'seemingly' to show that you've thought about the meaning of the text beyond the obvious.

Your inferences could be based on the general feeling you get from reading the text.

Think about the effect the writer wants to create...

Everything in a text has been carefully crafted by the writer, so look for clues that reveal their intentions. Demonstrate that you understand what the writer is showing you, not just what they're telling you.

Spelling, Punctuation and Grammar

There are lots of marks available in these exams for correct use of spelling, punctuation and grammar, or SPaG for short. These pages should help you to avoid the most common SPaG errors...

SPaG is **Especially Important** for the **Writing** questions

1) It's important that you use correct <u>spelling</u>, <u>punctuation</u> and <u>grammar</u> in all of your answers.

2) However, it's particularly important for the <u>writing questions</u> (question 5 on <u>both</u> papers), as they will test your ability to write <u>accurately</u> and <u>clearly</u> — which includes good <u>SPaG</u>.

3) Here are some tips to help keep your writing as <u>accurate</u> as possible.

Here are some **Spelling** hints

1) Avoid <u>common spelling mistakes</u>, like 'their', 'they're' and 'there' or 'where', 'were' and 'wear'.

2) Remember that '<u>affect</u>' is a <u>verb</u>, e.g. 'the simile affects the mood of the text', but '<u>effect</u>' is a <u>noun</u>, e.g. 'the interruption has a shocking effect on the reader'.

3) Always <u>write</u> words out in <u>full</u> — avoid <u>abbreviations</u> like 'etc.' and 'e.g.', and <u>don't</u> use text speak.

4) Make sure any <u>technical terms</u>, like 'metaphor' or 'onomatopoeia', are spelt correctly.

5) Make sure any <u>information</u> taken from the <u>extract</u>, such as the writer's name, is spelt correctly.

Use **Full Stops**, **Colons** and **Semi-colons** correctly

1) Make sure you've used <u>full stops</u> at the <u>end of sentences</u> and <u>question marks</u> at the <u>end of questions</u>.

2) Don't confuse <u>colons</u> and <u>semi-colons</u>:

- Colons can be used to introduce a <u>list</u> or if you want to add a piece of information that <u>explains</u> your sentence.
- <u>Semi-colons</u> can separate longer phrases in a <u>list</u>, or they can be used to <u>join</u> two sentences together — as long as both puntences are about the <u>same thing</u> and <u>make sense</u> on their own.

Spelling, Punctuation and Grammar

Use **Commas** properly

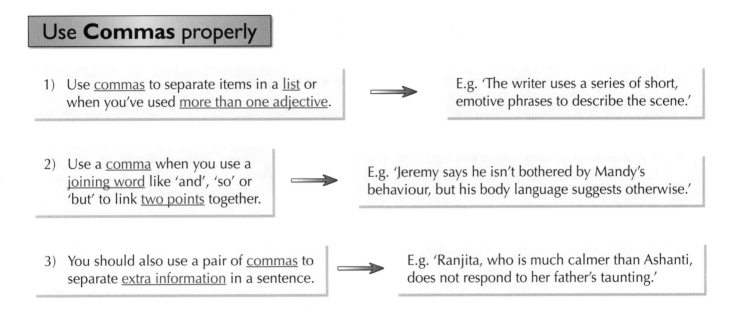

1) Use commas to separate items in a list or when you've used more than one adjective.

E.g. 'The writer uses a series of short, emotive phrases to describe the scene.'

2) Use a comma when you use a joining word like 'and', 'so' or 'but' to link two points together.

E.g. 'Jeremy says he isn't bothered by Mandy's behaviour, but his body language suggests otherwise.'

3) You should also use a pair of commas to separate extra information in a sentence.

E.g. 'Ranjita, who is much calmer than Ashanti, does not respond to her father's taunting.'

Follow this **Grammar** advice

1) Don't change tenses in your writing by mistake.

2) Don't use double negatives, e.g. 'There wasn't no reason' should be 'There wasn't any reason'.

3) Remember 'it's' (with an apostrophe) is short for 'it is' or 'it has'. 'Its' (without an apostrophe) means 'belonging to it'.

4) Never write 'should of' — it's always 'should have', 'would have', 'could have'.

5) Start a new paragraph for each new point. Show that it's a new paragraph by starting a new line and leaving a gap or indent before you start writing.

Check over your **Work** when you've finished

1) Try to leave a few minutes at the end of the exams to check your work.

2) There might not be time to check everything thoroughly. Look for the most obvious spelling, punctuation and grammar mistakes.

3) Start by checking your answers to the writing questions (question 5 on both papers), as these are the ones where you get the most marks for accuracy.

Spelling, Punctuation and Grammar

This is how you should **Correct** any **Mistakes**

- If you find a <u>spelling mistake</u>, put <u>brackets</u> around the word, <u>cross it out</u> neatly with <u>two lines</u> through it and write the correction <u>above</u>.

- If you've written something which isn't clear, put an <u>asterisk</u> (*) at the end of the sentence. Put another asterisk at the end of your work, and write what you mean beside it.

- If you realise you should have started a <u>new paragraph</u>, put // to show where it <u>starts</u> and write "(para)" in the margin.

- If you find you've <u>missed out</u> a word or two, put a "∧" where the words should go, then write them in <u>above</u> the line.

Make corrections as **Neatly** as possible

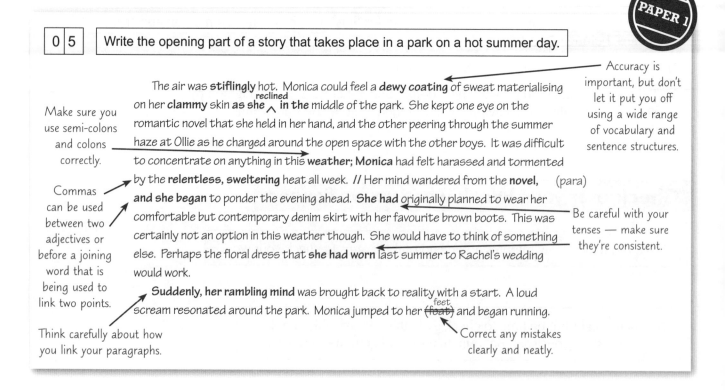

| 0 | 5 | Write the opening part of a story that takes place in a park on a hot summer day. |

PAPER 1

Accuracy is important, but don't let it put you off using a wide range of vocabulary and sentence structures.

The air was **stiflingly** hot. Monica could feel a **dewy coating** of sweat materialising on her **clammy** skin **as she** ∧ (reclined) **in the** middle of the park. She kept one eye on the romantic novel that she held in her hand, and the other peering through the summer haze at Ollie as he charged around the open space with the other boys. It was difficult to concentrate on anything in this **weather; Monica** had felt harassed and tormented by the **relentless, sweltering** heat all week. // Her mind wandered from the **novel,** (para) **and she began** to ponder the evening ahead. **She had** originally planned to wear her comfortable but contemporary denim skirt with her favourite brown boots. This was certainly not an option in this weather though. She would have to think of something else. Perhaps the floral dress that **she had worn** last summer to Rachel's wedding would work.

Suddenly, **her rambling mind** was brought back to reality with a start. A loud scream resonated around the park. Monica jumped to her (feet) ~~feat~~ and began running.

Make sure you use semi-colons and colons correctly.

Commas can be used between two adjectives or before a joining word that is being used to link two points.

Think carefully about how you link your paragraphs.

Be careful with your tenses — make sure they're consistent.

Correct any mistakes clearly and neatly.

Make sure you can spell some more complex words...

You need to use a wide range of vocabulary and sentence types in your writing, but you also need to make sure you use these correctly, with accurate SPaG. Try to find a balance between accuracy and imagination.

Revision Summary

At the end of most sections in this book, you'll find pages like this one. They're important, so don't skip them.

You've read the section, but do you know it? Here's where you find out — right here, right now.

- Try these questions and <u>tick off each one</u> when you <u>get it right</u>.
- When you've done <u>all the questions</u> under a heading and are <u>completely happy</u> with it, tick it off.

Planning, P.E.E.D. and Writing Well (p.9-13) ☑

1) True or false?
   You should make a detailed plan for every question in these exams.

2) What does P.E.E.D. stand for?

3) Give three ways that you could develop a point.

4) In your longer answers, how many of your points should be backed up with evidence from the text?
   a) A few of them
   b) About half of them
   c) Some of them
   d) All of them

5) Write down two different types of evidence that you could give from a text.

6) Which of these words and phrases could you use to link paragraphs in an exam answer?
   a) secondly   b) safe to say   c) in addition to this d) conversely

Reading with Insight (p.14-15) ☑

7) Give two examples of things you could comment on to show that you are reading with insight

8) What does 'inference' mean?

9) Give an example of a phrase you could use to show that you've made an inference.

Spelling, Punctuation and Grammar (p.16-18) ☑

10) Which of the following sentences is correct?
    a) I think the writer's use of metaphors in this extract is very effective.
    b) I think the writer's use of metaphors in this extract is very affective.

11) Does the following sentence use a semi-colon correctly?
    Gazing out of the open window; Tomek dreamt of the day when he would be free from revision.

12) Give three uses of commas.

13) What is a double negative?

14) Where is the grammatical error in the following sentence?
    You could of used a better paragraph structure to improve your answer.

15) When checking your answers for SPaG errors, which ones should you check first?

16) Write down the correction symbols for the following situations:
    a) When a new paragraph should start
    b) When a word or two is missing
    c) When something isn't clear

Information and Ideas

These two pages will help you with assessment objective 1 (see p.2). This page is about picking out information from a text, and the next page is about summarising information from two different texts.

Information and ideas can be **Explicit** or **Implicit**

1) The first thing you need to be able to do in order to <u>analyse</u> a text is to <u>understand</u> the basic things it's <u>telling you</u>.

2) This will help you to pick up some <u>easy marks</u> for <u>paper 1, question 1</u> and <u>paper 2, question 1</u>.

3) The information and ideas you need to pick out will either be <u>explicit</u> or <u>implicit</u>.

4) <u>Explicit</u> information is <u>clearly written</u> in the text.

> *Last weekend,*
> *it rained a lot.* → The text states that it rained, so we <u>know</u> that it rained.
> We also know <u>how much</u> it rained — "a lot."

5) <u>Implicit</u> information needs a little more <u>detective work</u> — you'll need to work it out from what is said in the text.

> *The castle was dark,*
> *decrepit and freezing cold.* → In this sentence, it is <u>implied</u> that the author doesn't
> like the castle very much, but this isn't stated outright.

Underline the **Relevant Facts** as you **Read** the text

PAPER 1

| 0 | 1 | Read again the first part of the source, lines 1 to 9. |

List **four** things from this part of the text about Brian's school.

The facts that you use in your answer must come from the part of the text mentioned in the question.

If a question asks you to 'list' something, all you need to do is find the information in the text. You don't need to analyse it at all.

> Brian had hated school. He often thought back to the dreary <u>breezeblock walls</u>, the <u>freezing classrooms</u> and the <u>constant drone</u> of the <u>centuries-old plumbing</u>.
>
> St Mary's had been the closest school to Brian's house, but that was an all-girls school. This meant that every morning Brian had had to withstand the torment of a fifteen-minute bus journey across town to <u>Beeches Hall</u> — the <u>boys' school</u>. This bus journey would have been perfectly tolerable had it not been for the driver: a peculiar, unpleasant man with a severely erratic driving style.

As you read the relevant part of the text, underline the facts that you will use to answer the question.

Make sure your facts are linked to the topic the question asked about.

A   **Brian's school** was called "Beeches Hall".

B   Its **classrooms were very cold**.

C   Brian's school had **"dreary breezeblock walls"**.

D   **The plumbing was noisy.**

You can paraphrase parts of the text...

... or you can quote directly from it.

This fact isn't explicitly written in the text, but it is implied.

Information and Ideas

You'll also need to **Summarise** information

1) Paper 2, question 2 will ask you to pick out information and ideas on the <u>same topic</u> from two <u>different texts</u>.

2) You'll then need to <u>summarise</u> the <u>similarities</u> or <u>differences</u> in what you've picked out.

3) You'll also need to <u>back up</u> your points with examples from the text.

4) <u>Linking words</u> are essential for writing about similarities and differences, as they show that you've made a <u>comparison</u>.

To show similarities:	
• Similarly	• Likewise
• Equally	• Also

To show differences:	
• Whereas	• Although
• However	• But

These are a few examples of linking words, but there are plenty more.

Make Links between the texts

PAPER 2

0	2	Use details from both sources. Write a summary of the differences between Andrew and Richard.

Look out for obvious differences between the two texts, e.g. Andrew's and Richard's ages, but don't just limit yourself to <u>explicit</u> details.

Source A — 20th century diary

Friday 21 March 1947
What a truly miserable afternoon. Daddy shouted at me just for being late to school. "You should be more responsible now you're thirteen, Andrew!" he was yelling. He even said he had half a mind to stop wasting his money on my private education. I know he's angry, but I think his outburst was a bit of an overreaction.

Source B — 19th century diary

Saturday 12 September 1868
Today was Richard's 16th birthday party, but it was not such a celebration after all. Richard sat quietly all evening, his hands folded in his lap, as Father ranted about how the party was a waste of the little money we have. Richard only broke his silence to acknowledge Father's tirade with a respectful "Yes, Sir".

Use linking words to show that you've thought about how the texts are similar or different.

Richard's body language has shown the reader something about his personality.

Andrew is willing to challenge ideas, as he remarks that his father has overreacted. **His defensive tone suggests** that he feels he knows better than his father. **In contrast**, Richard seems much meeker and less cheeky. **He sits quietly with "his hands folded in his lap"**, referring to his father as "Sir", even though he's shouting at him. This is perhaps a result of the fact that their situations are very different: Richard is a nineteenth-century boy from a family with "little money", whereas Andrew is a twentieth-century boy who has had an expensive **"private education"**.

You can make more perceptive observations by commenting on the tone of the texts.

Use quotes to support the comparisons you make.

If you master these skills you can pick up some easy marks...

You'll need good observation skills for these kinds of questions. Comment on the explicit differences between the texts, but don't forget to write about implicit ideas too — things that are implied by the writer.

Audience

In the exams, you'll need to think about the audience — the intended readers of the text.

Writers aim their work at **General** or **Specific** audiences

1) The writer will always have a <u>group of people</u> in mind when they write — this is their <u>audience</u>.

2) The audience of a text can be quite <u>general</u>, e.g. adults, or more <u>specific</u>, e.g. parents with children under the age of 3.

3) Some texts will have <u>more than one</u> audience, e.g. children's books will try to appeal to the <u>kids</u> who read them, but also to the <u>parents</u> who will <u>buy</u> them.

The **Content** gives you clues about the **Audience**

Sometimes you can work out <u>who</u> the target audience is by the text's <u>content</u> (subject matter):

This latest model is a beautiful car. Its impressive engine can send you shooting from 0-60 mph in less than 6 seconds. It's a great buy for anyone currently looking at competitor models in this range.

This text is clearly aimed at someone who's interested in <u>high-performance cars</u>, and probably someone who wants to <u>buy</u> one.

Ruben Corsanqui's new musical is a delight. It showcases the very best of his lyrical talents, and the choreography is stunning. We anticipate that these tickets will sell out as soon as they go on general release.

This text is clearly aimed at someone who has an interest in <u>musical theatre</u>. It might also be aimed at someone who is thinking of <u>seeing</u> a show.

Audience

Vocabulary can tell you about the Age of the audience

The vocabulary (choice of words) can tell you about the target audience's age group:

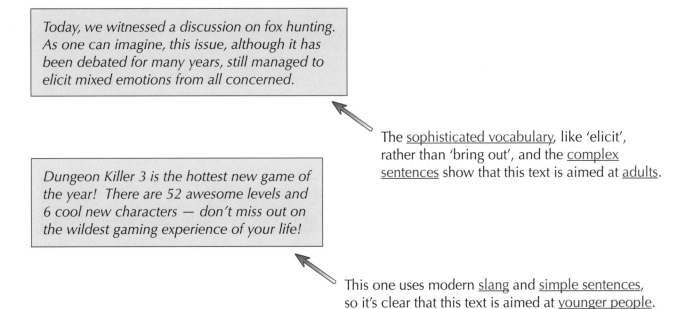

> Today, we witnessed a discussion on fox hunting. As one can imagine, this issue, although it has been debated for many years, still managed to elicit mixed emotions from all concerned.

The sophisticated vocabulary, like 'elicit', rather than 'bring out', and the complex sentences show that this text is aimed at adults.

> Dungeon Killer 3 is the hottest new game of the year! There are 52 awesome levels and 6 cool new characters — don't miss out on the wildest gaming experience of your life!

This one uses modern slang and simple sentences, so it's clear that this text is aimed at younger people.

Language can tell you about the audience's Understanding

The language can also give you clues about the target audience's level of understanding:

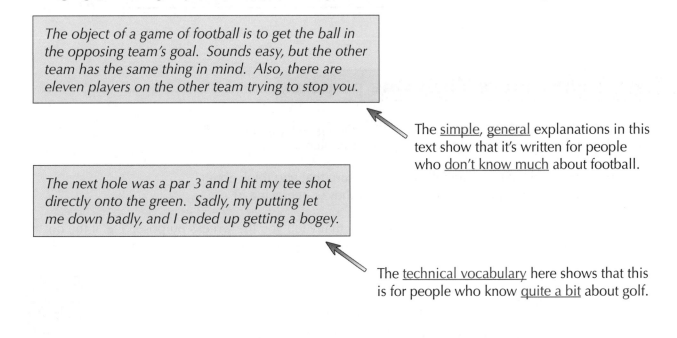

> The object of a game of football is to get the ball in the opposing team's goal. Sounds easy, but the other team has the same thing in mind. Also, there are eleven players on the other team trying to stop you.

The simple, general explanations in this text show that it's written for people who don't know much about football.

> The next hole was a par 3 and I hit my tee shot directly onto the green. Sadly, my putting let me down badly, and I ended up getting a bogey.

The technical vocabulary here shows that this is for people who know quite a bit about golf.

The audience is one of the first things you should look for in a text...

You need to work out who the intended audience of a text is so that you can discuss the writer's purpose, the techniques they use and how successful they are. Keep the audience in mind throughout your answer.

Writer's Purpose

Every text you come across in your English Language exams will have been written for a reason.

There are **Four Common Purposes** of writing

1) The <u>purpose</u> of a text is the <u>reason</u> that it's been written — what the writer is <u>trying to do</u>.

2) Most texts are written for <u>one</u> of these reasons:

To Argue or Persuade
- They give the writer's <u>opinion</u>.
- They get the reader to <u>agree</u> with them.

To Inform
- They <u>tell</u> the reader about something.
- They help the reader to increase their <u>understanding</u> of a subject.

To Entertain
- They are <u>enjoyable</u> to read.
- They make the reader <u>feel</u> something.

Pages 26-29 tell you how to spot a text's purpose, and how you can discuss this in the exam.

To Advise
- They <u>help</u> the reader to <u>do something</u>.
- They give <u>instructions</u> on what to do.

Texts can have **More Than One** purpose

1) Lots of texts have <u>more than one</u> purpose, though. E.g. a biographical text could be written to both <u>inform</u> and <u>entertain</u> its audience.

2) In the exams, read the texts carefully and make sure that you think about <u>what</u> the writers are trying to <u>achieve</u> (and <u>how</u> they're achieving it).

3) Look out for super helpful exam questions that actually <u>tell you</u> the writer's purpose. E.g. if the question asks you about how the writer uses language to <u>influence</u> the reader, you know it's about <u>persuading</u>:

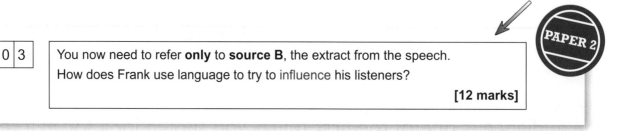

| 0 | 3 |

You now need to refer **only** to **source B**, the extract from the speech.
How does Frank use language to try to influence his listeners?

[12 marks]

PAPER 2

Writer's Purpose

Purpose is **More Obvious** in **Non-fiction** texts

1) The purpose of most <u>non-fiction</u> texts is usually quite <u>obvious</u>. For example:

If a speech is trying to <u>argue</u> a particular point of view, the writer might make this very <u>clear</u> to make the argument more <u>powerful</u>.

Forcing all students to take A-Levels would be a horrendous idea — it would be frustrating, pointless and demoralising for many of our young people.

2) Look out for texts where it might be <u>less obvious</u>, though. For example:

A <u>magazine article</u> is primarily written to <u>entertain</u> its audience, so it might use a <u>chatty</u> tone to engage the reader. This might make it <u>less obvious</u> that it's also trying to <u>argue</u> a particular point of view.

Here at CelebLife, we're marvelling at how soapstar Gemma Rodriguez manages to nail her festival get-up every time. This stylish lady is certainly working this summer's must-have dungarees and crop T-shirt look.

3) A piece of fiction's most obvious purpose is to <u>entertain</u>, but writers sometimes use entertainment to achieve <u>another purpose</u>.

Lots of fiction texts are <u>entertaining</u> stories on the surface, but they can contain <u>another message</u>. The writer might want to <u>argue</u> their own point of view or <u>inform</u> the reader about something.

The Underground closures were an unwelcome obstacle to Jeremy when he finally managed to leave the house. As he began the long walk to his next nearest station, he wondered why these 'essential works' always seemed to be most essential on a bank holiday.

You need to know the writer's purpose to write a good answer...

Always make sure you consider a text's purpose. If there's more than one purpose to a text, write about them both. And if you can write about how one purpose is used to achieve another, that's even better.

Informative Texts

Informative texts (like this book, in fact) always have something they're trying to tell you.

Informative writing Tells you something

1) When writing an informative text, the writer's aim is to pass on <u>knowledge</u> to the reader as <u>clearly</u> and <u>effectively</u> as possible.

Have a look back at p.22-23 for more on audience.

2) They will adapt their <u>language</u> to match their intended <u>audience</u>, e.g. they <u>might</u> need to write for different <u>age groups</u>, or for people with different <u>levels of understanding</u>.

3) Purely informative texts will present information in a <u>balanced</u> and <u>factual</u> way. They will contain lots of <u>facts</u> and <u>figures</u>, but no <u>opinions</u>.

4) Some informative texts might also be <u>arguing</u> a particular viewpoint, though. For example:

> Many newspapers <u>carefully pick</u> information that supports a particular political party. Even though a newspaper article may not say outright what its opinion is, it can still be <u>biased</u>.

Bias is when a piece of writing is influenced by the opinion of its author — see page 55.

Read the passage Carefully

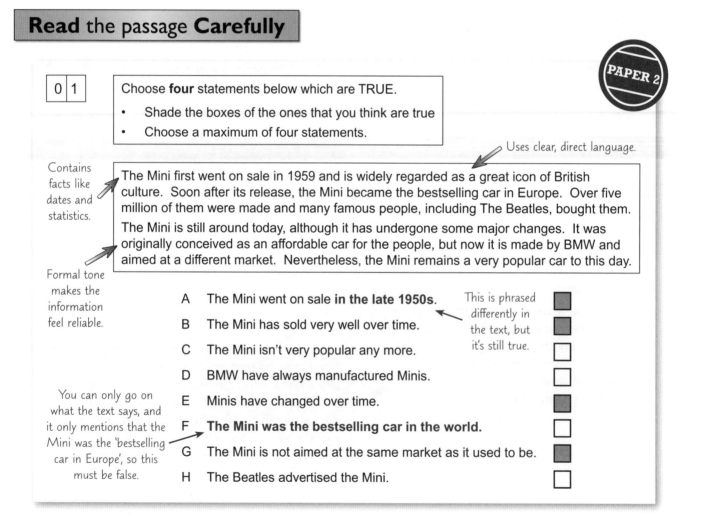

PAPER 2

0 1 Choose **four** statements below which are TRUE.
- Shade the boxes of the ones that you think are true
- Choose a maximum of four statements.

Uses clear, direct language.

Contains facts like dates and statistics.

The Mini first went on sale in 1959 and is widely regarded as a great icon of British culture. Soon after its release, the Mini became the bestselling car in Europe. Over five million of them were made and many famous people, including The Beatles, bought them.

The Mini is still around today, although it has undergone some major changes. It was originally conceived as an affordable car for the people, but now it is made by BMW and aimed at a different market. Nevertheless, the Mini remains a very popular car to this day.

Formal tone makes the information feel reliable.

A   The Mini went on sale **in the late 1950s**.

B   The Mini has sold very well over time.

This is phrased differently in the text, but it's still true.

C   The Mini isn't very popular any more.

D   BMW have always manufactured Minis.

E   Minis have changed over time.

You can only go on what the text says, and it only mentions that the Mini was the 'bestselling car in Europe', so this must be false.

F   **The Mini was the bestselling car in the world.**

G   The Mini is not aimed at the same market as it used to be.

H   The Beatles advertised the Mini.

Look at some examples of informative writing as practice...

You need to be able to recognise informative writing and explain how it's being used. If the information is biased, make sure you comment on that. It will show the examiner that you've really thought about the text.

Entertaining Texts

Entertaining texts make you feel something. You need to be able to explain how they do this.

Entertaining writing aims to be Enjoyable to read

1) Entertaining writing is the sort of thing you'd read for <u>pleasure</u>, e.g. literary fiction.

2) Unlike informative texts, they contain <u>few facts</u>. Instead, they try to make you <u>feel</u> something, like <u>scared</u>, <u>excited</u>, or <u>amused</u>.

3) Entertaining writing is often very <u>descriptive</u>, and uses <u>narrative techniques</u> to make texts more enjoyable to read (see p.56+60).

4) Writers also use <u>structural techniques</u> to create entertaining texts (see p.61-65). E.g. lots of <u>short</u>, <u>punchy</u> sentences can be used to make a text feel more <u>exciting</u>.

> Writers might use entertaining writing to <u>engage</u> a reader when they have <u>another</u> purpose in mind. E.g. travel books are <u>entertaining non-fiction</u>, but they're also <u>informative</u>.

Think about **What** makes the text entertaining

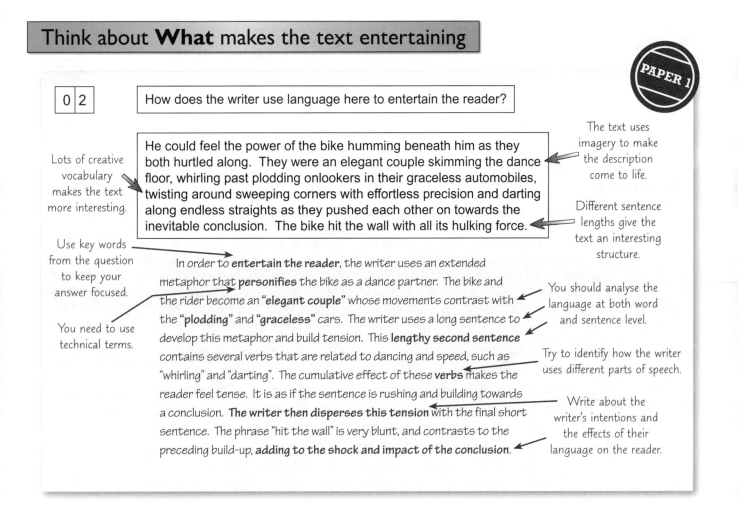

PAPER 1

| 0 | 2 | | How does the writer use language here to entertain the reader? |

He could feel the power of the bike humming beneath him as they both hurtled along. They were an elegant couple skimming the dance floor, whirling past plodding onlookers in their graceless automobiles, twisting around sweeping corners with effortless precision and darting along endless straights as they pushed each other on towards the inevitable conclusion. The bike hit the wall with all its hulking force.

Lots of creative vocabulary makes the text more interesting.

The text uses imagery to make the description come to life.

Different sentence lengths give the text an interesting structure.

Use key words from the question to keep your answer focused.

You need to use technical terms.

In order to **entertain the reader**, the writer uses an extended metaphor that **personifies** the bike as a dance partner. The bike and the rider become an **"elegant couple"** whose movements contrast with the **"plodding"** and **"graceless"** cars. The writer uses a long sentence to develop this metaphor and build tension. This **lengthy second sentence** contains several verbs that are related to dancing and speed, such as "whirling" and "darting". The cumulative effect of these **verbs** makes the reader feel tense. It is as if the sentence is rushing and building towards a conclusion. **The writer then disperses this tension** with the final short sentence. The phrase "hit the wall" is very blunt, and contrasts to the preceding build-up, **adding to the shock and impact of the conclusion.**

You should analyse the language at both word and sentence level.

Try to identify how the writer uses different parts of speech.

Write about the writer's intentions and the effects of their language on the reader.

Many entertaining texts also have other purposes...

Entertaining writing really helps to keep readers interested. So even if a writer's main purpose is to inform, argue, persuade or advise, they might still want to make their writing entertaining so the reader enjoys it.

Texts that Argue or Persuade

When you're writing about a text that argues or persuades, you need to be able to say exactly how it does this.

Arguing and Persuading are Similar

1) When people write to argue, they want to make the reader agree with their opinion. They use clear and forceful language to get their points across, and they might use facts and figures to back up points.

2) Persuasive writing tries to get the reader to do something, such as support a charity. It does this with techniques including emotive language that aims to make the reader sympathise with their cause.

3) When writing to persuade, writers might sometimes be more subtle about their aims and opinions, e.g.:

> *It is clear that this is a good school, and that people who attend it do well.* ⟶ This writer uses the phrase 'It is clear' to make their opinion sound like fact. This can make the writing sound more informative, when actually it's persuasive.

4) When writing to argue or persuade, writers often use rhetorical devices such as hyperbole, repetition or rhetorical questions (see p.54).

Explain the Effects of the writer's choice of Language

PAPER 2

| 0 | 3 | | How does the writer use language here to influence the reader? |

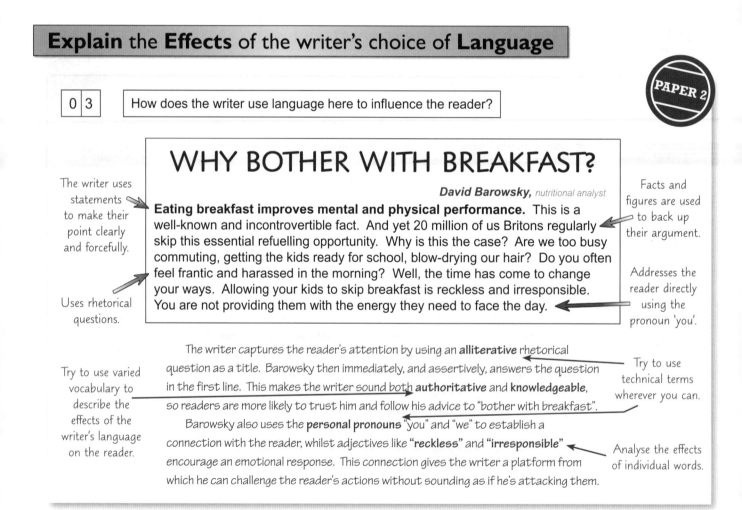

The writer uses statements to make their point clearly and forcefully.

Uses rhetorical questions.

WHY BOTHER WITH BREAKFAST?

David Barowsky, nutritional analyst

Eating breakfast improves mental and physical performance. This is a well-known and incontrovertible fact. And yet 20 million of us Britons regularly skip this essential refuelling opportunity. Why is this the case? Are we too busy commuting, getting the kids ready for school, blow-drying our hair? Do you often feel frantic and harassed in the morning? Well, the time has come to change your ways. Allowing your kids to skip breakfast is reckless and irresponsible. You are not providing them with the energy they need to face the day.

Facts and figures are used to back up their argument.

Addresses the reader directly using the pronoun 'you'.

Try to use varied vocabulary to describe the effects of the writer's language on the reader.

The writer captures the reader's attention by using an **alliterative** rhetorical question as a title. Barowsky then immediately, and assertively, answers the question in the first line. This makes the writer sound both **authoritative** and **knowledgeable**, so readers are more likely to trust him and follow his advice to "bother with breakfast".

Barowsky also uses the **personal pronouns** "you" and "we" to establish a connection with the reader, whilst adjectives like **"reckless"** and **"irresponsible"** encourage an emotional response. This connection gives the writer a platform from which he can challenge the reader's actions without sounding as if he's attacking them.

Try to use technical terms wherever you can.

Analyse the effects of individual words.

Texts that argue or persuade may well come up in paper 2...

If a writer is trying to argue a point or persuade you to do something, they're trying to make you see things from their point of view. It'll be one-sided, with carefully chosen evidence that supports their point of view.

Texts that Advise

When writing to advise, a writer uses reassuring and easily understandable language to guide their reader.

Writing to **Advise** sounds **Clear** and **Calm**

1) When writing to <u>advise</u>, writers want their readers to <u>follow their suggestions</u>.

2) The tone will be <u>calm</u> and <u>less emotional</u> than writing that argues or persuades.

3) The advice will usually be <u>clear</u> and <u>direct</u>. For example, it might use:

> • <u>Vocabulary</u> that matches the audience's <u>subject knowledge</u>.
>
> • <u>Second person</u> pronouns (e.g. 'you') to make the advice feel <u>personal</u>.
>
> • A <u>logical structure</u> that makes the advice <u>easy to follow</u>.

4) The register (see p.43) may be <u>formal</u>, e.g. in a letter from a solicitor offering legal advice, or <u>informal</u>, e.g. in a magazine advice column.

Writing to **Advise** looks **Like This**

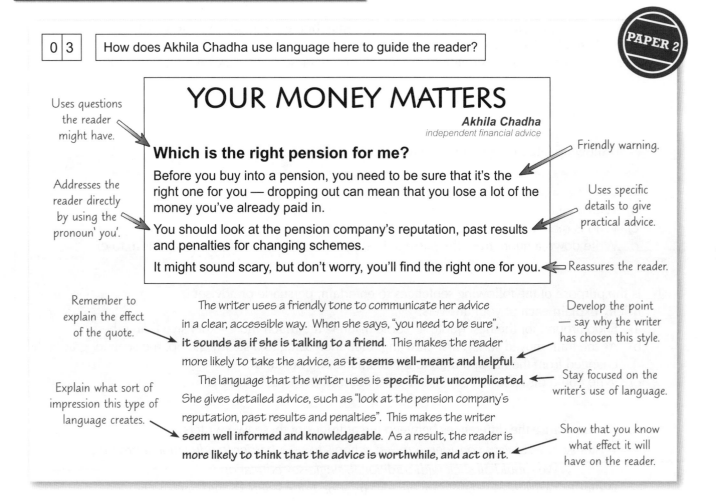

| 0 | 3 | How does Akhila Chadha use language here to guide the reader? |

PAPER 2

Uses questions the reader might have.

Addresses the reader directly by using the pronoun' you'.

YOUR MONEY MATTERS

Akhila Chadha
independent financial advice

Which is the right pension for me?

Before you buy into a pension, you need to be sure that it's the right one for you — dropping out can mean that you lose a lot of the money you've already paid in.

You should look at the pension company's reputation, past results and penalties for changing schemes.

It might sound scary, but don't worry, you'll find the right one for you.

Friendly warning.

Uses specific details to give practical advice.

Reassures the reader.

Remember to explain the effect of the quote.

Explain what sort of impression this type of language creates.

The writer uses a friendly tone to communicate her advice in a clear, accessible way. When she says, "you need to be sure", **it sounds as if she is talking to a friend**. This makes the reader more likely to take the advice, as **it seems well-meant and helpful**.

The language that the writer uses is **specific but uncomplicated**. She gives detailed advice, such as "look at the pension company's reputation, past results and penalties". This makes the writer **seem well informed and knowledgeable**. As a result, the reader is **more likely to think that the advice is worthwhile, and act on it**.

Develop the point — say why the writer has chosen this style.

Stay focused on the writer's use of language.

Show that you know what effect it will have on the reader.

Learn to spot the common features of texts that advise...

Texts that advise can be written for many different audiences, but a lot of the features will stay the same. Look at whether the language is formal or informal — it'll vary depending on the subject and audience.

Warm-Up Questions

To help you to digest everything you've read so far, here's a page of warm-up questions. The questions shouldn't take you too long, but try to write a few sentences for each one. You can check your answers in the back of the book to see how you're getting on. Then, when you're ready, have a look at page 31.

Warm-Up Questions

1) Read the short passage below.

> Dani approached the roller coaster with wide eyes. Her friend Amara had offered to give £20 to charity if Dani agreed to ride the biggest roller coaster in the park — a towering steel beast with four loops and six corkscrew turns. Her stomach churned at the thought.

   Are the following statements true or false?
   a) Dani is nervous about going on the roller coaster.
   b) It was Dani's idea to get sponsored to go on the ride.

2) Read the short passage below.

> "We're going to be late, Rakesh," warned Rita, biting her thumbnail nervously.
> "We'll be fine!" insisted Rakesh from the depths of his wardrobe. After a moment he emerged, triumphantly holding his favourite leather jacket aloft.
> Rita glared pointedly at her watch, then at Rakesh, who grinned.
> "We'll be fine," he repeated, trying on the jacket and admiring his reflection in the full-length mirror.
> "It's bad enough that we have to go to this reunion at all, and now we're going to show up late too," complained Rita. "This is all your fault."

   a) Which character is reluctant to go to the reunion?
   b) Which character cares most about time management?
   c) Who is the more confident character in the passage?
   d) Write down a quote from the passage to support each of your answers to parts a) to c).

3) Is the purpose of the following sentences to entertain, persuade or advise?
    Briefly explain each of your answers.
    a) Shop around for the best quote — some insurers are much more expensive than others.
    b) As the train moved south, first crawling, then increasing to a steady gallop, the scenery gradually changed from the flat and drab to the dramatic and beautiful.
    c) Who could disagree with the fact that children should eat healthily?

4) Briefly summarise the differences between the attitudes of these two writers.
    Writer A: *"I've always considered mixed schools to be a barrier to educational progress. We should all stick with traditional, single-sex education."*
    Writer B: *"Mixed-sex schools are clearly superior, but parents should have a choice."*

Exam-Style Questions

Now you've learnt some theory, it's time to put it into practice with these exam-style questions. They're very similar to the ones you'll see in the real AQA English Language exams. You should try to do them without looking back at this section for help. You can mark yourself using the answers in the back of the book.

Q1   Read the following extract from a novel.

List **four** facts from the text about George.

> The doorbell rang. Someone must have answered it, because moments later I heard George's nasal tones in the hallway.
> "So lovely to be here!" he cried, his voice carrying easily across the living room.
> "Did you invite him?" I hissed, staring desperately at Rosa.
> "I could hardly leave him out," she said coolly. "It would have been too obvious."
> He entered the room. His garish purple suit and elaborate hairstyle made him stand out sharply from the other guests. "George, darling," Rosa cooed. "You made it."
> "Rosa!" he said, presenting her with a bottle of cheap-looking wine. "And Freddie," he said to me with a smirk, extending a greasy hand adorned with several gaudy rings. "Good to see you."
> "You too," I said, forcing a smile and letting go of his hand quickly. "Drink?"
> "Oh, go on then," said George, "I'd love a nice whisky, if you have any?"
> "Nothing but the best for you, George," I replied through gritted teeth.

Q2   Read the following extracts. Source A is from a housekeeping magazine written in the 19th century, and Source B is a newspaper article that was written in the 21st century.

Use details from **both** sources. Write a summary of the differences between the views given in Source A and Source B.

Source A

The secret to a harmonious marriage lies in the willingness of the wife to be amenable to the needs of the husband.

A good wife will not pester her husband, nor will she bore him with gossip or domestic trivialities. Instead, she will endeavour to be sweet and charming, always fulfilling his needs. If he wishes to complain, she should listen; if he seeks quiet, she should be silent. The home is her sphere, and she should strive to make it a haven for him, in which he need not lift a finger.

Source B

In the 21st century, a marriage is a partnership of equals. Today, it is common for both members of a couple to work full-time. This means that it is essential for domestic responsibilities to be shared evenly too. Whilst housework was once considered the domain of women, most women today would spurn the idea that they should work full-time and take sole care of a home. Men are just as capable of cleaning and cooking as women, and fortunately many modern husbands have realised this crucial fact.

Exam-Style Questions

Q3 Read the following extract from a review of a holiday park.

> You would need a fortnight to try all the activities at Lowbridge Park. From abseiling to zorbing, the park offers a mind-boggling range of activities. I was only there for a long weekend, so I had to prioritise!
>
> I began with a pony trek. Although it drizzled the entire morning, it was a great way to explore the woodland. In the afternoon I debated between rock climbing and mountain biking. I settled on the former, primarily to stay out of the rain!
>
> The next day, the weather was much better, so my choice fell between canoeing and kayaking. I settled for a kayak and headed out on the lake, which was simply stunning early in the morning, clear, calm and blue. The good weather lasted into the afternoon, which meant that I was lucky enough to go paragliding. What an exhilarating experience!
>
> The next morning, I decided to finish my weekend with a spot of archery. Alas, I'm no Robin Hood, but the instructor was patient and funny, and I did improve a little over the course of the morning.

Choose **four** statements below which are TRUE.

- Shade the boxes of the ones that you think are true
- Choose a maximum of four statements.

A   The writer went mountain biking. ☐

B   On the second day, the writer got up early. ☐

C   The writer had time to try everything. ☐

D   The writer enjoyed the pony trek. ☐

E   The weather stayed sunny all weekend. ☐

F   You can abseil at Lowbridge Park. ☐

G   The writer liked the archery instructor. ☐

H   The writer went kayaking down a river. ☐

Q4 Read the following extract from an advice leaflet about an election.

How does the writer use language to advise the reader?

> ## It's Decision Time — But Who Do I Vote For?
>
> Unless you've been living under a rock for the past month, you'll probably have noticed that there's an election coming up. Deciding who to vote for can be a daunting task, but it's also an important one. Luckily, there's plenty of help out there.
>
> Firstly, you need to be well-informed on the principles and policies that each party stands for. If you start to feel overwhelmed by all the political lingo in their leaflets, don't panic — have a look online, where there are plenty of websites that break it down for you.
>
> It's also a good idea to look into the candidates in your constituency. They represent you in parliament, so you'll want to vote for someone who has a strong voice, and who will stand up for what your area needs.
>
> It's true — choosing who to vote for isn't easy. However, if you take the time to do a bit of research, you will be able to make the right decision for you.

Writer's Viewpoint and Attitude

Paper 2 is all about writers' viewpoints and attitudes, especially question 4.

Viewpoint and Attitude are Different to Purpose

1) A writer's purpose is what they're trying to do, but their viewpoint (or attitude) is what they think about the topics that they're writing about.

2) You can work out what a writer's viewpoint might be by looking for clues in the language, tone, style and content of a text. For example:

> *I urge you to visit this truly unique and hidden valley — you must see such beautiful scenery at least once in your life.*

This text's purpose is to persuade its audience to visit a place. The author's viewpoint is their belief that the valley is beautiful and that it should be visited. The writer uses emotive adjectives and an upbeat tone to convey their viewpoint.

Use the writers' Tone to make Inferences about Attitude

PAPER 2

0 4 Compare how the two writers convey their different attitudes to manners and politeness.

Source A — 19th century etiquette guide

The way you behave when out in society is paramount. It is essential that you show the highest level of social refinement possible. For example, if someone offers you their hand, take it. Always remove your hat when entering a building. Be punctual to all social events to which you are invited.

Source B — 21st century newspaper article

Anyone who's ever taken a ride on the London Underground will know that there are some real nuisances out there. All too often, I've seen people refusing to give their seat up to an elderly passenger. I mean, it's just common courtesy, isn't it? Is it really so difficult to just be a little more civil towards other people?

Try to make your observations as perceptive as possible. Examiners will be really impressed if you can pick out subtle differences between the writers' attitudes.

The authors of both sources largely agree that being polite is important. However, there are **subtle differences** in their attitudes. The author of source A focuses on etiquette in specific situations. They use a **confident, assured tone**, which is created by the use of **imperative verbs** such as "take" and "remove". They also give their advice using the **pronoun** "you", which makes the text sound more like a series of commands than a piece of advice. These things suggest that their ideas about "refinement" are very strict.

By contrast, the author of source B has a more laid-back attitude towards the need for "common courtesy". Rather than telling the reader how to behave as in source A, they use an example and rhetorical questions to make the reader think about why people should be "more civil". **This is possibly because source B is from the 21st century, whereas source A was written in the 19th century** — a time when etiquette was considered to be much more important.

Looking at the writer's tone is usually a good place to start.

Use technical terms to discuss the different methods both writers use to convey their attitudes.

This is a useful phrase to use when you're linking the two texts.

Think about the reasons why their attitudes differ — think about when and why they were written.

Comment on how attitudes are conveyed...

You need to go beyond just what the writer's saying and think about how they're expressing their viewpoint. For example, even if two writers have the same opinion, one might express it more strongly than the other.

Literary Fiction

In paper 1, you'll be given an extract from a piece of literary fiction, and you need to be able to analyse it.

Literary fiction **Entertains** the reader

1) Literary fiction, such as a novel or short story, is written to <u>entertain</u>. It might do this by affecting the reader's <u>emotions</u>, describing the <u>atmosphere</u> of a place, using an intriguing <u>structure</u> or developing the <u>personality</u> of a <u>character</u>.

See section 3 for more on all these language and structural features.

2) All literary fiction has a <u>narrator</u>. It's most often either a <u>first-person</u> (uses 'I' and 'we') or <u>third-person</u> (uses 'he', 'she' and 'they') narrator.

3) Literary fiction uses lots of <u>descriptive</u> and <u>figurative</u> language (e.g. metaphors, similes, analogy and personification) to capture the reader's <u>imagination</u>.

4) Literary fiction is also <u>structured</u> to interest the reader — texts will often build the <u>tension</u> towards a dramatic climax, or they might use <u>repetition</u> and varied <u>sentence structures</u> to change the <u>pace</u> of a text.

5) <u>Dialogue</u> is also often used to move the plot along and give insight into the <u>thoughts</u> and <u>feelings</u> of different characters.

Look Closely at the Language used in a text

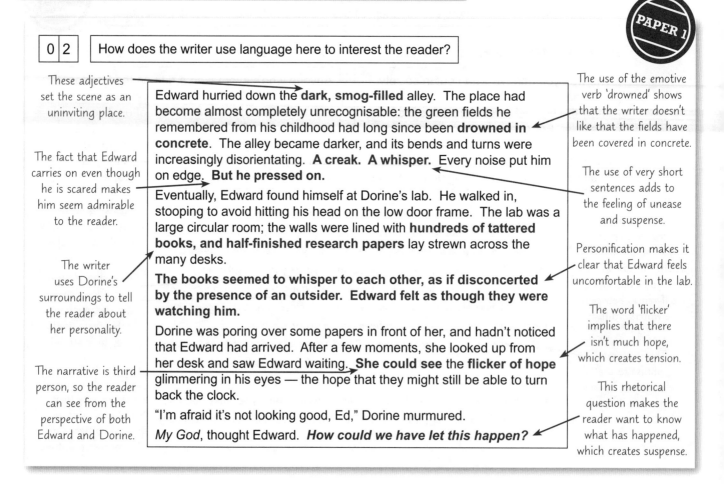

PAPER 1

| 0 | 2 | | How does the writer use language here to interest the reader? |

These adjectives set the scene as an uninviting place.

The fact that Edward carries on even though he is scared makes him seem admirable to the reader.

The writer uses Dorine's surroundings to tell the reader about her personality.

The narrative is third person, so the reader can see from the perspective of both Edward and Dorine.

Edward hurried down the **dark, smog-filled** alley. The place had become almost completely unrecognisable: the green fields he remembered from his childhood had long since been **drowned in concrete**. The alley became darker, and its bends and turns were increasingly disorientating. **A creak. A whisper.** Every noise put him on edge. **But he pressed on.**

Eventually, Edward found himself at Dorine's lab. He walked in, stooping to avoid hitting his head on the low door frame. The lab was a large circular room; the walls were lined with **hundreds of tattered books, and half-finished research papers** lay strewn across the many desks.

The books seemed to whisper to each other, as if disconcerted by the presence of an outsider. Edward felt as though they were watching him.

Dorine was poring over some papers in front of her, and hadn't noticed that Edward had arrived. After a few moments, she looked up from her desk and saw Edward waiting. **She could see** the **flicker of hope** glimmering in his eyes — the hope that they might still be able to turn back the clock.

"I'm afraid it's not looking good, Ed," Dorine murmured.

My God, thought Edward. ***How could we have let this happen?***

The use of the emotive verb 'drowned' shows that the writer doesn't like that the fields have been covered in concrete.

The use of very short sentences adds to the feeling of unease and suspense.

Personification makes it clear that Edward feels uncomfortable in the lab.

The word 'flicker' implies that there isn't much hope, which creates tension.

This rhetorical question makes the reader want to know what has happened, which creates suspense.

You need to practise writing about extracts from literary fiction...

You're always going to have to answer some questions about a piece of literary fiction — it makes up the whole reading section of paper 1. That means you're going to need to know all of this stuff really well.

Literary Non-Fiction

Now it's time for literary non-fiction. This is the focus of paper 2 ('Writers' Viewpoints and Perspectives').

Literary non-fiction is **Entertaining** but **Factual**

1) Literary non-fiction texts use <u>literary styles</u> and <u>techniques</u>, but they are based on <u>facts</u> or <u>real events</u>.

2) Non-fiction texts such as <u>biographies</u>, <u>autobiographies</u>, and <u>travel writing</u> will often be written in a similar style to literary fiction.

3) They are written to <u>inform</u> the reader about something, but the writer uses a literary style to make it <u>entertaining</u> too. For example, they might use <u>descriptive</u> language and <u>dialogue</u> to make the information more <u>interesting</u> to the reader.

Have a look back at the previous page to remind yourself about literary style.

4) Literary non-fiction is almost always written in the <u>first person</u>, which adds a sense of <u>personality</u> to the text, helping to <u>engage</u> the reader.

Literary non-fiction tries to **Engage** the **Reader**

PAPER 2

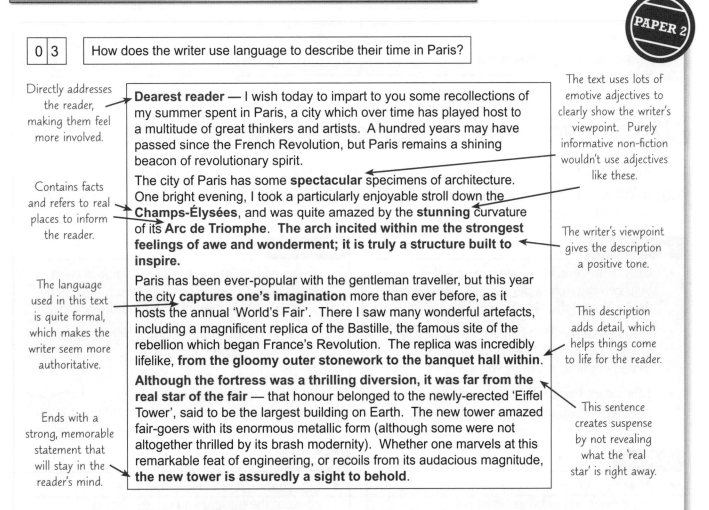

0 3 | How does the writer use language to describe their time in Paris?

Directly addresses the reader, making them feel more involved.

Contains facts and refers to real places to inform the reader.

The language used in this text is quite formal, which makes the writer seem more authoritative.

Ends with a strong, memorable statement that will stay in the reader's mind.

The text uses lots of emotive adjectives to clearly show the writer's viewpoint. Purely informative non-fiction wouldn't use adjectives like these.

The writer's viewpoint gives the description a positive tone.

This description adds detail, which helps things come to life for the reader.

This sentence creates suspense by not revealing what the 'real star' is right away.

Dearest reader — I wish today to impart to you some recollections of my summer spent in Paris, a city which over time has played host to a multitude of great thinkers and artists. A hundred years may have passed since the French Revolution, but Paris remains a shining beacon of revolutionary spirit.

The city of Paris has some **spectacular** specimens of architecture. One bright evening, I took a particularly enjoyable stroll down the **Champs-Élysées**, and was quite amazed by the **stunning** curvature of its **Arc de Triomphe**. **The arch incited within me the strongest feelings of awe and wonderment; it is truly a structure built to inspire.**

Paris has been ever-popular with the gentleman traveller, but this year the city **captures one's imagination** more than ever before, as it hosts the annual 'World's Fair'. There I saw many wonderful artefacts, including a magnificent replica of the Bastille, the famous site of the rebellion which began France's Revolution. The replica was incredibly lifelike, **from the gloomy outer stonework to the banquet hall within.**

Although the fortress was a thrilling diversion, it was far from the real star of the fair — that honour belonged to the newly-erected 'Eiffel Tower', said to be the largest building on Earth. The new tower amazed fair-goers with its enormous metallic form (although some were not altogether thrilled by its brash modernity). Whether one marvels at this remarkable feat of engineering, or recoils from its audacious magnitude, **the new tower is assuredly a sight to behold.**

Literary non-fiction is not as complicated as it might sound...

Don't let the phrase "literary non-fiction" worry you — it's just a category that describes any text that is factual, but is written in an entertaining way. Have a read of the texts on pages 81 and 85, for example.

19th-Century Texts

In paper 2, you'll always be given a 19th-century non-fiction text. Here's some information about the period.

19th-century Writing is often quite Formal

1) 19th-century texts can sound a bit <u>different</u> to more modern texts, but you should still be able to <u>understand</u> what's going on.

2) A lot of the texts will use a more <u>formal register</u> (see p.43) than modern writing, even if the <u>audience</u> is quite <u>familiar</u> (see next page for an example of this).

In the exam, any words in the text that aren't used today will be defined for you in a glossary.

3) The sentences may be <u>quite long</u> and the <u>word order</u> can sometimes be different to modern texts. Try not to worry about this — just <u>re-read</u> any sentences you can't make sense of at first. Here are a couple of examples:

Then, Albert being gone and we two left alone, Edward enquired as to whether I might accompany him on a stroll in the garden. ⟹	This sentence is written using a <u>formal</u> register, e.g. it uses 'enquired' instead of 'asked'. It might seem a bit <u>confusingly phrased</u> too, but 'Albert being gone and we two left alone' is just <u>another way</u> of saying 'Albert had gone and the two of us were left alone.'

I believe it necessary to abandon this foul enterprise. ⟹	Sometimes it can seem as if a word has been <u>missed out</u> — modern writers would probably put 'is' after 'it' in this sentence.

19th-century Society was Different to today

1) Knowing about 19th-century <u>society</u> will help you to <u>understand</u> the text better in the exam.

2) It will also help you to compare the <u>viewpoints</u> and <u>perspectives</u> of writers from different <u>time periods</u> (which you need to do for paper 2, question 4).

Social Class

- Early 19th-century society was <u>divided</u> between the rich <u>upper classes</u> (who owned the land) and the poorer <u>working classes</u>.

- Throughout the 19th century, the <u>Industrial Revolution</u> was creating opportunities for more people to make more <u>money</u>.

- This meant that the <u>middle classes</u> grew in <u>number</u> and <u>influence</u> throughout the century.

Education

- In the <u>early</u> 19th century, <u>few</u> children went to school. Children from poor families often <u>worked</u> to help support their families instead.

- In the <u>late</u> 19th century, <u>education reforms</u> made school <u>compulsory</u> for all young children.

- <u>Rich</u> families often sent their children to <u>boarding school</u>, or hired a <u>governess</u> to live with the family and teach the children at <u>home</u>.

Women

- After they got married, most women were expected to be in charge of looking after the <u>home</u> and <u>children</u>.

- Women didn't have as many <u>rights</u> as men — they couldn't <u>vote</u> in elections and they often didn't <u>control</u> their own money and property.

Religion

- <u>Christianity</u> had a big influence — most of the <u>middle</u> and <u>upper classes</u> attended <u>church</u> regularly.

- However, <u>science</u> was beginning to challenge religious ideas, e.g. Darwin's theory of <u>evolution</u> questioned the Bible's account of <u>creation</u>.

19th-Century Texts

Have a look at this piece of 19th-century Writing

This is a letter written to Princess (later Queen) Victoria of the United Kingdom by her uncle, King Leopold I of Belgium. In it, Leopold describes his new wife, Louise Marie.

The tone is affectionate but the register is formal — this is common in 19th-century letters.

Being 'virtuous' was an important quality in 19th-century society — it means having strong morals.

This shows the 19th-century viewpoint of what was valued in upper class women.

You might come across a tricky phrase or sentence. Use the context and the rest of the sentence to work out what's going on. Here, Leopold suggests that Louise Marie doesn't try very hard at playing the harp.

19th-century texts often phrase things differently — here, a modern writer might have said "I should end this letter here."

Laeken, 31st August 1832.

MY DEAREST LOVE,—You told me you wished to have a description of your new Aunt. I therefore shall both mentally and physically describe her to you.

She is extremely gentle and amiable, her actions are always guided by principles. She is at all times ready and disposed to sacrifice her comfort and inclinations to see others happy. She values goodness, merit, and **virtue** much more than beauty, riches, and amusements. With all this she is highly informed and very clever; **she speaks and writes English, German and Italian**; she speaks English very well indeed. In short, my dear Love, you see that I may well recommend her as **an example for all young ladies**, being Princesses or not.

Now to her appearance. She is about Feodore's* height, her hair very fair, light blue eyes, of a very gentle, intelligent and kind expression. A Bourbon** nose and small mouth. The figure is much like Feodore's but rather less stout. **She rides very well**, which she proved to my great alarm the other day, by keeping her seat though a horse of mine ran away with her full speed for at least half a mile. **What she does particularly well is dancing.** Music unfortunately she is not very fond of, though she plays on **the harp**; **I believe there is some idleness in the case**. There exists already great confidence and affection between us; she is desirous of doing everything that can contribute to my happiness, and I study whatever can make her happy and contented.

You will see by these descriptions that though my good little wife is not the tallest Queen, **she is a very great prize which I highly value and cherish**...

Now it is time I should finish my letter. Say everything that is kind to good Lehzen***, and believe me ever, **my dearest Love**, your faithful Friend and Uncle,

LEOPOLD R.

Upper class women were educated in European languages in the 19th century.

Upper class women were considered to be accomplished by their ability in things like riding, dancing, playing music and speaking languages.

Women were often seen as belonging to their husbands.

Superlatives (e.g. 'kindest', 'most gracious') are common in 19th-century writing.

Glossary

* Feodore — Victoria's half-sister, Princess Feodora

** Bourbon — the Bourbons were the French royal family

*** Lehzen — Princess Victoria's governess, Louise Lehzen

You will definitely have to analyse a 19th-century text in paper 2...

It's important to make sure you're comfortable reading and understanding 19th-century texts. These pages might look more like History than English, but they'll help you to improve some of your answers in paper 2.

Worked Answer

Here's a sample question with a worked answer for you to have a look at. Watch and learn...

Q1 Read the following extracts. Source A is an extract from a diary written in the 19th century, and Source B is from a speech written in the 21st century.

Source A
Dear Diary —

I've had quite a day today! Daddy and I took a trip to see the new steam train, which was being exhibited in James Square. It was fascinating — a clanking, grinding steel colossus, shiny as a new penny, with a great puff of steam that emerged from its funnel and curled into the summer sky. I've never seen the like — and to think, Daddy says one day they may be able to carry people from one end of the country to the other! I for one cannot wait.

Source B
Residents of Station Crescent! I know that you, like me, are plagued day-in, day-out with the sounds, smells and sights of the railway. Like me, many of you moved here at a time when three or four trains a day passed by, barely disturbing us at all. And like me, you've seen our area systematically invaded by a non-stop army of trains, impacting our quality of life — not to mention the price of our homes. The time has come to take a stand against the relentless growth of the railways.

Compare how the writers convey their different attitudes towards rail transport.

In your answer, you should:

- compare their different attitudes
- compare the methods they use to convey their attitudes
- support your ideas with quotations from both texts.

figurative language — "shiny as a new penny" in A, army metaphor in B
rhetorical devices in B — aims to persuade. A is more descriptive e.g. "curled" bit.
exclamation mark for excitement in A but for emotive effect in B
A wants more trains, B wants fewer trains

You don't need to make a detailed plan for this type of question, but quickly jotting down your ideas (like this) can be helpful.

This is a great opening sentence. It makes a clear point that is focused on the question.

The writers of both sources use figurative language to convey their attitudes to rail transport. In Source A, the train is "shiny as a new penny". This simile suggests that the writer feels the train is exciting because it's so new. In contrast, the figurative language in Source B shows the writer's frustration with trains. He uses a metaphor to compare them to a "non-stop army", which makes them seem like a relentless and aggressive nuisance.

This answer identifies a language technique and then explains its effect.

Use linking words and phrases to show that you're making a comparison.

To make this into a top level paragraph, you could mention why they might have these different attitudes by referring to the contexts of the sources.

Worked Answer

It's good to think about how the writer has conveyed their attitude through <u>structure</u>, as well as through language.

This quote does <u>support</u> the point, but it would be better to make it much <u>shorter</u> and then explain its effect more <u>specifically</u>.

The attitudes in Source B are conveyed using rhetorical devices. The writer <u>repeats</u> the phrase "like me" to get the audience on side. The writer also uses direct address, such as "Residents of Station Crescent", to suggest that the audience are a united team, who are able to work together to change things. In Source A <u>the attitudes are conveyed using</u> descriptive language, such as <u>"a great puff of steam that emerged from its funnel and curled into the summer sky"</u>. This shows how impressed the writer is by the new trains, feeling they are almost magical.

Phrases like this keep your answer <u>focused</u> on the second bullet point in the question — <u>how</u> attitudes are conveyed...

Both of the writers use exclamation marks to make their attitudes clear. In Source A, they are used by the writer to emphasise their <u>excited attitude</u> to the steam train. On the other hand, in Source B, the writer uses an exclamation mark to show his dedication to the cause and to persuade the audience to agree that <u>the trains are a problem</u>.

...and phrases like these focus on the <u>first</u> bullet point (<u>what</u> the attitudes are and how they're <u>different</u>).

The examiner will want to see that you can analyse the effect of individual words and <u>phrases</u>.

The writer in Source A hopes that there will be more trains. They "cannot wait" for the trains to be able to carry people from one end of the country to the other, and <u>the phrase "I for one"</u> implies that the author believes other people will feel the same. In Source B, the attitude is very different. This writer wants there to be fewer trains, because there used to be "three or four" and they use <u>the phrase "relentless growth"</u> to suggest to the audience that further expansion poses a real danger to the community.

Each <u>paragraph</u> in this answer makes a <u>new comparison</u> between the writers' attitudes. This shows a <u>clear understanding</u> of the differences.

- This is a good answer. It clearly compares the writers' attitudes (which covers the first bullet point) and it also discusses the writers' methods (which covers the second bullet point).

- To get the very top marks, this answer could be improved by:

  - using the different contexts of the sources to comment on why the attitudes might be different.

  - pointing out more subtle differences in the attitudes, e.g. the writer in Source A is writing about seeing one train on one particular day, whereas the writer in Source B is writing about living alongside multiple trains every day.

  - making sure that all the quotations are really precise.

Exam-Style Questions

Now that you've seen an example answer, have a go at these exam-style questions for yourself.

Q1   Read the following extracts. Source A is from a letter written in the 19th century, and Source B is from a newspaper article written in the 20th century.

Source A

Dear Miss Tinsham,

I read with concern your recent article on the new wave of art reaching British shores. With all due respect, I see it as nothing short of an abomination. It is created with a flagrant disregard for the conventions and traditions of classical art. These 'artists' seem not to have learnt from their predecessors, but instead insist on violating their canvasses with an assault of colour, which to view, in perfect honesty, is simply excruciating.

Source B

The London art scene has rarely been so exciting. We are seeing a real influx of artists who aren't afraid to throw off the iron shackles of 'traditional art' and champion self-expression. They're rule breakers, not intimidated by the giants of the past. They're revolutionaries, constantly looking forward, never back. Only by pushing the boundaries of modern art are we going to see any progression in the medium. When art conforms, it stagnates, and these new experimenters understand that.

Compare how the writers convey their different attitudes towards art.

In your answer, you should:

* compare their different attitudes
* compare the methods they use to convey their attitudes
* support your ideas with quotations from both texts.

Q2   Read the following extract from a novel.

Annie went from room to room, shaking her head at the disarray. The house looked as if it had been burgled. In the living room, a bookcase had been thrown onto the floor, and paperbacks were scattered chaotically across the carpet. In the kitchen, the floor was a treacherous landscape of smashed crockery and broken glass.

Annie frowned and headed cautiously up the stairs, following the crashing sounds into the master bedroom. Lucas stood with his back to her. His hair was a frantic mess, his movements manic as he pulled every item of clothing out of his wardrobe and launched them behind him. He was muttering frenetically under his breath.

"Lucas," Annie said calmly. He span around, surprised by her presence. His wide eyes were wild, beads of sweat had appeared on his forehead and his cheeks were red.

"I can't find it," he said. "I've looked everywhere. It's lost. They'll kill me."

"Don't be ridiculous. They're not going to kick you out just because you've lost your key to the clubhouse," said Annie, her arms folded.

"What would you know about it?" said Lucas, his eyes flashing in annoyance. "They're obsessed with not letting any outsiders in. If they find out I've lost it... I'm doomed. Finished. Condemned."

A student, having read this extract said "The writer is successful in bringing Annie and Lucas alive for the reader. You feel as if you can identify with both characters."

To what extent do you agree?

In your response, you could:

* write about your own impressions of Annie and Lucas
* evaluate how the writer has created these impressions
* support your opinions with quotations from the text.

Revision Summary

It's time for another Revision Summary. If you know your stuff, it will be very quick to complete.

- Try these questions and <u>tick off each one</u> when you <u>get it right</u>.
- When you've done <u>all the questions</u> under a heading and are <u>completely happy</u> with it, tick it off.

Thinking About the Information, Ideas, Audience and Purpose (p.20-25) ☑

1) What is the difference between explicit and implicit information?
2) Write down three examples of words or phrases you could use to show that you're making a comparison in an exam answer.
3) Name three things you can look at to work out who a text's audience is.
4) What audience is this Complete Revision and Practice book aimed at?
5) List four common purposes of a piece of writing.

Different Types of Text (p.26-29) ☑

6) Give two examples of an informative text.
7) Can an informative text be biased? How?
8) Which of these techniques might a writer use to make a text entertaining?
   a) an engaging opening
   b) descriptive language
   c) lots of facts
   d) different sentence lengths
9) Write down three rhetorical techniques that might be used to argue or persuade.
10) How is the tone of writing that advises usually different from writing that argues or persuades?
11) True or false? *Texts that advise are always written in a formal register.*

The Writer's Viewpoint in Different Texts (p.33-37) ☑

12) What is the difference between the writer's viewpoint and the writer's purpose?
13) Give three things you could look at in a text to work out what the writer's viewpoint is.
14) What is the main purpose of literary fiction?
15) What is literary non-fiction?
16) Write down whether the following texts are literary fiction or literary non-fiction.
   a) the autobiography of a retired professional cricketer
   b) a short story about a trip to the seaside
   c) a piece of travel writing about Rome
   d) an opinion piece in a broadsheet newspaper
17) Is the register of a 19th-century text likely to be formal or informal?
18) Write down whether the following statements are true or false.
   a) Christianity had a big influence on people's lives in the 19th century.
   b) After they got married, most 19th-century women were expected to go out to work.
   c) Poor children were often sent away to boarding schools in the 19th century.
   d) Early 19th-century society was divided into the upper classes and working classes.
   e) Women didn't have as many rights as men in the 19th century.

Tone

Tone can sometimes be difficult to describe, but it comes through in the text's language.

Tone is the General Feeling created by the text

1) A writer's tone is the <u>feeling</u> the words are written with, which creates a particular <u>mood</u> and shows what the writer's <u>attitude</u> is. For example, the tone of a text might be:

- happy or sad
- serious or funny
- sombre or light-hearted
- emotional and passionate or cool and logical

2) The main way to identify a text's tone is by looking at the <u>language</u>. For example, if a writer has used <u>informal</u> language, the tone might be quite <u>personal</u> or <u>familiar</u>, but <u>formal</u> language would suggest a more <u>serious</u> or <u>distant</u> tone.

Think of a writer's tone as being like someone's tone of voice when they're talking.

3) <u>Punctuation</u> can also give you a clue about tone. For example, if there are lots of exclamation marks, that might suggest that the tone is very <u>emotional</u> or <u>passionate</u>.

4) Tone can reflect the <u>purpose</u> of a text (e.g. informative texts usually have a serious tone) or the <u>audience</u> (e.g. a playful tone might suggest a younger audience).

Look closely at Language to Work Out a text's Tone

PAPER 1

| 0 | 4 | A student, having read this section of the text, said: "It seems like the character is in a scary place. Reading the text made me feel uneasy." To what extent do you agree? |

The adjectives used help to create the foreboding tone.

Phillipa stood on the cold, dark street, peering up at the abandoned hotel. Large wooden boards stood impassively across most of the window frames, sentries to the stillness and silence within, guarding the eerie presence of the dilapidated building.

Despite her misgivings, she pushed gently on the front door, and it crept open with an arthritic creak. As she tiptoed over the threshold, small clouds of dust wheezed out of the carpet where she put her feet.

The sinister tone is gripping for the reader, which keeps the text entertaining.

Don't forget to mention how much you agree or disagree with the statement.

Remember to use technical terms wherever possible.

I **strongly agree** with the student's statement. The heavily foreboding tone, created by **adjectives** such as "abandoned", "eerie" and "dilapidated", and **reinforced** by the **personification** of the "wooden boards" as silent "sentries", gives the passage a tense atmosphere. The **reader shares** in the fear and anxiety of the character, as you feel that something shocking could happen at any moment. The imagery of something cold and emotionless watching over the character **makes you feel** her vulnerability and fear for what might happen next.

Mention the combined effect of different features of the text.

You need to make sure you refer back to the statement for questions like this.

Some tones are easier to spot than others...

Sometimes, the tone of a text will be obvious. But watch out for texts that are written with an ironic or sarcastic tone — the words might not mean exactly what they seem to at first (take a look at pages 52-53).

Style and Register

Every text you come across will be written in a particular style, using a particular register...

Style is How the text is Written

1) A text's style is the overall way in which it's written, which includes language choices, sentence forms and structure.

2) There are lots of different styles you might encounter. E.g. cinematic, where the text is written as if the reader is watching a film, or journalistic which is a balanced way of writing reported news.

3) Register is the specific language (choice of words) used to match the writing to the social situation that it's for. Different situations require different registers, for example:

> If you wrote a letter to your local MP to ask them to stop the closure of a local leisure centre, you might use a formal register (e.g. 'the closure will have a detrimental effect'). This is because the audience is an authority figure that you don't know.

> If you wrote a letter to your friend to tell them about the leisure centre closure, you might use an informal register (e.g. 'it'll be rubbish when it shuts'). This is because the audience is someone you're familiar and friendly with.

Register can be thought of as a part of style.

4) Look out for how writers adapt their style and register to suit the purpose and the audience they are writing for.

Write about Style and Register when Analysing Language

PAPER 2

| 0 | 3 | How does the writer use language here to appeal to a younger audience? |

Uses non-Standard English e.g. 'ain't.

> I mean, come on, snowboarding is by far the coolest, craziest sport out there. Who's gonna argue with that? Here at SportFreakz magazine, we know what it's all about when it comes to extreme sports, and we can tell you that there ain't nothing else that gets the adrenaline pumping more than jumping on a board and flying down some snow-covered slopes.
> Ski season's upon us, guys. So book a flight, grab your board and get out to the Alps before all that snow melts! You just know you wanna!

The text is full of colloquial language, e.g. 'come on'.

The use of the second person makes it seem more personal.

Give examples to show what makes the register informal and youthful.

The text uses an informal, youthful register, with non-Standard English such as **"ain't nothing else"**, and colloquial language like **"come on"**, **"gonna"** and **"wanna"**. These contribute to the text's conversational style, which is likely to appeal to a younger audience because **it mirrors the way they might actually speak**. I think this would make younger people more likely to identify with the writer, and **therefore trust their opinion and be more interested in what they have to say**.

Discuss how the style creates the desired effect on the reader.

Develop your point with the overall effect of the text.

You need to comment on how style and register are created...

Style has to do with language and vocabulary, structure, tone... so think about how the style is built up from all these different features. You also need to think about the text's register and how it's been achieved.

Words and Phrases

Writers choose their words very carefully to produce a desired effect, and you need to comment on this.

Writers use a range of Word Types

It's important to be able to identify the types of words that a writer is using.
Have a look at the definitions below to remind you:

Nouns are naming words — they might refer to a person, place, thing or idea, e.g. sister, pen, art.

A pronoun is a word that replaces a noun, e.g. he, she, it, them.

Possessive pronouns are pronouns that show ownership, e.g. his, hers, ours, theirs.

Verbs are action words, e.g. think, run, swim, shout.

Adjectives describe a noun or pronoun, e.g. happy, clever, interesting.

Adverbs give extra information about verbs, e.g. quickly, loudly, accidentally.

Words and Phrases can be used to achieve Different Effects

1) For the reading questions (1-4 on both papers), you need to pay close attention to the reasons why a writer has used particular words or phrases.

Analysing the connotations of words is a way of 'reading with insight'. There's more on this on pages 14-15.

2) Words can have subtle implications beyond their obvious meaning — these are called 'connotations'. For example:

Pedro *shut* the door.

Pedro *slammed* the door.

⟶ When the verb 'shut' is used, it doesn't imply anything about Pedro's emotions. The verb 'slammed' has a similar meaning to 'shut', but it gives the impression that Pedro is angry or tense.

I *sniggered* when I saw Peter's costume.

I *chuckled* when I saw Peter's costume.

⟶ The verbs 'sniggered' and 'chuckled' both mean the writer laughed, but 'sniggered' has a slightly nastier connotation — as if the writer is making fun of Peter.

3) Words are often chosen to achieve particular effects. For example:

my dear reader

your beloved pet

⟶ Phrases that use the possessive determiners 'my', 'your' and 'our' help to establish familiarity between the writer and the reader.

Determiners are words that help to identify nouns — in this case, they show who the noun belongs to.

a *fundamentally* flawed proposition

a *totally* unbelievable situation

⟶ Some phrases use intensifiers to make the text seem more emotive and powerful. Intensifiers are adverbs like 'very', 'really' or 'extremely' that are used alongside strong adjectives to provide emphasis.

Words and Phrases

Words **Work Together** to create **Cumulative Effects**

1) Writers can use the words from a specific semantic field (the words associated with a particular theme or topic) to convey an idea to the reader. For example:

> *Dessert was simply divine; a cloud-like puff of pastry that was lighter than an angel's wing.* ⟶ Here, the semantic field of heaven is used to make something sound appealing.

2) Keep an eye out for situations where particular types of words are repeated, e.g. sentences with lots of adjectives or paragraphs with lots of verbs.

3) You could comment on the cumulative effect of particular types of words — show you've thought about how the words in the text work together to create tone or affect the reader in some way, e.g.

> *Adjectives like 'electrifying', 'thrilling', 'tense' and 'intriguing' create a cumulative effect of excitement.*

> *The adverbs 'jovially', 'readily' and 'pleasantly' combine to create an impression of enjoyment.*

Try to pick out **Significant Words** and **Phrases**

PAPER 2

| 0 | 3 | How does the writer use language here to influence the reader? |

Adjectives like 'magical', 'beautiful', 'balmy', 'glistening' and 'sumptuous' have an alluring cumulative effect — they create a calming atmosphere.

Watch out for repeated grammatical constructions — they give the text emphasis.

Phrases that use possessive determiners establish familiarity with the reader and make the text more persuasive.

The list of three verbs — 'relax', 'recline' and 'indulge' — gives the text a convincing tone and makes the offer sound inviting.

Imperatives like 'sit back' and 'let us' give the text an authoritative tone, whilst the words 'perhaps' and 'maybe' give the impression that the reader has a choice.

A PICTURE-PERFECT PICNIC

Bijoux Birthdays invite you to celebrate **your special day** in style. Join us for a **magical** evening of entertainment on the **beautiful** banks of the River Fairer. Let us help you to **relax** in the **balmy** atmosphere of a warm summer's evening, **recline** next to the **glistening** waters and **indulge** in the most **sumptuous** of picnics. **We can** tailor your evening to suit you. **We can** provide a refreshing feast for your senses. **We can** transport you to another place and time. Just **sit back** and **let us** do all the work. All you need to do is relax.

We have a large selection of menus for you to choose from, as well as a whole host of different entertainment acts — **maybe** you'd like a string quartet, or **perhaps** you'd be more interested in a circus act? Whatever your tastes, rest assured that we will be able to accommodate you.

If you're planning a celebration, Bijoux Birthdays really is the only choice.

Comments like "this is an adjective" aren't quite good enough...

The technical grammar of words and phrases is important, but don't just point it out — you need to analyse its effects. Think about why certain words and phrases have been used and what impression they create.

Warm-Up Questions

Before you answer the exam-style questions on the right, give these ones a go as a handy warm-up.

Warm-Up Questions

1) Is the tone of each of the following sentences sentimental, detached or upbeat?
   a) Investigators have recently confirmed that DNA found at the scene of the burglary matches that of suspect Fergus Maybach.
   b) I had a riot helping out at the birthday party — who would've guessed that kids were the perfect audience for my magic tricks?
   c) As he stared across the bay where they had first met, he remembered vividly the tinkle of her laughter and the floral scent of her hair.

2) Which of the sentences in question 1 is written in a journalistic style?

3) What is the tone of the following text? Explain your answer.

   > At this point I was starting to get a tad — how shall I put it? — cheesed off. It's one thing being patient, accepting the fact that things don't always go to plan and that now and then delays just happen. It's quite another to be told, after paying good money for a ticket to Town A, that for no good reason you're taking a little detour through Village B, River C and Swamp D. I was finding it more and more difficult to follow what I had figured was the local way of dealing with difficulties — smiling and pretending to find the grim industrial scenery interesting. It wasn't.

4) Rewrite each of the following sentences so that they are in a formal register.
   a) Sorry, we don't take credit cards!
   b) Check you've got the proper kit to hand before you go any further.

5) Write down the noun, verb and adverb in this sentence: "Bella approached us excitedly."

6) Explain the different connotations of the underlined words in the sentences below.
   "Just go," she <u>whispered</u>.
   "Just go," she <u>spat</u>.

7) a) Is the semantic field of the passage below i) Shakespeare, ii) money or iii) shellfish?
   b) What impression does this create of the narrator?

   > I wasn't interested in seeing my sister's school Shakespeare play, but I couldn't afford to miss being at the theatre that night. The owner of DigTech was going to be there watching his daughter, and I was desperate to sell him my latest design idea. I decided to buy myself some extra time by locking him inside the gents toilets with me during the interval. A bit drastic, perhaps, but you have to cash in on this sort of opportunity.

8) What is the cumulative effect of the verbs in this sentence?
   The wind barged across the barren, open moorland and threw itself against the stoic stone walls of the cottage, wrenching the window shutters from their frames.

Exam-Style Questions

Here are a couple of exam-style questions for you to have a go at. Keep in mind the theory you've just been reading about in this section — the writer's use of tone, style, register, and words and phrases.

Q1 Read the following extract from an adventure holiday brochure.

> If you're up to your neck in revision, the promise of a long summer holiday might be the only thing keeping you going. For most students, the dream will be of lazy days spent with mates, maybe playing video games, or getting a bit of a tan down the park. There's nothing wrong with wanting a break. You've earned it. But here at Adventure Action, we can give you the chance to do something unforgettable with your summer.
>
> If you're aged 15 to 18, you could spend four weeks on one of our incredible adventure and conservation programmes at breathtaking locations around the world. You could trek through dense rainforest in Peru, to help build primary schools in isolated villages. You could take a flight over ancient glaciers to volunteer at a remote bear sanctuary in Alaska. Or you could earn a scuba-diving certificate whilst working in a marine biology lab in The Bahamas. Our programmes are tailored to give you a fantastic experience, where you can bag loads of new skills and be a part of something important.
>
> **Adventure beyond the usual this summer. Apply to Adventure Action today.**

How does the writer use language to appeal to the reader?

Q2 Read the following extract from a piece of fiction.

> She raised an eyebrow at him icily. Her mouth was a stern, straight line. It did not twitch.
> "Please," he pleaded, "it was a mistake. It won't happen again."
> Her silence was stone cold. He began to wring his hands fretfully. He could feel the sweat prickling like needles on the back of his neck. The seconds crawled by excruciatingly as he waited for her to say something, anything. He briefly considered speaking, but was too fearful of aggravating her further.
> "Evidently," she said at last, "you can no longer be trusted." The only emotion in her voice was disdain.
> His breath caught painfully in his chest; he knew the worst was coming.
> "I have no use for people I cannot trust," she continued. "You are dismissed. Leave now. Resign your post. Never let me see your face again. Understood?"
> Trembling, he managed a clumsy nod.
> "Good. Now get out."
> He turned and, dragging his feet like a condemned man, left the room.

How does the writer use language to present the two characters?

You could include the writer's choice of:

- words and phrases
- language features and techniques
- sentence forms.

Metaphors and Similes

Metaphors and similes are both types of imagery — writers use them to help readers imagine things vividly.

Metaphors and Similes are Comparisons

1) Metaphors and similes describe one thing by <u>comparing</u> it to something else.

> <u>Metaphors</u> describe something by saying that it <u>is</u> something else.   →   *His gaze <u>was</u> a laser beam, shooting straight through me.*

> <u>Similes</u> describe something by saying that it's <u>like</u> something else. They usually use the words <u>as</u> or <u>like</u>.   →   *Walking through the bog was <u>like</u> wading through treacle.*

2) They help writers to make their <u>descriptions</u> more creative and interesting.

3) Metaphors usually create a <u>more powerful image</u> than similes, because they describe something as if it <u>actually were</u> something else.

4) Metaphors and similes are most commonly used in <u>literature</u> and <u>literary non-fiction</u>.

See pages 34-35 for more on literature and literary non-fiction.

You should Comment on the Effect of Metaphors and Similes

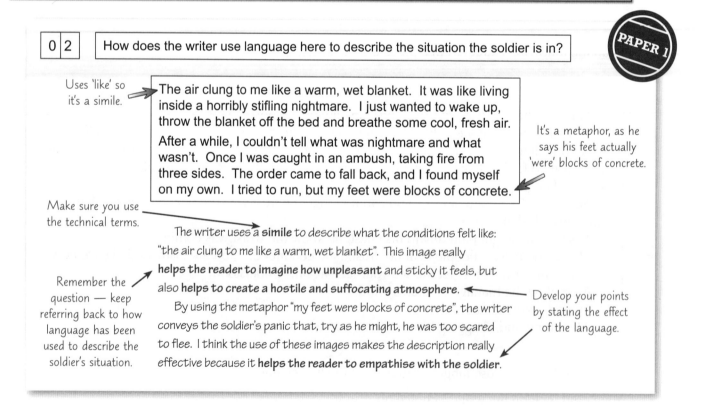

| 0 | 2 | | How does the writer use language here to describe the situation the soldier is in? |

PAPER 1

Uses 'like' so it's a simile.

> The air clung to me like a warm, wet blanket. It was like living inside a horribly stifling nightmare. I just wanted to wake up, throw the blanket off the bed and breathe some cool, fresh air.
>
> After a while, I couldn't tell what was nightmare and what wasn't. Once I was caught in an ambush, taking fire from three sides. The order came to fall back, and I found myself on my own. I tried to run, but my feet were blocks of concrete.

It's a metaphor, as he says his feet actually 'were' blocks of concrete.

Make sure you use the technical terms.

The writer uses a **simile** to describe what the conditions felt like: "the air clung to me like a warm, wet blanket". This image really **helps the reader to imagine how unpleasant** and sticky it feels, but also **helps to create a hostile and suffocating atmosphere.**

Remember the question — keep referring back to how language has been used to describe the soldier's situation.

By using the metaphor "my feet were blocks of concrete", the writer conveys the soldier's panic that, try as he might, he was too scared to flee. I think the use of these images makes the description really effective because it **helps the reader to empathise with the soldier.**

Develop your points by stating the effect of the language.

These are two language features that are definitely worth learning...

Picking out metaphors and similes will help you to closely analyse the effect of language used in the exam texts. You might need to write about them on paper 1, questions 2 and 4, and paper 2, questions 3 and 4.

Analogy

Writers often use analogies when they're writing to argue or persuade.

Analogies are **Really Fancy Comparisons**

Analogies are like extended similes (see p.48) — they also often use the word 'like'.

1) An analogy <u>compares</u> one idea to another to make it easier to <u>understand</u>.

2) Analogies provide <u>powerful</u> and <u>memorable</u> images. They can be more <u>familiar</u> or more <u>shocking</u> than the original idea, which makes it easier for the reader to <u>grasp the point</u>. For example:

> *Deforestation is happening at an incredible speed. An area of rainforest equal to twenty football pitches is lost every minute.* ⟹ By <u>comparing</u> the area to football pitches, the writer makes it easier to <u>visualise</u> the scale of the problem.

> *Hoping your exams will go OK without opening your books is like hoping to win the lottery without buying a ticket.* ⟹ By <u>comparing</u> the chances of success to an impossible situation, the writer <u>emphasises</u> how unlikely it is.

3) Analogies are common in <u>non-fiction</u> texts that are trying to <u>argue</u> a point or <u>persuade</u>, as they can help to get the writer's viewpoint across <u>clearly</u> and <u>forcefully</u>.

Think about **Why** the writer has used an **Analogy**

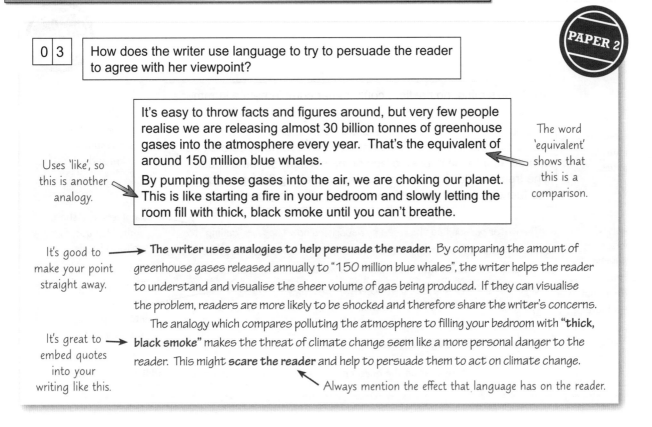

PAPER 2

| 0 | 3 | How does the writer use language to try to persuade the reader to agree with her viewpoint? |

It's easy to throw facts and figures around, but very few people realise we are releasing almost 30 billion tonnes of greenhouse gases into the atmosphere every year. That's the equivalent of around 150 million blue whales.

By pumping these gases into the air, we are choking our planet. This is like starting a fire in your bedroom and slowly letting the room fill with thick, black smoke until you can't breathe.

Uses 'like', so this is another analogy.

The word 'equivalent' shows that this is a comparison.

It's good to make your point straight away. → **The writer uses analogies to help persuade the reader.** By comparing the amount of greenhouse gases released annually to "150 million blue whales", the writer helps the reader to understand and visualise the sheer volume of gas being produced. If they can visualise the problem, readers are more likely to be shocked and therefore share the writer's concerns.

The analogy which compares polluting the atmosphere to filling your bedroom with **thick,** *It's great to* → **black smoke"** makes the threat of climate change seem like a more personal danger to the *embed quotes* reader. This might **scare the reader** and help to persuade them to act on climate change. *into your writing like this.* *Always mention the effect that language has on the reader.*

Don't worry if you haven't heard of analogies before...

Writers use analogies to make their points clearer and easier to understand. They can also make a piece of writing more interesting — think about how you could use them in the writing section of your exams.

Personification

Personification is another technique that you could comment on in questions about language.

Personification is describing a Thing as a Person

1) Personification describes something as if it's a <u>person</u>. This could be in the way something <u>looks</u>, <u>moves</u>, <u>sounds</u> or some other aspect of it. For example:

Describing an object as if it were alive	**Describing an abstract idea as if it were alive**	**Describing an animal as if it were a person**
The desk groaned under the weight of the books.	*Fear stalked the children with every step they took.*	*The cunning fox smiled with a self-satisfied grin.*

2) Personification makes a description <u>more vivid</u> (so it '<u>comes to life</u>' for the reader).

3) It can also help to give a sense of the <u>viewpoint</u> or <u>attitude</u> of the <u>writer</u> or <u>character</u>:

> *Military helicopters prowled the city, their menacing mechanical voices threatening to stamp out the smallest sign of activity.* ⟹ This shows that the writer feels that the helicopters are an <u>intimidating</u> presence.

Try to think of other ways you could use personification in your own writing.

Think about How personification Improves a Description

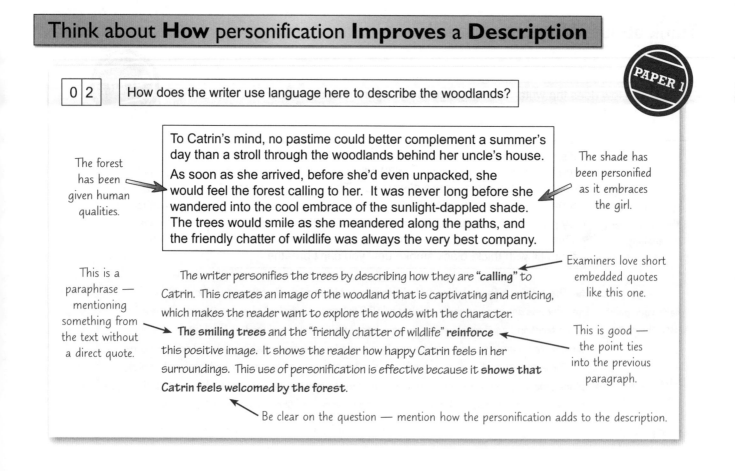

PAPER 1

0 2   How does the writer use language here to describe the woodlands?

The forest has been given human qualities.

> To Catrin's mind, no pastime could better complement a summer's day than a stroll through the woodlands behind her uncle's house. As soon as she arrived, before she'd even unpacked, she would feel the forest calling to her. It was never long before she wandered into the cool embrace of the sunlight-dappled shade. The trees would smile as she meandered along the paths, and the friendly chatter of wildlife was always the very best company.

The shade has been personified as it embraces the girl.

This is a paraphrase — mentioning something from the text without a direct quote.

The writer personifies the trees by describing how they are **"calling"** to Catrin. This creates an image of the woodland that is captivating and enticing, which makes the reader want to explore the woods with the character. **The smiling trees** and the "friendly chatter of wildlife" **reinforce** this positive image. It shows the reader how happy Catrin feels in her surroundings. This use of personification is effective because it **shows that Catrin feels welcomed by the forest**.

Examiners love short embedded quotes like this one.

This is good — the point ties into the previous paragraph.

Be clear on the question — mention how the personification adds to the description.

Remember, it's not just objects that can be personified...

Personification is not always easy to spot, especially when an abstract idea is personified. When you're writing about personification, concentrate on why the writer's used it and what effect it has on the reader.

Alliteration and Onomatopoeia

As well as learning about what alliteration and onomatopoeia are, make sure you can spell them.

Alliteration and Onomatopoeia are about how words Sound

1) Alliteration and onomatopoeia use the <u>sounds</u> of words to create an <u>effect</u>:

> <u>Alliteration</u> is when words that are close together begin with the <u>same sound</u>.
>
> *PM's panic!*   *Close call for kids*

> <u>Onomatopoeic</u> words <u>sound like</u> the noises they describe.
>
> *thud   squish   smash   crackle   hiss*

2) <u>Alliteration</u> helps a writer to grab a reader's <u>attention</u>.

3) It's often used for <u>emphasis</u> and to make key points more <u>memorable</u>.

4) <u>Onomatopoeia</u> makes descriptions more <u>powerful</u> — it appeals to the reader's sense of <u>hearing</u>, which helps them <u>imagine</u> what the writer is describing.

Alliteration and onomatopoeia Keep Readers Interested

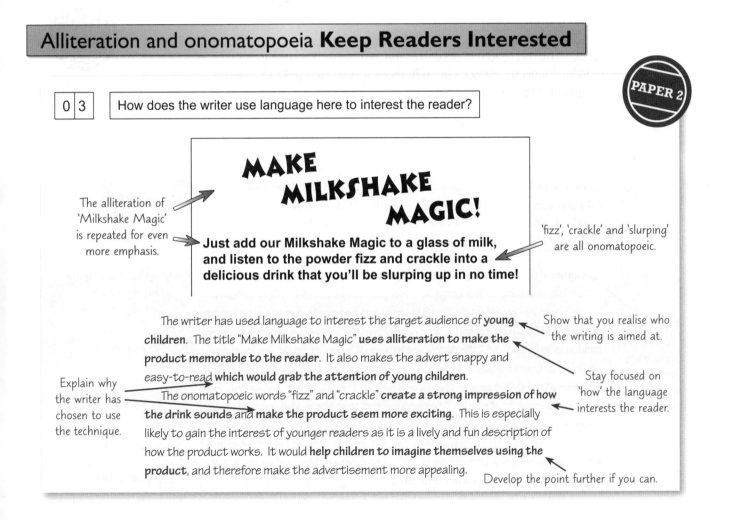

| 0 | 3 | How does the writer use language here to interest the reader? |

PAPER 2

The alliteration of 'Milkshake Magic' is repeated for even more emphasis.

MAKE MILKSHAKE MAGIC!

Just add our Milkshake Magic to a glass of milk, and listen to the powder fizz and crackle into a delicious drink that you'll be slurping up in no time!

'fizz', 'crackle' and 'slurping' are all onomatopoeic.

The writer has used language to interest the target audience of **young children**. The title "Make Milkshake Magic" **uses alliteration to make the product memorable to the reader**. It also makes the advert snappy and easy-to-read **which would grab the attention of young children**. The onomatopoeic words "fizz" and "crackle" **create a strong impression of how the drink sounds and make the product seem more exciting**. This is especially likely to gain the interest of younger readers as it is a lively and fun description of how the product works. It would **help children to imagine themselves using the product**, and therefore make the advertisement more appealing.

Explain why the writer has chosen to use the technique.

Show that you realise who the writing is aimed at.

Stay focused on 'how' the language interests the reader.

Develop the point further if you can.

Think about using these techniques in your own writing...

You need to be able to write about the effects of alliteration and onomatopoeia in the reading sections of both papers, but you could also consider using them in the fiction and non-fiction writing sections.

Irony

Irony can be important for the tone of a piece of writing, so make sure you're comfortable commenting on it.

Irony is **Saying** the **Opposite** of what you **Mean**

1) Irony is when the <u>literal meaning</u> of a piece of writing is the exact <u>opposite</u> of its <u>intended meaning</u>.

2) The reader can tell the writer is being ironic from the <u>context</u> of the writing.

3) Writers often use irony to express their viewpoint, but it helps to make what they're saying more <u>humorous</u> or <u>light-hearted</u>.

> *It was pouring down with rain — perfect weather for a barbecue.* ⟶ The <u>context</u> (the rainy weather) shows that the writer actually means that it was <u>terrible</u> weather for a barbecue.

Irony can sometimes be a **Little Tricky** to **Spot**

PAPER 1

| 0 | 4 | A student, having read this section of the text, said: "The writer makes the character's feelings really clear. It feels as if you really get to know her". To what extent do you agree? |

Clara sat on her lounger at the edge of the pool, thinking of all the poor souls still trapped in the office. She'd been asked to travel to Spain for work. Stay hunched over her cramped, stuffy desk in London or work in this paradise? A very difficult decision indeed.

As the sun rose higher in the sky and the temperature crept up, she thought of dreary, cloudy London. "It's a tough job," she thought to herself, "but somebody's got to do it."

You can tell she is being ironic because of the context — she describes it as a 'paradise' so it can't have been a 'difficult decision'.

I agree with the first part of this statement, though Clara's feelings are potentially open to misinterpretation. Her comments about a "difficult decision" and a "tough job" are negative if read literally, **but the context makes it clear that they should be taken ironically**. She clearly prefers being in Spain. Her office in London is "cramped", and the people are "trapped", whereas Spain is a "paradise". The irony emphasises just how happy she is by highlighting this contrast.

I also strongly agree with the second part of the student's statement. Her ironic tone shows that she isn't too serious, but that she is also perhaps quite unsympathetic. The contrast between her situation and that of the "poor souls" in the London office shows that whilst she is "thinking of all" of them, she is most interested in how pleasant her situation is. **As a reader, this makes me unsure as to whether I like her character or not.**

Don't forget to mention how much you agree or disagree with the statement.

Make sure you clearly explain why the language is ironic.

A further personal response is a good way to develop your answer.

To work out if something is ironic, look at the context...

It might seem confusing that exactly the same words can mean completely opposite things, but the context usually makes it fairly clear when a writer is trying to be ironic — otherwise it wouldn't be very effective.

Sarcasm

There is a subtle difference between sarcasm and irony — have a look at this page.

Sarcasm is **Nastier** than **Irony**

1) <u>Sarcasm</u> is language that has a <u>mocking</u> or <u>scornful</u> tone. It's often intended to <u>insult someone</u> or <u>make fun</u> of them, or to show that the writer is <u>angry</u> or <u>annoyed</u> about something.

2) Sarcastic writing usually uses <u>irony</u> — but the tone is more <u>aggressive</u> and <u>unpleasant</u>.

> *The food took 90 minutes to arrive, which was just brilliant. I can think of no better way to spend a Saturday evening than waiting around for a plate of mediocre mush.*

The writer's used <u>irony</u> and a <u>sarcastic</u> tone to show his <u>frustration</u> and <u>anger</u> — it's meant to <u>insult</u> the restaurant that kept him waiting.

3) <u>Satire</u> is a kind of writing that uses sarcasm to <u>make fun</u> of a particular person or thing — it's often used in <u>journalism</u> and <u>reviews</u>.

Explain How you can tell a comment is **Sarcastic**

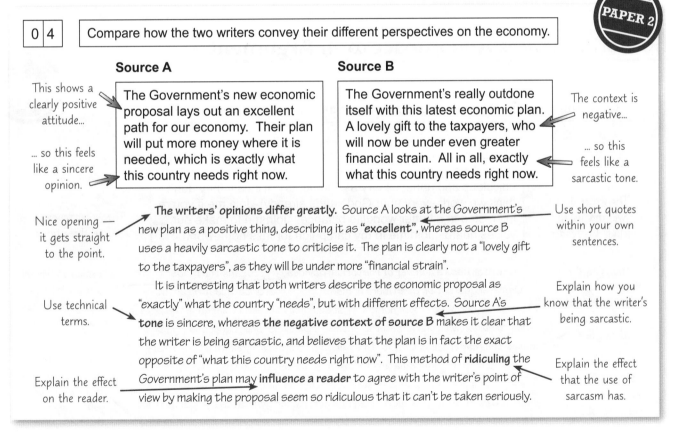

04 | Compare how the two writers convey their different perspectives on the economy.

PAPER 2

Source A

This shows a clearly positive attitude...

The Government's new economic proposal lays out an excellent path for our economy. Their plan will put more money where it is needed, which is exactly what this country needs right now.

... so this feels like a sincere opinion.

Source B

The Government's really outdone itself with this latest economic plan. A lovely gift to the taxpayers, who will now be under even greater financial strain. All in all, exactly what this country needs right now.

The context is negative...

... so this feels like a sarcastic tone.

Nice opening — it gets straight to the point.

The writers' opinions differ greatly. Source A looks at the Government's new plan as a positive thing, describing it as **"excellent"**, whereas source B uses a heavily sarcastic tone to criticise it. The plan is clearly not a "lovely gift to the taxpayers", as they will be under more "financial strain".

Use short quotes within your own sentences.

Use technical terms.

It is interesting that both writers describe the economic proposal as "exactly" what the country "needs", but with different effects. Source A's **tone** is sincere, whereas **the negative context of source B** makes it clear that the writer is being sarcastic, and believes that the plan is in fact the exact opposite of "what this country needs right now". This method of **ridiculing** the

Explain how you know that the writer's being sarcastic.

Explain the effect on the reader.

Government's plan may **influence a reader** to agree with the writer's point of view by making the proposal seem so ridiculous that it can't be taken seriously.

Explain the effect that the use of sarcasm has.

Sarcasm is often used to ridicule someone or something...

Sarcasm can be quite an unpleasant technique to use, but it's also a very effective one. Remember to explain <u>how</u> you know that a piece of writing is sarcastic, and also explain the effect of the sarcasm.

Rhetoric

Rhetorical techniques make language more persuasive. Lots of speeches use rhetoric, for example (see p.86).

There are **Lots** of **Rhetorical Techniques**

Think about how other techniques (e.g. alliteration, sarcasm) could be used as rhetorical devices.

1) <u>Rhetorical questions</u> require no answer — they make readers <u>engage</u> with the text and realise the answer <u>for themselves</u>. This makes the reader feel like they're making up their <u>own mind</u>, when actually the writer is trying to make them think a certain way.

> *Is it right that footballers are paid such vast sums of money?*

2) Writers often use a <u>list of three</u> words or phrases to <u>emphasise</u> the point they're making. They often repeat three adjectives.

> *The cross-country run is <u>painful</u>, <u>pointless</u> and pure <u>evil</u>.*

3) <u>Hyperbole</u> is intentional exaggeration. It's used to make a point very <u>powerfully</u>.

> *We had to wait <u>forever</u> for the food to arrive.*

4) <u>Antithesis</u> is a technique where <u>opposing</u> words or ideas are presented <u>together</u> to show a <u>contrast</u>.

> *Just a <u>small</u> donation from you could have <u>huge</u> consequences for others.*

5) <u>Parenthesis</u> is when an <u>extra</u> clause or phrase is inserted into a complete sentence. Parenthesis can be used in many ways, such as to add <u>extra</u> <u>information</u> or to <u>directly address</u> the reader.

> *This issue, <u>as I'm sure you all agree</u>, is of the highest importance.*

Rhetorical devices **Add Impact** to an **Argument**

PAPER 2

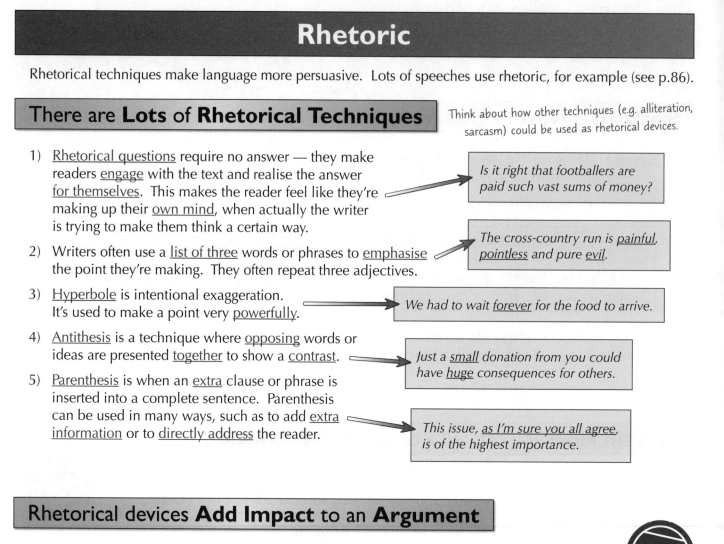

| 0 | 3 | How does the writer use language to argue their point about homework? |

Here's some hyperbole.

The writer uses 'we' and 'us' to include the reader.

This plan to give students across the country more homework is shocking. Can it really be fair to set us even more ridiculous and unnecessary assignments? It's as if they don't think we work every hour God sends already! Join me if you're interested in a better work/life balance. Join me to make our voices heard. Join me in my campaign for less homework!

This is a rhetorical question.

The writer repeats 'join me' three times.

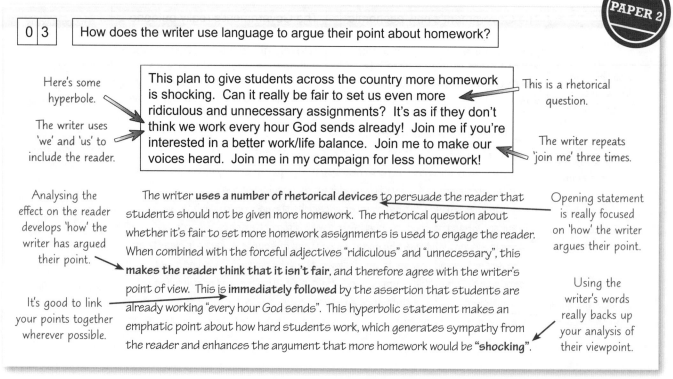

Analysing the effect on the reader develops 'how' the writer has argued their point.

It's good to link your points together wherever possible.

The writer **uses a number of rhetorical devices to persuade the reader that** students should not be given more homework. The rhetorical question about whether it's fair to set more homework assignments is used to engage the reader. When combined with the forceful adjectives "ridiculous" and "unnecessary", this **makes the reader think that it isn't fair**, and therefore agree with the writer's point of view. This is **immediately followed** by the assertion that students are already working "every hour God sends". This hyperbolic statement makes an emphatic point about how hard students work, which generates sympathy from the reader and enhances the argument that more homework would be **"shocking"**.

Opening statement is really focused on 'how' the writer argues their point.

Using the writer's words really backs up your analysis of their viewpoint.

Lots of political speech writers use rhetoric...

Remember, there are lots of different types of rhetorical techniques — this page just tells you about some of the most common ones. Make sure you analyse the effect of a rhetorical technique if you spot one.

Bias

If a text is biased, it doesn't give a balanced view — the writer's opinion affects the writing.

Biased writing is Affected by the Writer's Opinions

1) Biased writers don't usually lie, but they don't give the <u>full picture</u>.

2) Sometimes the writer <u>won't mention</u> something that opposes their viewpoint, or they'll <u>exaggerate</u> something that supports it.

3) Biased writing also often uses <u>generalisations</u> — sweeping statements that aren't necessarily true.

4) Bias isn't always <u>obvious</u>, or even <u>deliberate</u>. Biased writers often <u>seem</u> to be talking in a neutral, factual way — while actually only presenting one point of view.

5) You need to be able to <u>recognise</u> bias, so that you don't mistake opinion for fact.

6) Look out for bias in non-fiction texts like <u>newspaper articles</u> and <u>reviews</u>.

Bias Weakens a writer's Argument

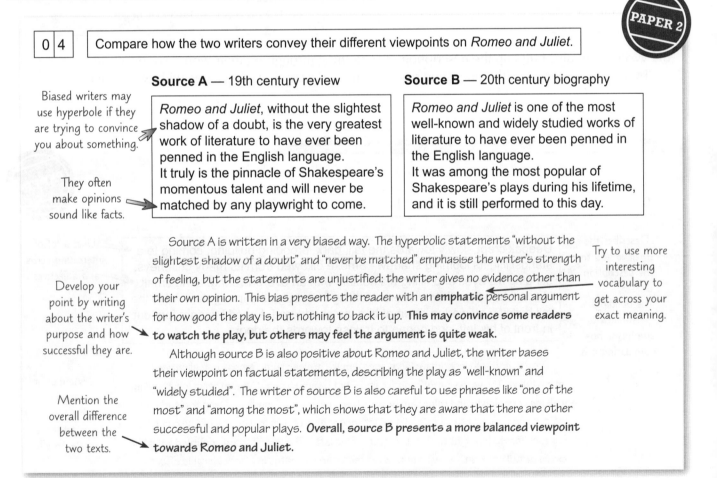

PAPER 2

| 0 | 4 | Compare how the two writers convey their different viewpoints on *Romeo and Juliet*. |

Biased writers may use hyperbole if they are trying to convince you about something.

They often make opinions sound like facts.

Source A — 19th century review

Romeo and Juliet, without the slightest shadow of a doubt, is the very greatest work of literature to have ever been penned in the English language. It truly is the pinnacle of Shakespeare's momentous talent and will never be matched by any playwright to come.

Source B — 20th century biography

Romeo and Juliet is one of the most well-known and widely studied works of literature to have ever been penned in the English language. It was among the most popular of Shakespeare's plays during his lifetime, and it is still performed to this day.

Develop your point by writing about the writer's purpose and how successful they are.

Mention the overall difference between the two texts.

Source A is written in a very biased way. The hyperbolic statements "without the slightest shadow of a doubt" and "never be matched" emphasise the writer's strength of feeling, but the statements are unjustified: the writer gives no evidence other than their own opinion. This bias presents the reader with an **emphatic** personal argument for how good the play is, but nothing to back it up. **This may convince some readers to watch the play, but others may feel the argument is quite weak.**

Although source B is also positive about Romeo and Juliet, the writer bases their viewpoint on factual statements, describing the play as "well-known" and "widely studied". The writer of source B is also careful to use phrases like "one of the most" and "among the most", which shows that they are aware that there are other successful and popular plays. **Overall, source B presents a more balanced viewpoint towards Romeo and Juliet.**

Try to use more interesting vocabulary to get across your exact meaning.

Always ask yourself whether a text is biased...

A good way to spot bias is when the writer presents their opinion as fact (by saying something confidently), but giving no evidence for it. This weakens their argument — they could be saying something ridiculous.

Descriptive Language

You'll find descriptive language in both literary fiction and literary non-fiction texts.

Descriptive Language makes text Interesting

1) Writers use descriptive <u>techniques</u> and <u>vocabulary</u> so that the reader gets a really clear <u>image</u> in their mind of what the writer's describing. It makes the text more <u>interesting</u>, <u>dramatic</u> and <u>convincing</u>.

2) <u>Descriptive techniques</u> include <u>imagery</u> such as metaphors, similes and personification (see p.48-50).

3) Writers often give <u>descriptions</u> based on their five <u>senses</u> (what they can <u>see</u>, <u>smell</u>, <u>hear</u>, <u>touch</u> or <u>taste</u>).

4) Another sign of descriptive language is when the writer uses lots of <u>adjectives</u> — describing words like 'huge' or 'fiery' that give a specific <u>impression</u> of something.

5) Writers might also use interesting <u>verbs</u>, such as 'saunter' instead of 'walk' to make their descriptions really <u>specific</u>.

The sun was setting over the sea. *The view from the beach was incredible.*	This example relies on the reader to picture <u>for themselves</u> what a nice sunset might look like.
The salty sea air whooshed around me as the dark-orange sun melted into the horizon, dyeing the cobalt sky a deep crimson.	This one uses interesting <u>adjectives</u> and <u>verbs</u> to help the reader to picture and even 'feel' what's going on.

6) Writers can also <u>build up</u> the description of something <u>throughout</u> their work. For example, by writing sentences with <u>contrasting</u> descriptions or descriptions that <u>agree</u> with each other.

Talk about the Effects of Specific Words

PAPER 1

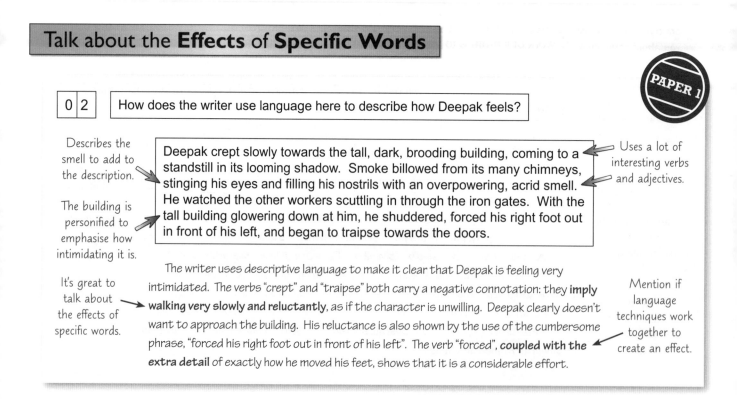

| 0 | 2 | How does the writer use language here to describe how Deepak feels? |

Describes the smell to add to the description.

The building is personified to emphasise how intimidating it is.

Deepak crept slowly towards the tall, dark, brooding building, coming to a standstill in its looming shadow. Smoke billowed from its many chimneys, stinging his eyes and filling his nostrils with an overpowering, acrid smell. He watched the other workers scuttling in through the iron gates. With the tall building glowering down at him, he shuddered, forced his right foot out in front of his left, and began to traipse towards the doors.

Uses a lot of interesting verbs and adjectives.

It's great to talk about the effects of specific words.

The writer uses descriptive language to make it clear that Deepak is feeling very intimidated. The verbs "crept" and "traipse" both carry a negative connotation: they **imply walking very slowly and reluctantly**, as if the character is unwilling. Deepak clearly doesn't want to approach the building. His reluctance is also shown by the use of the cumbersome phrase, "forced his right foot out in front of his left". The verb "forced", **coupled with the extra detail** of exactly how he moved his feet, shows that it is a considerable effort.

Mention if language techniques work together to create an effect.

You will definitely come across descriptive language in your exams...

Look out for descriptive language in both the literary fiction extract in paper 1 and the literary non-fiction in paper 2. Make sure you write about the effect it has, focusing on the specific words and phrases used.

Warm-Up Questions

Use these warm-up questions to test your knowledge of language techniques, then have a go at some of the exam-style questions on the next two pages. Ready, set, write...

Warm-Up Questions

1) What impression is created by this metaphor?
   The glassy eye of the lake watched us in silent judgement.

2) Read the texts below. How does the use of an analogy in the second text make it more effective?

   > *A running tap wastes around 6 litres of water for every minute it's left running.*

   > *A running tap wastes the equivalent of seventeen cups of tea for every minute it's left running.*

3) Write down whether each of the sentences below use personification, alliteration or onomatopoeia. Then explain the effect that the technique creates.
   a) The computer grumbled into life, before smugly informing me that it required six hours of updates.
   b) The buzz and chatter of the students ruined the tranquillity of the scene.
   c) Bag a Bargain at Brigson's — Portsmouth's Premier Pig Farm!

4) Briefly explain the difference between irony and sarcasm.

5) Is the following text sarcastic? Explain your answer using an example from the text.

   > Oh yeah, Ivan is a brilliant secretary — I especially appreciate the way he keeps forgetting to bring a pen and steals mine instead. And he's reorganised our files into a brand new system, which only he can understand — that's really made our lives easier.

6) For each sentence below, name the rhetorical technique and then explain its effect.
   a) Far from the sandwich heaven I'd been hoping for, I found myself in sandwich hell.
   b) I urge you, dear readers, to avoid this new restaurant at all costs.
   c) There's nothing worse than rain during an outdoor theatre performance.

7) Explain why the following text is biased. Use evidence from the text to support your answer.

   > By far the best hobby for young people is the card game "cribbage". All young people from the ages of eight to eighteen adore playing cribbage.

8) Write a paragraph about the effect of some of the descriptive language in the text below.

   > The air smelt of scorched grass. I could feel the blistering sun burning into my skin as I trudged slowly through the prickly, dry vegetation, my heavy load cutting cruel lines into my drooping shoulders. In the distance, the air shimmered in waves with the heat. I felt as if I were underwater, constantly being pulled back by the tidal drag of the temperature, every step an effort, every breath a trial.

Exam-Style Questions

To answer these exam-style questions, you need to draw on all of your knowledge about language techniques — have a quick glance back at pages 48-56 to refresh your memory, then get stuck into this lot.

Q1 Read the following extract from a piece of fiction.

> The landscape was dull steel. The sea was grey, the sky was grey and the mountains in the distance were grey. And we were grey too. Our meagre rations of bread and nameless slop had left us sallow-faced, with dark rings under our eyes. We huddled together nervously, like mice in a cage. A thin layer of snow carpeted the tundra already. It was only September; there would be plenty more snow to come. The wind whipped at our cheeks and we shivered.
>
> The soldiers were smoking by the hut, casting sideways glances at us once in a while, to make sure that we weren't doing anything foolish, like trying to escape. Eventually they trampled on their cigarettes and marched over to us — wolves in military uniform, coming to snarl at lambs.
>
> "There's work to do!" the officer in charge barked, clapping his gloved hands and then gesturing to the crates we'd unloaded. "Come on! Get a move on!" He fired his orders like cannon balls, and we dispersed frantically to do as he said. "If they're not all unpacked by nightfall, no one eats."

How does the writer use language to present the characters?

You could include the writer's choice of:

- words and phrases
- language features and techniques
- sentence forms.

Q2 Read the following extract from a piece of travel writing.

> The streets of Kuala Lumpur are a labyrinth of lost lanes, back-streets, dead-ends and alleys, which twist and turn and double back on themselves, constantly trying to bewilder the unaccustomed traveller. An apparently infinite series of haphazard side streets break out from the main street of the Chinatown area, like snakes winding across the desert. On every corner hang the pungent but irresistible smells of food stalls offering a cornucopia of exotic cuisines. Heavy trucks rumble past impatiently, whilst thousands of scooters whine and buzz like a swarm of bees, honking horns and hurling out exhaust fumes that stubbornly stagnate in the desperately hot air. The heat is relentless. Even standing still in the shade I can feel the sweat gathering on my forehead.
>
> In search of a bit of peace from the incessant heat and choking fumes, I make my way to the city centre park. Here, neat pathways wind their way leisurely through immaculate green lawns. On every side of the park, glimmering steel skyscrapers tower into the sky, peering down at the people walking below. It's like being surrounded by a giant metal rainforest, thronging with life.

How does the writer use language to convey their feelings about Kuala Lumpur?

Exam-Style Questions

Q3 Read the following extracts. Source A is from a letter written in the 19th century, and Source B is from a review posted on a travel website in the 21st century.

Source A

Dear Jane,

 I have arrived at my lodgings in Ware. They are satisfactory, if not impressive — the room must once have been decorated in good taste, but alas, it is the good taste of a bygone age. Nevertheless, the room is clean, tidy and of a good size. As I had expected, the mattress was not of the standard I am accustomed to (nor, for that matter, was the limited refreshment offered by the kitchens), but for a short stay, it will suffice.

Source B

The room smelt like its window hadn't been opened for about a century. The wallpaper was peeling. The carpet was a battlefield between all sorts of suspicious stains. Given the state of the rest of the room, I doubted that the 'fresh' bedding was clean, but it was the mattress that really drew my attention — it was like something from a Victorian prison cell, barely a few inches thick.

Compare how the writers convey their different attitudes to their rooms.

In your answer, you should:

- compare their different attitudes
- compare the methods they use to convey their attitudes
- support your ideas with quotations from both texts.

Q4 Read the following extract from a short story.

 "Howard, you made it!" Percy beamed, ushering me through the doors of his mansion. "Come in, come in — you don't want to miss a minute of this party; I promise you, it's my best yet!"

 He hastened me through the marble hallway towards the ballroom. I could already hear the thumping of music and the hum of voices. As the golden doors were opened, the noise hit me like a wave. The room was thronged with hundreds of guests, and they were all joking, laughing, making introductions. Their voices wove together into a single, undulating buzz of talk. Beyond their voices was the exuberant playing of the live band; drums and saxophones adding bass and melody to the already throbbing noise. There were other sounds too — the clinking of glasses, the occasional popping of champagne corks followed by cheers.

 And the colours! The men were all in tuxedos, cutting sharp lines of white and black, while the women were shimmering in silks of every colour — emerald and scarlet, gold and violet, cobalt and cerise. Lights glittered from the chandeliers, sparkling on the women's jewellery and the martini glasses and the silverware. The ballroom had become a never-ending kaleidoscope of wealth.

A student, having read this extract said "The writer of this extract uses descriptive language very successfully. The reader really feels like they're at the party with Howard."

To what extent do you agree?

In your response, you could:

- write about your own impressions of the scene
- evaluate how the writer has created these impressions
- support your opinions with quotations from the text.

Narrative Viewpoint

Literary texts will always have a narrator — a voice that is telling the story.

The **Narrative Viewpoint** is usually quite **Easy** to spot

1) A <u>first-person narrator</u> tells the story using words like 'I', 'we' and 'me'. A first-person narrator is often one of the <u>characters</u>, telling the reader <u>directly</u> about their feelings and experiences.

> *I stood on the fringes of the stage, waiting my turn, fear coursing through my veins.* → A first-person narrator establishes a <u>stronger</u>, more <u>personal</u> connection with the reader.

2) A <u>second-person narrator</u> tells the story using words like 'you'. A second-person narrator talks as if the reader ('you') <u>is</u> one of the characters.

> *You turn your head to see her walking towards you. Your heart begins to race.* → A second-person narrator makes the reader '<u>feel</u>' what the character is feeling.

3) A <u>third-person narrator</u> is not one of the characters. They tell the story using words like 'he' and 'she' to talk <u>about</u> the characters.

> *Jo's elated expression could mean only one thing: she had got a place at medical school.* → A third-person narrator has a more <u>detached</u> viewpoint.

Some third-person narrators are omniscient — they know what all the characters are thinking. Others are limited — they only know what one character is thinking.

4) When writing about a narrator, think about how <u>reliable</u> they are. You might not be able to <u>trust</u> them fully if they <u>don't know something</u>, or if they're trying to <u>affect</u> the reader in some way.

Think about how the **Narrator Presents** the **Characters**

PAPER 1

| 0 4 | A student, having read this extract, said: "Alice is clearly a very annoying character." To what extent do you agree? |

Uses 'she' and is separate to the characters, so it's a third-person narrator.

> Faiza was walking down the corridor when she noticed that Alice was walking towards her. Faiza sighed, rolled her eyes and braced herself.
> "Hi Faiza!" chirped Alice, with her typically exhausting optimism, "I hope I'll see you at the party later!"
> Faiza's face contorted into an obviously forced smile as she nodded sharply.

Think carefully about how the narrator's perspective is being used to affect the reader.

I agree with the student's evaluation. The writer has used the narrator's perspective to **present Alice as unlikeable, despite her actions**. Everything she does is positive: she is bright, friendly, optimistic and simply invites Faiza to a party. The narrator presents her optimism as "typically exhausting" though, so her actions come across to the reader as tiresome, rather than positive. **This is reinforced by the narrator's heavy focus on Faiza's expressions**, which all betray her personal dislike for Alice: she "rolled" her eyes and had a "forced smile".

Link your points together to give a really detailed analysis of what the writer has done.

Get to know these different narrative viewpoints...

It can be quite easy to forget about the narrator, because they're often not one of the characters directly involved in the story. But try to think about how they talk, and whether you can trust what they tell you.

Structure — Whole Texts

Whole text structure is all about the order that writers present events and ideas to the reader.

Structure is important for Fiction and Non-fiction

1) Structure is the way a writer organises their ideas within a text.

2) In non-fiction texts, writers will use structure to help them achieve their purpose. This might be to:

> - Build their argument to a powerful conclusion.
> - Reinforce the persuasive elements of their text through repetition.
> - Set out an informative text in a clear and balanced way.
> - Order their advice in a logical and easy-to-follow way.

3) In fiction texts, writers will structure their work in a way they think will entertain the reader. For example, story writing could have a linear or non-linear structure:

> Texts with a linear structure are arranged chronologically — events are described in the order in which they happened and the text flows naturally from beginning to middle to end.

> Texts with a non-linear structure are ordered in a way that makes the text interesting, rather than in chronological order. They might include things like flashbacks, changes in perspective or time shifts.

4) Linear texts tend to build towards some form of climax, whilst non-linear texts might begin with a dramatic moment and work backwards from there.

5) Whenever you write about structure, you need to show how the writer has used structure to produce a particular effect on the reader.

Writers use structure to Focus the Reader's Attention

1) One of the easiest ways to write about structure is to think about how the writer is directing your attention as you read. There are lots of ways a writer can do this, for example:

> - The writer might draw the reader in by describing something general, then narrow their focus down to something more specific.
> - The writer could describe things along a journey and make you feel as if you are travelling with them. This might involve moving from the outside to the inside or just from one place to another.
> - A text might start with description and then move on to dialogue. This would shift your focus from setting to characters.
> - Often, a writer will use a new paragraph to start a new topic. This could be a smooth transition or it could have a jarring effect that draws the reader's attention to a particular part of the text.
> - In non-fiction texts, the writer will usually use paragraphs to lead you from their introduction, through their main points and onto their conclusion.

2) Often, descriptive writing will show rather than tell the reader what to focus on. For example, it might move the reader's attention from one place to another, acting like a camera shot does in a film. This type of writing is often called cinematic writing.

Structure — Whole Texts

The **Narrative Viewpoint** will **Affect** the **Structure**

1) The <u>narrator</u> controls what the reader <u>sees</u> and what <u>information</u> they <u>receive</u>.

2) The narrator might <u>withhold</u> some information to create <u>tension</u>, or they could <u>skip</u> over certain parts of a story because they are <u>biased</u>.

3) Different <u>narrators</u> will have different <u>effects</u> on the <u>structure</u> of a text:

> • A <u>third-person</u> narrator (see page 60) will often have an <u>overall</u> view of the story, and so the structure might <u>skip around</u> to cover lots of <u>different</u> events.
>
> • For texts with a <u>first-person</u> narrator, the structure will probably <u>follow</u> that character's experiences quite <u>closely</u>.

4) Look out for texts that have <u>more than one</u> narrator. This might mean that the structure <u>jumps around</u> or alternates between the different <u>perspectives</u>.

5) Some texts use a <u>frame</u> narrative — this is when one story is presented <u>within</u> another. For example, the writer might use one character to <u>narrate</u> a story to <u>another</u> character. This allows the writer to move between <u>multiple settings</u> and sets of <u>characters</u>.

Explain what **Effect** the text's **Structure** has on the **Reader**

0 3

For paper 1, question 3, it will say where in a text the extract is from. Make sure you bear this in mind when writing your answer.

> You now need to think about the **whole** of the **source**.
> This text is from the opening of a novel.
> How has the writer structured the text to interest you as a reader?

Think about the overall structure of the text as you read. Try to identify any perspective shifts or other obvious structural features.

> The mountain looked a little mysterious in the half-light of the dusky evening. Its snow-capped peak stood alert, bathing in the dying embers of the setting sun. From there, my eye was drawn to the narrow path that wound its way precariously down past the dark woods and craggy outcrops of the mountain face. I traced the weaving path all the way down, until it vanished behind the spire of a magnificent church that loomed over the town nestled at the foot of the mountain.
>
> This was the town of my youth.
>
> This was the town where I had taken my first steps. This was the town where I had been to school, where I had battled through those tough transition years of teenage angst and, finally, where I had first fallen in love. It was permeated with memories of childhood games and, later in my adolescence, secret late-night trysts.
>
> I crossed the road and entered the alley that would take me deeper into the warren of streets that wound their way around the foot of the imposing church. When I finally emerged into the square, I was assaulted by a barrage of sights and smells that instantly took me all the way back to my youth.

You can write about individual sentences, but for structure questions you must explain the effect they have on the text's overall structure.

Structure — Whole Texts

Immediately, I was back under the oak tree, crouching silently next to my best friend Mirela. We were hiding from James Cotton, and it was matter of grave honour that we preserved our hiding place. Back then, a game of hide and seek was no mere playground triviality, it was a fierce battle of the sexes, a passionately fought war between two equally resolute forces.

Both Mirela and I were fascinated with James: he was old for his age, smart and funny. Obviously, at that age, this fascination manifested itself as bitter hatred. The coyness would come later, along with the feelings of claustrophobia and a yearning for the big city. Mirela hadn't felt the same longing for the metropolis as I had, but she had discovered the coyness that would replace the naive and innocent feud. She had stayed here and built a life for herself; tomorrow morning I was to attend the wedding at which she would become Mrs Cotton.

The tolling of the church bells brought me back to the present with a start. I needed to hurry if I was to get to my parents' house before dinnertime. With a sigh of nostalgia, I began the final leg of my journey back to my former home.

This text contains time shifts — it has a non-linear structure.

The text is structured to control the reader's focus, directing their attention closely to interesting features of the setting and the narrator's past. At the start, it is as if the writer is describing how someone might look at a painting as she **draws the reader's attention** to the "snow-capped peak" of the mountain and "the dying embers of the setting sun". She then uses the "narrow path" as a device to **lead the reader's focus** "From there" to the town at the bottom. By **narrowing** the focus in this way, the writer is able to smoothly shift perspective. She does this using the **single sentence paragraph**, "This was the town of my youth", which shifts the reader's focus from the landscape to the narrator's account of her youth. This structure enables a transition from the impersonal to the personal **without making it obvious to the reader that their attention is being carefully controlled**.

Think about how the writer might have used cinematic techniques to focus the reader's attention.

You need to talk about the text as a whole, but you can also focus on how the writer has used individual paragraphs.

The structure includes a **time-shift** from the present, where the narrator is describing her return to the town, to the past and her memories of childhood. This shift is triggered by a "barrage of sights and smells" and reversed, in the final paragraph, by the "tolling of the church bells" that transports the narrator back to the present. The fact that the narrator's account of the past is framed by her experiences in the present **prevents it from having a jarring effect on the reader, so they are able to immerse themselves fully in the intriguing story of the narrator's past**. This is also helped by the fact that the town is used as a **link** between the passages that occur in the past and the passages that occur in the present.

A perspective shift could involve a shift in time or place or both.

Try to develop all your points by writing about the effects of different structural features on the reader.

This text has been structured to create a smooth flow of ideas. Other texts might use more obvious perspective shifts to deliberately draw the reader's attention to something.

The use of a first-person narrative voice also allows the writer to use structure to control the reader's focus. **The reader is taken on the same journey as the narrator, from moving around the town, to moving around her thoughts.** This gives the reader a steady trickle of information, as we learn about the setting, then its relation to the character, her youth and finally the complex reason for her return. This gradual supply of information keeps the reader interested and focused on what happens to her.

Recurring themes or ideas (called motifs) can be used to draw together various parts of a text or argument.

Always use examples to back up your points — you can use short quotes from the text or descriptions of the text.

Structure is used to have an effect on the reader, just like language...

You need to think about how the writer is using structure to direct your attention to certain things. Look out for things like cinematic techniques, perspective shifts, single sentence paragraphs and recurring ideas.

Sentence Forms

Writing about the effects of different sentence forms will earn you marks in questions about language. In structure questions, you need to talk about how individual sentences affect the overall structure of the text.

Sentences are made up of **Clauses**

1) A <u>clause</u> is a part of a sentence that has a <u>subject</u> and a <u>verb</u>. A clause usually <u>makes sense</u> on its own.

2) A <u>single clause</u> on its own is called a <u>simple sentence</u>.   The <u>subject</u> is the person or thing <u>doing</u> the verb.

> *The sky was grey and sombre.* ⟹ This is a single clause that is also a simple sentence. It has a <u>subject</u> ('The sky') and a <u>verb</u> ('was').

3) Simple sentences can be used to <u>explain</u> something <u>clearly</u> and <u>simply</u>. They are also often used to create a <u>sharp</u> or <u>abrupt</u> tone that keeps the reader <u>engaged</u> or creates <u>tension</u>.

4) A <u>compound sentence</u> has <u>two</u> main clauses, linked by a <u>conjunction</u> like 'or', 'but' or 'and'. <u>Both</u> clauses have to be able to make sense on their own. For example:

> *The sky was grey and sombre, and the rain lashed at our faces.* ⟹ Writers can use compound sentences to do things like <u>expand</u> on their initial statement, creating more <u>detailed</u> and <u>interesting</u> descriptions.

5) <u>Complex sentences</u> have <u>two</u> or more clauses, but only <u>one</u> of them needs to make sense on its own.

> *Above the sleepy town, the sky was grey and sombre.* ⟹ This is a complex sentence — 'Above the sleepy town' wouldn't work as a sentence on its <u>own</u>. This clause could go either <u>before</u> or <u>after</u> the main clause. Writers often <u>create interest</u> by using complex sentences to break up the <u>rhythm</u> of a text.

6) Writers use a variety of <u>sentence forms</u> to achieve different <u>effects</u> and keep the reader <u>interested</u>.

There are **Four Main Types** of sentence

1) Different <u>types</u> of sentences have different <u>purposes</u>:

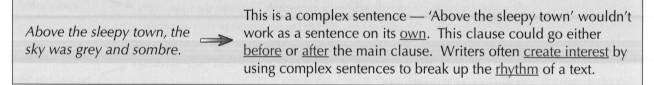

- <u>Statements</u> deliver <u>information</u>, e.g. 'The referee made the decision.' They can be found in all texts, but they are particularly common in <u>informative</u> texts like newspaper articles, reports and reviews.

- <u>Questions</u> ask the reader something, e.g. 'What would you do in my situation?' They don't always require an <u>answer</u> — sometimes they are just there to <u>encourage</u> us to <u>think</u> about something.

- <u>Orders</u>, or <u>commands</u>, tell us to <u>do</u> something, e.g. 'Consider the effects of this in the long-term.' They often use <u>imperative</u> verbs (verbs that give an instruction, like 'remember', 'think about' or 'go').

- <u>Exclamations</u> convey <u>strong emotions</u>, e.g. 'This is outrageous!' or 'This cannot be allowed to continue!' They usually end with an <u>exclamation mark</u>, and they're common in <u>persuasive</u> texts.

2) For the <u>reading questions</u>, it's a good idea to think about <u>how</u> and <u>why</u> writers have used particular <u>types</u> of sentence — bear in mind that different sentence types are suited to different <u>purposes</u>.

Sentence Forms

Writers use Different Sentence Forms to Interest the reader

1) Varying the <u>length</u> of sentences can create different <u>effects</u>. Here are a couple of <u>examples</u>:

These are just examples — the effects of different sentence lengths will vary from text to text.

> *The sky was growing darker. I couldn't see where I was going. I stumbled.* ⟶ Short simple sentences can be used to <u>build tension</u> or to create a <u>worried</u> and <u>confused</u> tone.

> *I waited excitedly at the foot of the stairs, listening to the footsteps above, thinking about the afternoon ahead, pacing the hall and counting down the minutes until we could set off.* ⟶ A longer, complex sentence could be used to give the impression of <u>time dragging</u>.

2) The <u>order</u> of words within sentences can also be chosen to create an <u>effect</u>. For example:

> *I had <u>never</u> seen such chaos <u>before</u>.*
 <u>Never before</u> had I seen such chaos. ⟶ Writers sometimes use <u>inversion</u> (<u>altering</u> the normal <u>word order</u>) to change the <u>emphasis</u> in a text. Here, inversion helps to emphasise the phrase '<u>Never before</u>'.

3) If you notice something about the way a writer has used sentences, don't just identify it — you need to <u>analyse</u> the <u>effects</u> to show how they <u>influence</u> the reader.

Comment on the Effects of different Sentence Forms

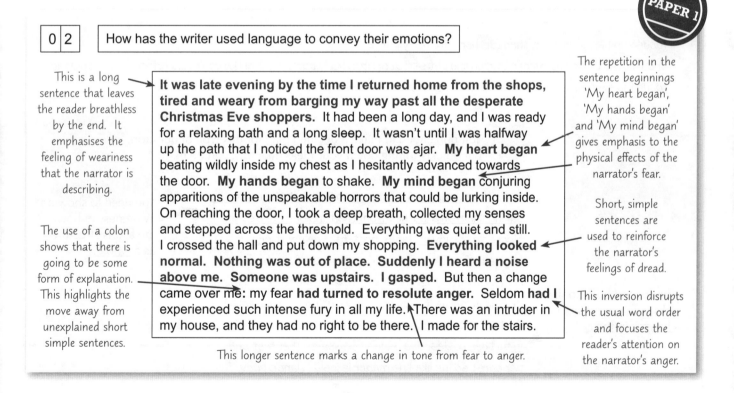

PAPER 1

0 2 | How has the writer used language to convey their emotions?

This is a long sentence that leaves the reader breathless by the end. It emphasises the feeling of weariness that the narrator is describing.

The use of a colon shows that there is going to be some form of explanation. This highlights the move away from unexplained short simple sentences.

It was late evening by the time I returned home from the shops, tired and weary from barging my way past all the desperate Christmas Eve shoppers. It had been a long day, and I was ready for a relaxing bath and a long sleep. It wasn't until I was halfway up the path that I noticed the front door was ajar. **My heart began** beating wildly inside my chest as I hesitantly advanced towards the door. **My hands began** to shake. **My mind began** conjuring apparitions of the unspeakable horrors that could be lurking inside. On reaching the door, I took a deep breath, collected my senses and stepped across the threshold. Everything was quiet and still. I crossed the hall and put down my shopping. **Everything looked normal. Nothing was out of place. Suddenly I heard a noise above me. Someone was upstairs. I gasped.** But then a change came over me: my fear **had turned to resolute anger.** Seldom **had I** experienced such intense fury in all my life. There was an intruder in my house, and they had no right to be there. I made for the stairs.

The repetition in the sentence beginnings 'My heart began', 'My hands began' and 'My mind began' gives emphasis to the physical effects of the narrator's fear.

Short, simple sentences are used to reinforce the narrator's feelings of dread.

This inversion disrupts the usual word order and focuses the reader's attention on the narrator's anger.

This longer sentence marks a change in tone from fear to anger.

Make sure you can write confidently about sentences...

It'll really help you in the language and structure questions if you can talk about the effects of different sentence forms. Spend some time learning the technical terms for different forms and types of sentences.

Worked Answer

Right, it's time for another worked answer...

Q1 Read the following extract. It is from the ending of a short story.

> The shot rang out. Jane powered off the blocks. The sound of the stadium had faded now, and only one thing mattered: putting one foot in front of the other, faster than she had ever done before. This was her race. She was born for this! Her blood pounded in her ears as she sprinted round the track.
>
> In the distance, the finish line was approaching. There were still two runners ahead of her. Faster! Jane urged herself on. Her legs burned. Her lungs screamed. But she was gaining on them. She overtook one. Still faster! At the last second, she overtook the final competitor and her foot came down first, landing triumphantly over the white line.
>
> Jane slowed to a halt, and doubled over with her hands on her knees as she gasped for breath. Wiping the sweat from her eyes, she looked up again at the stadium, and nearly cried with joy. Thousands and thousands of people were on their feet, cheering; they were waving flags and calling her name, smiles reaching from ear to ear. She could hardly believe it. All the months of hard training had paid off and she had achieved her lifelong dream: she had won a gold medal at the Olympics.

How has the writer structured the text to interest you as a reader?

You could write about:

- what the writer focuses your attention on at the beginning
- how and why the writer changes this focus as the extract develops
- any other structural features that interest you.

focus zoomed in on Jane, then further onto body parts

then moves on to the runners/finish line but still describes body parts — feel like you're experiencing it with Jane

focus moves to crowd after the race — see wider view of what's happening

You <u>don't</u> need to make a <u>detailed plan</u> for this type of question, but <u>quickly</u> jotting down your <u>ideas</u> (like this) can be helpful.

The second bullet point asks you to write about <u>changes</u> in <u>focus</u>.

<u>The extract is structured to interest the reader by</u> <u>taking them on a journey from the tension of the starting</u> <u>blocks to the joy of Jane's post-race celebrations</u>. It begins by focusing closely on Jane herself as she moves off the blocks. This shows the reader Jane's perspective, making it feel as if they are experiencing the race with her. As the first paragraph progresses, the writer <u>focuses</u> <u>in further</u>, to describe Jane's body parts (her feet and her ears), <u>so it's like the reader is inside Jane's body</u>.

You need to show an awareness of how the text is structured as a <u>whole</u>.

This is a good explanation, but to be even better, it could be <u>developed</u> by linking back to the question — putting the reader in Jane's position is a way of <u>interesting</u> the reader.

Worked Answer

This question type is all about the **effect** on the **reader**.

In the second paragraph, the writer's focus expands to describe what Jane can see ahead of her. <u>This gives the reader a wider view of the scene and helps them to understand what else is going on in the race.</u> This adds tension to the story, because the reader is made aware that Jane is near the end of the race and will need to run faster in order to win. The tense atmosphere makes the story more interesting for the reader.

Support your points with short quotations or references to the text.

Despite this description of the wider scene, the writer maintains a close focus on Jane herself. The writer describes Jane's physical experience of the race as "<u>Her legs burned. Her lungs screamed."</u> <u>As in the first paragraph</u>, the constant focus on individual body parts really helps to engage the reader by putting them in Jane's position, and showing how <u>her exhaustion has progressed from earlier in the extract</u>.

One way to <u>develop</u> a point is to <u>link</u> back to a point you made earlier.

This example is fine, but it could be much **shorter**.

In the final paragraph, the writer's focus moves to the crowd, who are all "<u>on their feet, cheering; they were waving flags and calling her name, smiles reaching from ear to ear."</u> This makes the text more interesting for the reader because they can see the larger view of the whole stadium and what is happening all around Jane. It helps the reader to imagine the powerful reaction from the crowd, as if they are in the stadium celebrating themselves. The <u>change in viewpoint from inside Jane's head to a pan round the stadium</u> shows the change in Jane's focus too.

This is called <u>cinematic writing</u> — you could use the technical term here.

- This answer has explored a variety of structural features — such as the writer's focus and changes in perspective — and explained their effects on the reader. It also backs up these points with suitable examples.

- To get the top marks, this answer could be improved by:
  - keeping quotations precise.
  - using a few more technical terms, e.g. narrative viewpoint, cinematic writing
  - making sure all points are fully developed by including a bit more detail.

Exam-Style Questions

You should know the drill by now — use these exam-style questions to help you practise for the real thing.

Q1 This is the ending to a short story. Joan is eighty-six years old, and one of the nurses from her care home has volunteered to take her to the beach.

> They arrived shortly before lunchtime. The seagulls squawked noisily overhead, swooping and circling, bright as doves against the blue sky. The nurse pushed the wheelchair down the boardwalk. Looking out over the sand and the grey-green sea, Joan was transfixed.
>
> The first time she had been to the beach was as a little girl, shortly before the war broke out. It had been a hot day. The beach was full of people sprawled on multicoloured deck chairs and picnic blankets, lending the scene a carnival feel. She remembered the smell of the water as she raced into the sea for the first time. She remembered the feeling of damp sand between her fingers and toes, and how the sea salt had dried into tiny crystals on her skin. Her mother had packed a picnic of hard-boiled eggs and potato salad. It had been the best day of her life so far, and as her father had bundled her into a towel, tired and sun-soaked, ready to go home, she had already been looking forward to the next visit.
>
> Now Joan watched the children race delightedly across the sand like she had done. Her nurse bought her fish and chips for lunch. Joan bought sticks of rock for her great-grandchildren. As the sun was going down, and they headed back to the car, Joan looked back over her shoulder. She knew there wouldn't be a next visit — but she didn't mind. She had seen the sea again.

How has the writer structured the text to interest you as a reader?
You could write about:

- what the writer focuses your attention on at the beginning
- how and why the writer changes this focus as the extract develops
- any other structural features that interest you.

Q2 Read the following extract. It is from the opening to a short story.

> The theatre hummed with expectant conversation as the spectators began to fill the stalls. The red velvet seats and gentle golden lighting gave the impression of being caught in the centre of a giant ruby. There was a magical feeling, as if everyone knew they were going to witness something spectacular that night, and eyes kept flickering over to the theatre drapes, wondering when the show would begin.
>
> Backstage, biting his fingernails down to the nail-bed, was the one they were all waiting for. Mikhail had been told by everyone he met that he was the greatest tenor of all time. Conductors had shed a tear when he sang, audiences had wept openly. But that never stopped him from feeling sick with nerves before a performance. What if his voice faltered? What if he forgot the words? What if he disappointed them all?
>
> "Sixty seconds to curtain," the stage manager called to him. Mikhail took a deep breath. His palms were damp with sweat. His legs felt like jelly. He didn't know if he was ready for this.

How has the writer structured the text to interest you as a reader?
You could write about:

- what the writer focuses your attention on at the beginning
- how and why the writer changes this focus as the extract develops
- any other structural features that interest you.

Revision Summary

If you've got to grips with the section, this page will be a breeze. Don't move on until you can do it all.

- Try these questions and <u>tick off each one</u> when you <u>get it right</u>.
- When you've done <u>all the questions</u> under a heading and are <u>completely happy</u> with it, tick it off.

Tone and Style (p.42-45) ☑

1) Are the following definitions for tone or style?
   a) This is the overall way in which the text is written.
   b) This is the feeling the words are written with. ☑

2) Would you expect the register of the following types of writing to be formal or informal?
   a) a job advert for the role of bank manager
   b) a newspaper article reporting on changes to the tax system
   c) an article about mountain biking on a website aimed at teenagers ☑

3) True or false?
   *In your English Language exams, you should comment on
   the effect of individual words and phrases in the text.* ☑

Language (p.48-56) ☑

4) What is the difference between a metaphor and a simile? ☑

5) Which of the following are metaphors and which are similes?
   a) He was as hairy as a dog.
   b) On the racetrack my sister was a whippet.
   c) You look like something the cat dragged in. ☑ ☑

6) Why might a writer give the weight of a cruise ship in elephants rather than in tonnes?

7) Ella says "the writer uses personification — he describes the young girl as if she were an animal."
   Why is Ella wrong? ☑

8) Choose an alliterative adjective to go with 'badger' to make the badger sound:
   a) attractive
   b) dangerous ☑

9) Write out three examples of onomatopoeic words. ☑

10) What is irony? ☑

11) What is the main thing you can look at to work out if a writer is being sarcastic? ☑

12) Name three rhetorical techniques. ☑

13) True or false? *It'll always be obvious if a text is biased.* ☑

14) Which word fills in the blank? *Writers often give descriptions based on the five _____.* ☑

Narrative Viewpoint and Structure (p.60-65) ☑

15) What are the three types of narrative viewpoint? Write down a brief definition for each one. ☑

16) What is a linear structure? ☑

17) Are the following sentences simple, compound or complex?
   a) Gazing longingly out to sea, the sailor dreamed of adventure.
   b) I waited for an hour, but he never arrived.
   c) She listened in shock to the news on the radio.
   d) The sun rose reluctantly, casting sombre shadows across the fields. ☑

18) What are the four main types of sentence? ☑

Writing with Purpose

All writing has a purpose, so you need to make it clear in both your fiction and non-fiction writing.

Structure your writing to Suit your Purpose

See pages 26-29 for more about writer's purpose.

1) The purpose of your writing might be to <u>inform</u>, <u>advise</u>, <u>argue</u> or <u>persuade</u>, or <u>entertain</u>. It could even be <u>more than one</u> of these.

2) For both papers, question 5 will let you know what the <u>purpose</u> of your writing needs to be.

3) Sometimes it will be <u>obvious</u>, e.g. in paper 2 you might be asked to write a letter to argue or persuade. It can be <u>less obvious</u> though, so sometimes you'll need to <u>work it out</u>, e.g. if you're asked to write a story for paper 1, your purpose would be to entertain.

4) Different purposes will need different <u>structures</u>, so you'll need to think about a <u>structure</u> that will help you achieve your purpose most effectively.

5) You can lay out your structure by writing a <u>plan</u>, so that it stays <u>consistent</u> throughout your answer:

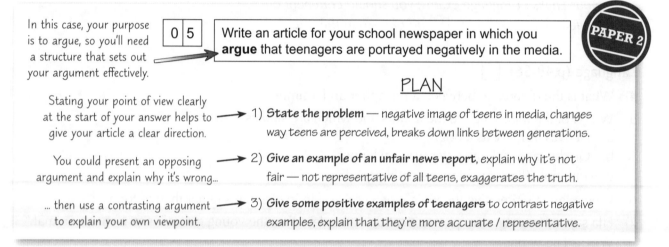

In this case, your purpose is to argue, so you'll need a structure that sets out your argument effectively.

0 5   Write an article for your school newspaper in which you **argue** that teenagers are portrayed negatively in the media.

PAPER 2

PLAN

Stating your point of view clearly at the start of your answer helps to give your article a clear direction.

→ 1) **State the problem** — negative image of teens in media, changes way teens are perceived, breaks down links between generations.

You could present an opposing argument and explain why it's wrong...

→ 2) **Give an example of an unfair news report**, explain why it's not fair — not representative of all teens, exaggerates the truth.

... then use a contrasting argument to explain your own viewpoint.

→ 3) **Give some positive examples of teenagers** to contrast negative examples, explain that they're more accurate / representative.

Choose your Tone, Style and Register to match your Purpose

1) In order to get good marks, you also need to show that you can <u>adjust</u> your <u>tone</u>, <u>style</u> and <u>register</u> to suit your purpose.

See p.42-43 for more on tone, style and register.

2) For example, a text written to <u>advise</u> might have an <u>objective</u>, <u>authoritative</u> tone:

Upon consultation with local residents, and in light of their strong opposition, this committee recommends that the proposal be withdrawn immediately.

→ This text uses a <u>formal</u> register and <u>complex</u> language to make its advice seem <u>reliable</u>.

3) A <u>persuasive</u> text needs to be more <u>subjective</u> (based on personal feelings). It might try to create a <u>personal</u> tone that involves the reader in a text:

See p.54 for some rhetorical techniques that help to achieve this.

Like me, you must be weary of the incessant criticism. We're intelligent young citizens who understand the issues threatening our planet. Why are we being ignored?

→ This text uses a <u>rhetorical question</u> and the pronouns 'you' and 'we' to <u>involve</u> and <u>persuade</u> its audience.

4) When you adjust your <u>writing</u> to suit your purpose, make sure you're still showing off your ability to use <u>sophisticated vocabulary</u>.

Writing with Purpose

Literary Fiction texts are often written to Entertain

0 5 You are entering a creative writing competition.
The winner will have their piece printed in a national newspaper.
Write the opening part of a story suggested by this picture:

The purpose will always be referred to in the question. In this case, you're writing the opening part of a story, so you're writing to entertain the reader.

The purpose is to entertain, so this story starts in the middle of the action to grab the reader's interest.

This uses complex sentences to keep the writing style varied.

I'd never in my life needed a break so badly. My airless writing room had begun to feel suffocating; so had the frustration of my unending writer's block. I gave up, threw down my pen, and went out for a walk.

Figurative language helps the reader to imagine the writer's feelings.

My **irritation evaporated** almost immediately into the crisp autumn air. **Buoyed** by the hope of finding inspiration amongst the fiery leaves that surrounded me, I **ambled** contentedly through the silence of the golden wood.

Unusual vocabulary makes your writing more interesting and enjoyable to read.

Non-fiction texts can have a Variety of Purposes

PAPER 2

0 5 'Cosmetic surgery is a psychologically damaging procedure that increases the pressure to achieve an unrealistic level of perfection. It should be banned.'
Write an article for a broadsheet newspaper in which you explain your point of view on this statement and persuade your readers to agree with you.

In this task, your purpose is to explain your point of view and persuade your readers.

If you're writing to persuade, you could structure your answer by stating an opposing opinion and then counteracting it.

Public consensus has long seen cosmetic surgery as a mere vanity project, a procedure dreamed up by the wealthy to aid their endless pursuit of perfection. **This seems somewhat unfair on the medical establishment.**
In truth, cosmetic surgery sits at the height of medical achievement. Far from being a symptom of a shallow society, cosmetic procedures are a solution: **they offer the chance of a new life.** Plastic surgery has the power to improve lives, something that has always been an important medical objective.
It is time for a sea-change in attitudes to plastic surgery — **it is no longer acceptable** for the world to view with scorn those who have chosen to specialise in the improvement of the human form.

Emotive phrases like this can help to make the audience sympathise with your viewpoint.

You need to use a confident, assured tone to be persuasive.

There are marks available for adapting your writing to fit a purpose...

Don't forget that writing can often have more than one purpose (see p.24) — make sure you think about all the reasons that you're writing, so that you can adapt your style and produce a high level answer.

Writing for an Audience

For each writing task, you'll need to think about your audience. Your audience is just anyone who's going to hear or read your writing — it doesn't mean you'll have to perform your work.

Work out **Who** your **Audience** is

1) For question 5 on both papers, you'll need to pay attention to the <u>audience</u> you're writing for.

2) In paper 1, the question will usually specify a <u>particular audience</u>:

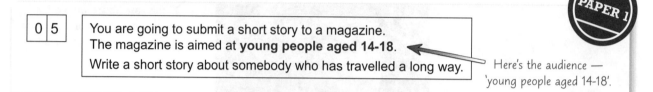

| 0 | 5 | You are going to submit a short story to a magazine.
The magazine is aimed at **young people aged 14-18**.
Write a short story about somebody who has travelled a long way. |

PAPER 1

Here's the audience —
'young people aged 14-18'.

3) In paper 2, you might need to work out from the <u>question</u> who your audience is. The <u>form</u> and <u>content</u> will give you some clues:

| 0 | 5 | 'Students should attend classes virtually. In today's digital society, it's illogical that students still have to leave the house to go to school.'
Write a broadsheet newspaper article in which you argue the case for or against this statement. |

PAPER 2

This statement is about schools, so the audience will be people interested in education, such as parents or teachers.

You're writing a broadsheet newspaper article, so your audience will mostly be well-educated adults.

Choose your **Tone**, **Style** and **Register** to match your **Audience**

1) Once you know who your audience is, you'll need to <u>adapt</u> your <u>tone</u>, <u>style</u> and <u>register</u> so that they're <u>appropriate</u> to the people who will be reading your writing.

2) For example, you might want to consider the <u>age</u> and level of <u>expertise</u> of your audience, as well as your <u>relationship</u> with them.

See p.42-43 for more on tone, style and register.

Age

- If you're addressing a <u>younger</u> audience, you might use a more <u>light-hearted</u> tone and a <u>less formal</u> register, with a <u>colloquial</u> or <u>chatty</u> style.

- A <u>formal</u>, <u>serious</u> register might work better for <u>older</u> audiences. You might also use a more <u>complex</u> style than you would for a younger audience.

Expertise

- Different audiences will have different levels of <u>expertise</u> in the subject you're writing about.

- For example, if you're writing a report for a panel of experts, your register should be more <u>formal</u>, with a style that uses more <u>specialised</u> language than if you were writing for a <u>general</u> audience.

Relationship with reader

- If you're writing to a <u>familiar</u> audience, such as your <u>year group</u> at school, you might use a <u>less formal</u> register, and a <u>friendly</u> tone.

- If you're writing to an <u>unknown</u> audience, it would be better to use an <u>impersonal</u> tone and a <u>formal</u> register.

3) You should always aim to show your <u>writing skills</u> to the examiner — even if you're writing <u>less formally</u> or for a <u>young audience</u>, you still need to make sure you include a <u>range</u> of <u>vocabulary</u> and <u>sentence types</u>.

Writing for an Audience

Literary Fiction texts need to Engage their Audience

`0 5` You are entering a creative writing competition.
The judges will be a panel of your teachers.
Write the opening part of a story about a character's birthday.

The audience for this question is your teachers.

For this task, your immediate audience is a panel of judges — you need to impress them by writing engagingly. Try surprising them with something unexpected, e.g. addressing the reader directly.

Amelia's eighteenth birthday had truly been a day like no other. It was the day she first met Jack: a tall, handsome stranger dressed in a naval uniform. **Don't be fooled by the intrusion of a charming stranger into this narrative. This is not a romance novel, and Amelia was not Cinderella.** Jack was her brother — her long-lost brother, who had left to join the Navy before she had been born, and who returned now with **the cowed despondence of a disgraced man.**

Amelia could never forget her mother's face as she had opened the door to greet another well-wishing neighbour, only to find her lost son hunched on the doorstep. Her features appeared to melt, losing all definition as they formed themselves into a canvas over which several emotions flashed. At first there was shock, which quickly became anger, then relief, and finally, remorse.

To impress teachers, you will need to use a formal, sophisticated register.

Non-fiction texts can use a Personal Tone

`0 5` 'Social media has provided a new way for us to interact with our peers. In turn, this has led to the creation of a new forum for bullying — the Internet.'
Write a speech to be given at your school, advising teenagers on how to cope with the threat of internet bullying.

In this task, you're writing for a teenage audience, so you'll need to adjust your tone, style and register accordingly.

You're writing to advise teenagers. Use words like "we" and "you" to establish a connection and give your advice calmly, without being patronising.

We are a generation that has been raised in the era of social media. Every day, most of us use some form of social media to broadcast our identities. **We're** telling the world, "This is who I am." That's why cyber bullying can be so upsetting — it can feel like your whole identity is being attacked.

There are many different ways to deal with online bullying. The first thing you need to do is report it. You can usually do this on the social media site itself, but if you don't feel comfortable doing this, you should talk to someone in person. Suffering in silence will only make things worse.

If you find you are the victim of persistent bullying, take steps to block the person who is bullying you from contacting you. It's also a good idea to record the bullying in some way — you could take a screenshot, or even just save the messages somewhere. This will make things much easier to report later.

Your tone should be helpful and friendly, but in this case your register should still be quite formal. Don't use any slang or text speak.

Show the examiner that you're aware of your audience...

In question 5 on both papers, the examiner will be looking carefully at how well-matched your answer is to your audience. Think carefully about your word choices, sentence structures and overall writing style.

Writing Stories

Story-writing is a task that might appear in paper 1, question 5. You might have to write a short story, or focus on writing a particular part, like the opening or the ending. It's a good idea to practise writing this type of text.

Grab your Reader's Attention from the Start

1) It's always a good idea to <u>start</u> your stories with an <u>opening sentence</u> that'll make your <u>reader</u> want to <u>carry on</u> reading. For example:

You could start with a <u>direct address</u> to the reader:

> *Everybody has a bad day now and again, don't they? Well, I'm going to tell you about a day that was much, much worse than your worst day ever.*

Or you could try a description of a particularly <u>unusual character</u>:

> *Humphrey Ward was, without a shadow of a doubt, the most brilliant (and most cantankerous) banana thief in the country.*

Try to avoid clichéd openings like 'Once upon a time'.

2) If you start your story in the <u>middle of the action</u>, it'll create a <u>fast-paced</u> atmosphere that makes the reader want to find out <u>what happens next</u>:

> *I couldn't believe it. He was gone. "He must be here," I thought to myself as I went through the shed, desperately throwing aside box after box. It was no use. Tanmay had run away, and it was all my fault.*

3) This example <u>explains</u> some of what's happening after a few sentences, which keeps up the <u>fast pace</u> of the narrative — so the story stays <u>interesting</u>.

4) You could also try <u>prolonging</u> the mystery to create <u>tension</u> in your narrative. Just make sure you <u>reveal</u> what's going on before it gets too <u>confusing</u> for your audience.

5) However you start your writing, you need to make sure it's <u>engaging</u> and <u>entertaining</u> for the reader — so whatever you do, don't <u>waffle</u>.

Try to Build the Tension from the Start

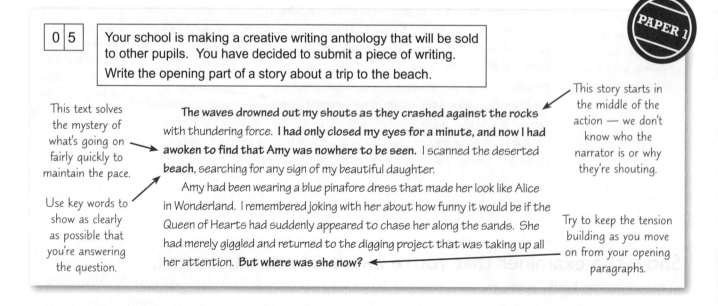

0 5 — Your school is making a creative writing anthology that will be sold to other pupils. You have decided to submit a piece of writing. Write the opening part of a story about a trip to the beach.

PAPER 1

This text solves the mystery of what's going on fairly quickly to maintain the pace.

Use key words to show as clearly as possible that you're answering the question.

The waves drowned out my shouts as they crashed against the rocks with thundering force. **I had only closed my eyes for a minute, and now I had awoken to find that Amy was nowhere to be seen.** I scanned the deserted **beach**, searching for any sign of my beautiful daughter.

Amy had been wearing a blue pinafore dress that made her look like Alice in Wonderland. I remembered joking with her about how funny it would be if the Queen of Hearts had suddenly appeared to chase her along the sands. She had merely giggled and returned to the digging project that was taking up all her attention. **But where was she now?**

This story starts in the middle of the action — we don't know who the narrator is or why they're shouting.

Try to keep the tension building as you move on from your opening paragraphs.

Writing Stories

Make your **Language** and **Narrative Viewpoint** fit the **Task**

1) Different <u>word choices</u> will have different <u>effects</u>, so you'll need to pick vocabulary that creates the right <u>tone</u> for your story. For example:

> *The door screeched open and I carefully entered the dingy cellar. Shadows cast by my torch leapt up at me through the gloom.*

⟹ Words like '<u>screeched</u>', '<u>dingy</u>' and '<u>gloom</u>' make this writing sound <u>spooky</u>.

> *I burst noisily through the thicket of trees and sprinted towards the shore. The men were still chasing me, bellowing threats.*

⟹ Words like '<u>burst</u>', '<u>sprinted</u>' and '<u>chasing</u>' make this writing sound <u>exciting</u> and <u>dramatic</u>.

2) You also need to think about what <u>narrative viewpoint</u> you're going to use (see p.60).

3) A <u>first-person narrator</u> uses the pronouns 'I' and 'we', as they're usually one of the <u>characters</u> in the story.

> *I quickly scanned the book for anything that might help. My heart was racing; I knew I needed to work fast.*

⟹ The first-person narrative makes things more <u>dramatic</u> by helping the reader to <u>imagine</u> the story is happening to them.

4) A <u>third-person narrator</u> uses words like 'he' and 'she' to talk <u>about</u> the characters from a <u>separate</u> viewpoint.

> *Shamil lit the bonfire carefully, then retreated back a few metres as the feeble fire began to crackle and spit.*

⟹ The narrator isn't part of the story. This creates <u>distance</u>, as the narrative voice and the characters are <u>separate</u> from each other.

Use **Descriptive Techniques** to make your text **Engaging**

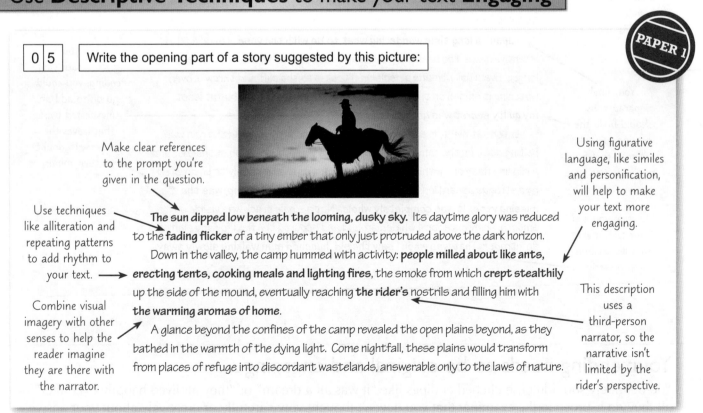

0 5 — Write the opening part of a story suggested by this picture:

PAPER 1

Make clear references to the prompt you're given in the question.

Using figurative language, like similes and personification, will help to make your text more engaging.

Use techniques like alliteration and repeating patterns to add rhythm to your text. ⟶

Combine visual imagery with other senses to help the reader imagine they are there with the narrator.

The sun dipped low beneath the looming, dusky sky. Its daytime glory was reduced to the **fading flicker** of a tiny ember that only just protruded above the dark horizon. Down in the valley, the camp hummed with activity: **people milled about like ants, erecting tents, cooking meals and lighting fires**, the smoke from which **crept stealthily** up the side of the mound, eventually reaching **the rider's** nostrils and filling him with **the warming aromas of home.**

A glance beyond the confines of the camp revealed the open plains beyond, as they bathed in the warmth of the dying light. Come nightfall, these plains would transform from places of refuge into discordant wastelands, answerable only to the laws of nature.

This description uses a third-person narrator, so the narrative isn't limited by the rider's perspective.

Writing Stories

It's **Important** to write a **Good Ending**

1) Whether you're asked to write the <u>end</u> of a story, or a <u>different part</u>, it's still important that you <u>finish it well</u> — you want to leave the examiner with a <u>great impression</u> of your writing abilities.

2) Here are some <u>examples</u> of different ways that you could <u>end</u> a story:

> - You could finish with an unexpected <u>plot twist</u> that will <u>shock</u> the reader.
> - You could show the <u>main character</u> coming to some kind of <u>realisation</u>.
> - You could create a <u>cliffhanger</u> ending by finishing with a <u>question</u>. This will leave the reader thinking about what will happen <u>next</u>.
> - You could have a <u>neat</u>, <u>happy ending</u> that will <u>satisfy</u> the reader.

3) If you find you're running out of time, think up a <u>quick ending</u> — make sure you show how the story ends, and finish with a short, <u>punchy</u> line.

4) Under absolutely no circumstances use the ending, "And it was all a <u>dream</u>."

Try to make your **Ending** as **Powerful** as possible

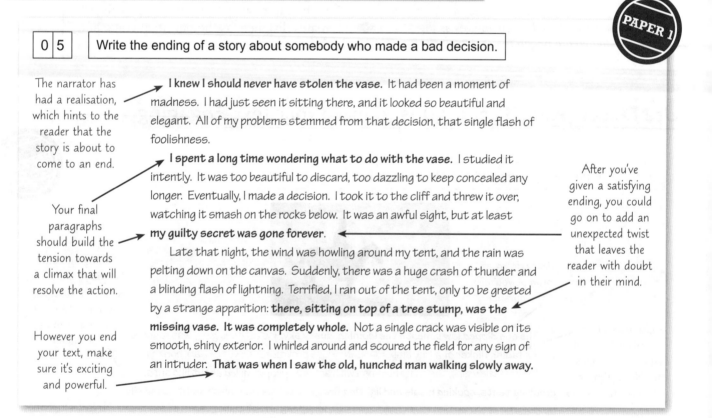

PAPER 1

| 0 | 5 | Write the ending of a story about somebody who made a bad decision. |

The narrator has had a realisation, which hints to the reader that the story is about to come to an end.

Your final paragraphs should build the tension towards a climax that will resolve the action.

However you end your text, make sure it's exciting and powerful.

I knew I should never have stolen the vase. It had been a moment of madness. I had just seen it sitting there, and it looked so beautiful and elegant. All of my problems stemmed from that decision, that single flash of foolishness.

I spent a long time wondering what to do with the vase. I studied it intently. It was too beautiful to discard, too dazzling to keep concealed any longer. Eventually, I made a decision. I took it to the cliff and threw it over, watching it smash on the rocks below. It was an awful sight, but at least **my guilty secret was gone forever.**

Late that night, the wind was howling around my tent, and the rain was pelting down on the canvas. Suddenly, there was a huge crash of thunder and a blinding flash of lightning. Terrified, I ran out of the tent, only to be greeted by a strange apparition: **there, sitting on top of a tree stump, was the missing vase. It was completely whole.** Not a single crack was visible on its smooth, shiny exterior. I whirled around and scoured the field for any sign of an intruder. **That was when I saw the old, hunched man walking slowly away.**

After you've given a satisfying ending, you could go on to add an unexpected twist that leaves the reader with doubt in their mind.

Your ending needs to be original and engaging...

You definitely shouldn't use clichéd endings like "it was all a dream" or "they all lived happily ever after" — all they do is prove to the examiner that you haven't thought very carefully or creatively about your answer.

Writing Descriptions

For paper 1, question 5 you could be asked to write a description. Your aim is to give your audience a detailed idea about a character or scene, so you'll need to use words to paint a vivid, interesting picture in their mind.

Descriptions are Detailed

1) Descriptions use strong <u>visual</u> language to create an <u>impression</u> of a person or place for the reader.

2) You <u>don't</u> need to include as much <u>plot</u> or <u>action</u> — focus mostly on <u>describing</u> the subject.

3) Even though there's no <u>plot</u>, you still need to <u>structure</u> your writing — e.g. you could start with a <u>general</u> description, then go on to describe some more <u>specific</u> details.

4) The purpose of a description is normally to <u>entertain</u> the reader, so you need to adapt your writing <u>style</u> accordingly, and keep your <u>language</u> interesting.

5) Descriptions need <u>detail</u>. For example, a <u>character</u> description might include:

- A character's <u>physical features</u>, e.g. hair colour, clothing.
- A character's <u>personality</u>, e.g. they could be funny, serious, reserved, extroverted.
- Any other particular <u>features</u> that reveal <u>more</u> about them, e.g. any nervous habits.
- Your <u>personal opinion</u>, e.g. what you like or dislike about them.

Use **Language** to describe a **Character** or **Scene**

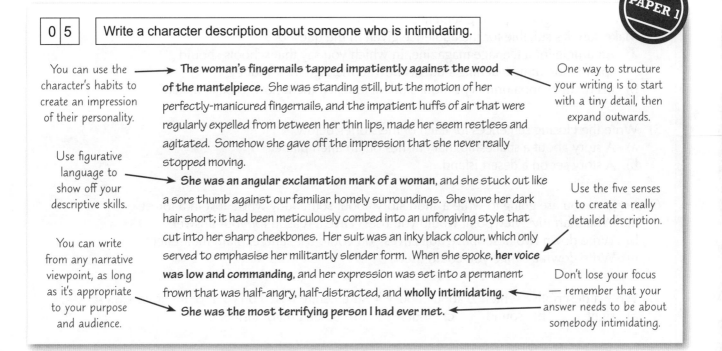

PAPER 1

| 0 | 5 | Write a character description about someone who is intimidating. |

You can use the character's habits to create an impression of their personality.

The woman's fingernails tapped impatiently against the wood of the mantelpiece. She was standing still, but the motion of her perfectly-manicured fingernails, and the impatient huffs of air that were regularly expelled from between her thin lips, made her seem restless and agitated. Somehow she gave off the impression that she never really stopped moving.

One way to structure your writing is to start with a tiny detail, then expand outwards.

Use figurative language to show off your descriptive skills.

She was an angular exclamation mark of a woman, and she stuck out like a sore thumb against our familiar, homely surroundings. She wore her dark hair short; it had been meticulously combed into an unforgiving style that cut into her sharp cheekbones. Her suit was an inky black colour, which only served to emphasise her militantly slender form. When she spoke, **her voice was low and commanding**, and her expression was set into a permanent frown that was half-angry, half-distracted, and **wholly intimidating.**
She was the most terrifying person I had ever met.

You can write from any narrative viewpoint, as long as it's appropriate to your purpose and audience.

Use the five senses to create a really detailed description.

Don't lose your focus — remember that your answer needs to be about somebody intimidating.

Try to use a good variety of descriptive language...

There are plenty of techniques to choose from here: metaphors, similes, alliteration, personification, the five senses, adjectives, repetition, onomatopoeia, hyperbole — the important thing is to use them engagingly.

Warm-Up Questions

Feeling chilly? No fear — these questions will get you feeling toasty in no time (when it comes to your English Language skills, that is). Use them as an introduction to the longer writing tasks on the next page.

Warm-Up Questions

1) Which of the following techniques are common in persuasive writing?
   a) an impersonal tone   b) rhetorical questions
   c) technical terms   d) emotive language

2) Rewrite the informative text below so that it persuades the reader to visit the church.

   Lyttlewich Church

   Situated in the rural village of Lyttlewich, Howtonshire, Lyttlewich Church is one of the oldest churches in the country: some parts of the church were built in 984 AD. The church receives thousands of visitors a year, and is particularly renowned for its artwork, which has recently been restored.

3) Rewrite each sentence below so that it's appropriate for an audience who have no expertise on the subject.
   a) Fertilisers provide phosphorous and potassium, which are essential for plant growth.
   b) The ossicle bones in the ear (the malleus, incus and stapes) are some of the smallest in the human skeleton.
   c) Roman legionaries used javelins and throwing-darts to defeat their enemies.

4) Write down a good opening sentence for each of the texts below.
   Make sure it's suitable for the audience given in the question.
   a) An article for a teenage magazine, in which you say that schools should spend more time teaching students how to manage their money.
   b) Instructions for a primary school student to teach them how to bake a cake.

5) Write the closing sentences for each of the stories below.
   a) A story about a spaceship that crashes on an alien planet.
   b) A story set on a desert island.

6) Imagine you are going to write a short story about somebody who's lost in a forest.
   a) What narrative viewpoint would you use? Give a reason for your answer.
   b) Write down two descriptive adjectives you could use, and explain their effect.
   c) Write down a simile you could use.

7) Write a descriptive sentence about a busy leisure centre based on each of the following senses.
   a) sight   b) sound   c) touch   d) smell and/or taste

8) You have been asked to write a description of a family member. Draw a spider diagram showing your ideas for things you might include.

Exam-Style Questions

These exam-style questions are like the fiction writing question — that's question 5 in paper 1. It's a good idea to make a quick plan for your answers, because there are marks in this question for well-organised writing.

Q1

> You have been asked to write a piece for a storytelling event at your local library. Your writing will be read aloud to an audience of adult library users.
>
> Write the beginning of a story about somebody who goes camping.

Q2

> You want to submit a piece of creative writing to be published in your local newspaper. The paper's editor will decide which submissions to publish.
>
> Write a short story that is set in your local area.

Q3

> You are going to enter a writing competition run by your school newspaper. The competition is being judged by your head teacher.
>
> Write a description suggested by this picture:
>
>

Writing Newspaper Articles

Paper 2, question 5 might ask you to write a newspaper article.

Newspaper articles Report Events and Offer Opinions

1) A newspaper's main purpose is to <u>inform</u> people about <u>current affairs</u> and <u>other topics</u> of interest.

2) Some newspaper articles <u>directly report</u> news. They convey <u>facts</u> about a <u>story</u> or <u>theme</u>, often using an <u>unemotional</u> tone and a <u>sophisticated</u> style to make the information seem <u>accurate</u> and <u>reliable</u>.

3) Other newspaper articles offer the <u>viewpoint</u> of the <u>writer</u> on a news story or theme. These are sometimes called <u>commentaries</u>, <u>columns</u>, <u>editorials</u> or <u>opinion pieces</u>.

You need to make sure that your own viewpoint comes across whichever type of article you write.

4) As well as <u>informing</u> the reader, <u>commentaries</u> try to <u>entertain</u> their audience by making readers engage with the <u>personality</u> of the writer.

Commentaries need to Engage their Audience

1) To grab the audience's <u>interest</u>, a commentary might use a <u>personal</u> tone and a <u>conversational</u> style to help convey the writer's opinions and personality.

> *It seems to me that this lot all need to take a deep breath and stop whinging. Nobody's going to bulldoze our green spaces any time soon — they'll have to spend 25 years making a planning application first.*

← This uses <u>colloquial</u> words to create a conversational style and <u>sarcasm</u> to convey the viewpoint of the writer.

2) <u>Rhetorical techniques</u> (see p.54) are commonly used in commentaries to help get the writer's opinions across forcefully and to encourage readers to <u>agree</u> with the writer.

> *What happened to the good old days, when the presence of a heap of spuds on the table at dinnertime brought delight all round? Has all this 'health food' nonsense made us forget our faithful starchy friend?*

← This uses <u>rhetorical questions</u> to engage and persuade the reader.

The Layout of an article is Important

Newspaper articles often use <u>layout features</u> to engage the reader's attention and convey information clearly.

Headlines tell you, very briefly, what an article is about. Headlines need to capture the audience's interest so that they carry on reading the article.

SECRET WEDDING FOR DUTTON DUO

Private ceremony for TV's cutest couple

By our showbiz reporter, Joe Snooping

Actors Simon Tremble and Katie Davies, stars of the TV series *Dutton Manor*, married yesterday at a secret ceremony in the Lake District.

LOVE AT FIRST SIGHT
According to insiders, the pair got together just three months ago and their engagement was only announced publicly last week. Thirty close friends and family, including several co-stars, joined them to celebrate, and pop sensation Al Blue performed at the reception.

DIRECTOR IS 'DELIGHTED'
Director of the series, Julian Parker, told The Daily Gossip that he was 'absolutely delighted' for the couple and added that they are 'perfect for each other'. However, he refused to comment on rumours that Simon's character in the show may be killed off when the new series begins in April.

COUPLE TO HONEYMOON IN CARIBBEAN
After their wedding, the couple jetted off on honeymoon to the beautiful island of Antigua. They will stay at a luxury beach resort for two weeks before returning to London to set up their new home.

Straplines are short statements that expand on the headline. They try to hook the reader, after the headline has got their initial interest.

Articles often start with a short paragraph that gives an overview of the story or theme.

Subheadings are used to split an article up. Each subheading briefly tells you what the next section of text is about, often in an interesting or humorous way.

Writing Newspaper Articles

Newspapers have Varying Audiences

1) Newspapers are broadly split into two types — <u>tabloids</u> and <u>broadsheets</u>.

2) <u>Tabloids</u> (such as *The Sun* and *The Mirror*) tend to focus on more <u>sensational</u> stories, making their news stories accessible and with a wide appeal.

3) <u>Broadsheets</u> (such as *The Telegraph* and *The Guardian*) are thought of as more <u>formal</u>, 'high-brow' journalism — focusing on what are thought to be more sophisticated topics.

4) Question 5 will tell you what <u>form</u> to write in, e.g. 'a broadsheet newspaper article' — make sure you adapt your <u>tone</u>, <u>style</u> and <u>register</u> to the right audience.

5) Most newspapers also publish articles on the <u>internet</u>. If you're asked to write a news article for an online audience, think about how your audience might be <u>different</u> (e.g. <u>younger</u> or with a different level of <u>understanding</u> about the subject), and <u>adapt</u> your writing to suit.

Make sure your Article gives Your Opinion

0 5 'You will never be able to get the real feel of a place by taking a guided tour. The true heart of any country lies off the beaten track.' Write an article for a broadsheet newspaper in which you explain your point of view on this statement.

This question is asking you to give your opinion on a topic.

PAPER 2

FORGET THE ROAD LESS TRAVELLED

Your headline needs to be short and punchy to engage the reader.

Pay no attention to those who tell you otherwise: guided tours are the best way to experience somewhere new.

Use a strapline to summarise the article in an interesting way.

At some point or other, we've all been faced with a travel snob: that particular breed of rough-and-tumble traveller who knows all about where to go, what to see and, most importantly, how to see it. **The travel snob** thinks that guided tours are for the uncultured bores of this planet. **The travel snob** believes in travel without a destination. **And yet, the travel snob** will always find time to tell you about a 'hidden gem' that only they can take you to.

You're giving an opinion, so your tone should be quite personal.

Use rhetorical devices like repetition to make your writing entertaining and persuasive.

You would think **someone so educated in the ways of the world** would have realised the irony by now — **travel snobs are themselves tour guides**. The places that they think are **'off the beaten track'** are transported, by their own recommendation, right onto 'the beaten track'. They are the one beating the track; they are leading the tourists away from their well-populated honeypot attractions into 'the heart of things'.

Make sure you link your answer to the prompt you're given in the question.

You can use a sarcastic tone to give your writing a sense of personality.

In the meantime, guided tours are often run by local people, who will frequently have a real treasure trove of local knowledge. **How can a throwaway recommendation from an outsider possibly surpass that?** Anybody who wants to see the true heart of a country must be guided by the people who live in it.

Opinion articles often combine a conversational style with complex sentences and vocabulary.

You need to get the style right in a newspaper article...

It's worth having a look at some real newspaper articles as part of your revision. You'll start to spot some patterns in the vocabulary and structure that they use, which will help you write better articles yourself.

Writing Leaflets

Leaflets need to give the reader lots of information in a clear, organised way.

Leaflets can have Varied Audiences and Purposes

1) Leaflets can have <u>any</u> purpose, but they're often used to <u>advise</u> (e.g. a leaflet advising the reader to open a savings account) or <u>persuade</u> an audience (e.g. to vote for a particular political party).

2) They can have a <u>general audience</u> (e.g. a leaflet about the importance of healthy eating) or a more <u>specific audience</u> (e.g. a leaflet advertising a particular museum or exhibition).

3) Leaflets need a <u>clear structure</u> to <u>break up</u> information. This could include:

- a clear title
- subheadings
- bullet points
- boxes around extra bits of information

> It's important to break up the information in a leaflet, but don't waste time in the exam trying to make it look pretty or drawing pictures.

4) Leaflets also need to <u>grab the reader's attention</u>, so that they <u>remember</u> all the information they're given. You can use <u>language techniques</u>, such as <u>lists of three</u> or <u>direct address</u>, to achieve this.

Organise your Leaflet in a Clear and Interesting way

PAPER 2

0 5 | 'Keeping fit as a student is too hard. Gym memberships and exercise equipment are too expensive for young people, and students don't have time to exercise.' Write the text for a leaflet in which you advise students about how to keep fit.

Use a title to catch the reader's attention.

KEEPING FIT THE EASY WAY

Exercise is important for your health, but as a student **your time and budget may be limited**. Fortunately, there are many cheap, simple, fun ways to keep fit.

You're writing for students, but you should still use a formal register and Standard English.

<u>Walk the walk</u>

Walking costs you nothing, and it doesn't require too much spare time. You could try:

Use interesting subheadings to organise your answer and hold the reader's interest.

- **Walking to a friend's house instead of asking your parents for a lift.**
- **Planning a longer route to a destination you already walk to.**
- **Getting off the bus or train a few stops early and walking the rest of the way.**

Use bullet points to break information up for the reader.

<u>Pedal power</u>

If you own a bike, cycling is an excellent way to keep fit. Look at your council's website to see if there are cycle routes nearby, or **plan a safe route on your local roads**.

Imperatives and direct address create a clear, confident tone.

<u>Dance the night away</u>

Alliteration and a list of three emphasise the variety of activities on offer.

Dancing can help to maintain your fitness and improve your coordination, regardless of your skill level. Try looking for tutorial videos on the Internet to help you learn.

<u>Your turn...</u>

These are just a few ideas; there are many more options available. Whether it's **skipping, skating or salsa**, there will certainly be something for you.

Short paragraphs can help to break up the information in a text.

You need to match your writing to the audience in the question...

Leaflets can be written for a wide variety of different audiences. Make sure your leaflet is adapted to the audience you're given in the question — choose a suitable writing style that uses appropriate language.

Travel Writing

Travel writing needs to effectively convey your feelings about the place you're writing about.

Travel Writing is Personal and Descriptive

1) Travel writing is an <u>account</u> of a writer's travels to a specific <u>place</u>.

2) If you're asked to produce some travel writing for paper 2, you'll need to convey your <u>thoughts</u> and <u>opinions</u> about the place you're writing about, as well as give some <u>information</u> about it.

3) A piece of travel writing can <u>entertain</u> the reader (e.g. if it's in a book or magazine), <u>inform</u> them (e.g. if it's in a travel guide), or <u>persuade</u> them to visit a destination.

4) However, it's usually written for a <u>combination</u> of these purposes, e.g. <u>travel guides</u> are often written to both <u>inform</u> and <u>entertain</u> the reader.

5) Travel writing usually has a <u>personal</u> tone, and it's almost always written in the <u>first person</u>. Try to write in a <u>conversational</u> style, but don't forget to use lots of <u>descriptive techniques</u> too.

Use Interesting Language to Convey your Opinions

PAPER 2

0 5 'New York is the city of dreams. There is no greater place on earth.' Imagine you have just visited New York. Write an article for a travel magazine in which you explain your point of view on this statement.

This question asks you to write a magazine article. It needs to be entertaining and informative, and could also persuade the reader to agree with your point of view.

An interesting, punchy title can help to grab your audience's attention.

Dismayed in Manhattan

Lucy Farthing says "no thanks" to New York.

I've travelled to many cities during my career as a travel writer, and it's fair to say that there are a few I'd rather have avoided. **None, however, have quite matched up to the levels of discomfort, disappointment and sheer frustration I experienced in the city of New York.**

I suspect my high expectations didn't help. Before embarking on my trip, I'd been regaled with stories from friends and family who'd already visited the place. **"It's the city of dreams"**, I was told; "the best city in the world!"

What I realised instead, somewhere between my fifth cup of overpriced coffee and my fourteenth hour-long queue, was that **New York is the city of nightmares**. Not only did it feel like the world's busiest city, it felt like the **noisiest**, too; by the end of my week there I found myself longing for the joys of silence and solitude. Maybe for some, New York is a city where dreams come true, but it was certainly far from the **inspiring haven** I had hoped to find.

Use personal pronouns like 'I' to make the tone of your writing more personal.

Link your answer back to the statement.

Try to use all five senses to create a sense of the atmosphere of the place.

Make your opinion on the statement very clear.

Use interesting language to make your text more entertaining.

You're allowed to disagree with the statement in the question...

You don't necessarily have to write positively about the place you're describing. It's fine to have a negative opinion, as long as you express it clearly and use the appropriate language, tone and style for your audience.

Writing Reports and Essays

Reports and essays use a similar tone and style, but they do have one difference — their typical audience.

Reports and Essays are Similar

1) Reports and essays should be <u>impersonal</u> and <u>objective</u> in tone. You'll need to go through the arguments <u>for</u> and <u>against</u> something, then come to a conclusion that demonstrates your <u>own point of view</u>.

2) Reports and essays should follow a <u>logical structure</u>. They need to have:

> • An <u>introduction</u> that sets up the <u>main theme</u>.
> • Well-structured <u>paragraphs</u> covering the <u>strengths</u> and <u>weaknesses</u> of the arguments.
> • A <u>conclusion</u> that ties things together and offers <u>your own</u> point of view.

3) The purpose of reports and essays is almost always to <u>inform</u>, but they often <u>advise</u> their audience too.

4) You need to make sure you write for the correct <u>audience</u> — <u>essays</u> usually have quite a <u>general</u> audience, but <u>reports</u> are normally written for a <u>particular</u> person or group of people.

Reports should Analyse and Advise

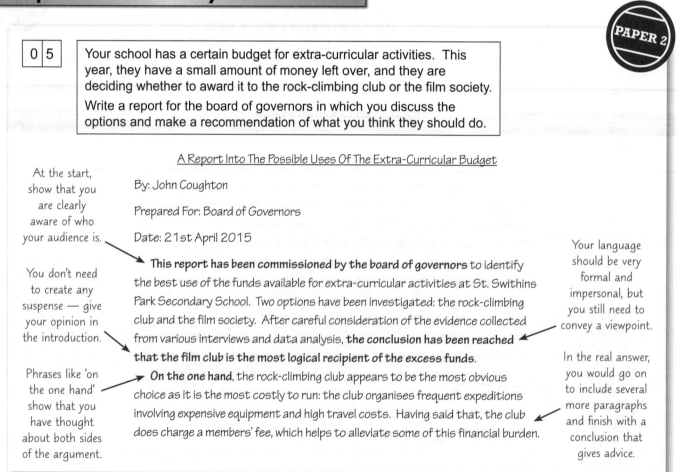

PAPER 2

| 0 5 | Your school has a certain budget for extra-curricular activities. This year, they have a small amount of money left over, and they are deciding whether to award it to the rock-climbing club or the film society. Write a report for the board of governors in which you discuss the options and make a recommendation of what you think they should do. |

A Report Into The Possible Uses Of The Extra-Curricular Budget

By: John Coughton

Prepared For: Board of Governors

Date: 21st April 2015

This report has been commissioned by the board of governors to identify the best use of the funds available for extra-curricular activities at St. Swithins Park Secondary School. Two options have been investigated: the rock-climbing club and the film society. After careful consideration of the evidence collected from various interviews and data analysis, **the conclusion has been reached that the film club is the most logical recipient of the excess funds**.

On the one hand, the rock-climbing club appears to be the most obvious choice as it is the most costly to run: the club organises frequent expeditions involving expensive equipment and high travel costs. Having said that, the club does charge a members' fee, which helps to alleviate some of this financial burden.

At the start, show that you are clearly aware of who your audience is.

You don't need to create any suspense — give your opinion in the introduction.

Phrases like 'on the one hand' show that you have thought about both sides of the argument.

Your language should be very formal and impersonal, but you still need to convey a viewpoint.

In the real answer, you would go on to include several more paragraphs and finish with a conclusion that gives advice.

Remember that paper 2 is called 'Writers' Viewpoints and Perspectives'

Reports and essays are quite simple to write — just make sure that you're being as objective, analytical and formal as possible. But you must make sure that you still show a viewpoint by coming to a conclusion.

Writing Reviews

People read reviews to find out the writer's opinion about something, so you need to express yours clearly.

Reviews should Entertain as well as Inform

1) A review is a piece of writing that gives an opinion about how good something is — it might be a book, a piece of music or even an exhibition.

2) Reviews can appear in lots of different publications. If you have to write a review in the exam, the question will usually tell you where it's going to appear.

3) The publication where your review appears will affect what kind of audience you're writing for and how you write. For example, a film review for a teen magazine could be funny and chatty, but a review of a Shakespeare play for a broadsheet newspaper should be serious and informative.

4) You should also pay attention to purpose. Your review could have several different purposes:

- Your review needs to entertain the reader.
- You also need to inform the reader about the thing you're reviewing, based on your own opinion.
- You might also need to advise the reader whether or not to see or do the thing you're reviewing.

5) Don't get too hung up on describing everything in minute detail — it's much more important that you give your opinion. Just keep your review engaging by focusing on the interesting bits and using sophisticated language.

Your review needs to Give an Evaluation

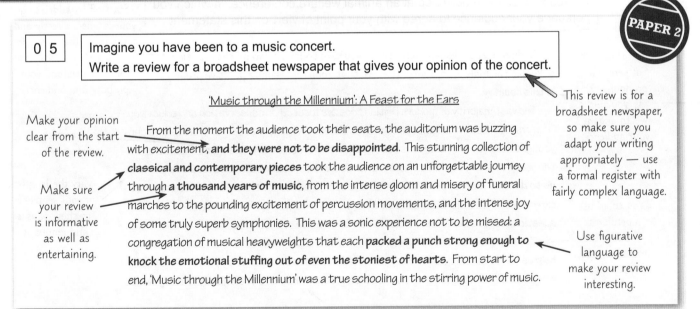

| 0 | 5 | Imagine you have been to a music concert. Write a review for a broadsheet newspaper that gives your opinion of the concert. |

PAPER 2

This review is for a broadsheet newspaper, so make sure you adapt your writing appropriately — use a formal register with fairly complex language.

'Music through the Millennium': A Feast for the Ears

Make your opinion clear from the start of the review.

Make sure your review is informative as well as entertaining.

From the moment the audience took their seats, the auditorium was buzzing with excitement, **and they were not to be disappointed**. This stunning collection of **classical and contemporary pieces** took the audience on an unforgettable journey through **a thousand years of music**, from the intense gloom and misery of funeral marches to the pounding excitement of percussion movements, and the intense joy of some truly superb symphonies. This was a sonic experience not to be missed: a congregation of musical heavyweights that each **packed a punch strong enough to knock the emotional stuffing out of even the stoniest of hearts**. From start to end, 'Music through the Millennium' was a true schooling in the stirring power of music.

Use figurative language to make your review interesting.

Your opinion needs to be very clear in a review...

Reviews are quite a nice thing to write — they're all about your opinions, which means you can say exactly what you think. You should try to express your thoughts clearly, and in a way that entertains the reader.

Writing Speeches

A speech needs to be powerful and moving. You should aim to have an emotional effect on your audience.

Speeches need to be Dramatic and Engaging

1) <u>Speeches</u> are often written to <u>argue</u> or <u>persuade</u>, so they need to have a <u>dramatic</u>, <u>emotional impact</u> on their audience.

2) One way to make a speech persuasive is to give it an effective <u>structure</u> — arrange your points so that they build <u>tension</u> throughout your answer, then end with an <u>emotive</u> or <u>exciting</u> climax.

3) You can use lots of <u>language techniques</u> to make your writing <u>engaging</u> and <u>persuasive</u>:

> *These accusations are hateful, hurtful and humiliating.* → <u>Alliteration</u> and the use of a <u>list</u> of three adjectives make this <u>sound</u> strong and angry.

Persuasive language techniques like these are known as rhetorical devices — see page 54.

> *Do we really have no other option? The current situation is a disgrace!* → <u>Rhetorical questions</u> and <u>exclamations</u> engage the reader and make your writing sound more like <u>spoken language</u>.

4) Remember that speeches are <u>spoken</u>, not read. Try to use techniques that are effective when they're spoken <u>out loud</u>.

Your speech should Make People Think

PAPER 2

> 0 5 'The practice of keeping animals in zoos cannot be allowed to continue. It is inhumane and encourages the use of animals as mere entertainment.' Write a speech to be delivered at an animal welfare conference, in which you persuade your audience to agree with your point of view on this statement.

Start off by addressing your listeners directly and announcing the reason for your speech — show that you've understood your purpose and audience.

Try to use lots of personal pronouns like 'I', 'you' and 'we' to engage your audience.

Ladies and gentlemen, I have called you here today to defend the practice of keeping animals in captivity. I believe that zoos represent a positive presence in this country.

The vast majority of modern British zoos are focused on conservation and education. To my mind, these important values are worth preserving. It is essential that we give our youngsters a sense of awareness about the world around them. **We must** impress upon the youth of today the need to protect endangered species and habitats. **Zoos can help us to do this.** Modern zoos offer extensive opportunities for these kinds of educational experiences: there are interactive exhibitions, talks from conservationists and live question-and-answer forums that will help to educate our young people.

You could use repetition to increase the dramatic impact of your speech.

Zoos can help us inspire a generation with the importance of conservation. **Zoos can help us** raise awareness of environmental issues. **Zoos can help us** by providing a space in which we can work together to build a **safer, greener and more ecologically friendly world.**

The word 'must' creates a confident tone.

Vary the lengths of your sentences to show pauses and emphasis.

Use rhetorical devices like lists of three to make your argument sound more forceful.

Practise using some rhetorical devices in your writing...

There are plenty of famous speeches throughout history — you could try looking at some of the techniques they use. Your speech doesn't have to impress a crowd of people, but it does have to impress the examiner.

Writing Letters

Letters are always addressed to a particular person or group of people. This means that they have very specific audiences, so it's very important that you tailor your letter to suit that audience.

Letters need to Start and End correctly

1) If you're asked to write a <u>letter</u>, look at the <u>audience</u> to decide how <u>formal</u> your register should be.

2) If the letter is to someone you <u>don't</u> know well, or to someone in a position of <u>authority</u>, keep it <u>formal</u> with a <u>serious</u> tone. This means you should:

- Use <u>formal greetings</u> (e.g. 'Dear Sir/Madam') and <u>sign-offs</u> (e.g. 'Yours sincerely' if you've used their name, 'Yours faithfully' if you haven't).
- Use <u>Standard English</u> and <u>formal vocabulary</u>, e.g. you could use phrases like 'In my opinion...' or 'I find this state of affairs...'.

Letters often start with the address of the sender, the address of the recipient and the date.

3) If the letter is to someone you <u>know</u>, or someone who <u>isn't</u> in a position of authority, you might use a more <u>conversational</u> style, although it should still be fairly <u>formal</u>. This means you should:

- Start with your reader's <u>name</u>, e.g. 'Dear Paul', and <u>sign off</u> with 'best wishes' or 'warm regards'.
- Make sure you still write in <u>Standard English</u> (so no <u>text speak</u> or <u>slang</u>) and show the examiner that you can use interesting <u>vocabulary</u> and <u>sentence structures</u>.

State your Viewpoint clearly

PAPER 2

0 5   You have read a newspaper article which states:
'International travel is not worth the cost.'
Write a letter to the newspaper in which you argue for or against this statement.

Bristol, 22nd February

Formal language like this helps to set the right tone for your letter and shows that you've understood your audience.

This letter is for somebody in a position of authority, so it uses a formal greeting and sign-off.

Dear Sir or Madam,

    I **read with dismay your recent article regarding international travel.** As a regular traveller myself, **I strongly disagree with your assertion that international travel is not worth the cost**. The benefits of international travel far outweigh the expenses incurred: it broadens the mind, adds to your wealth of experience and heightens your awareness of the world around you.

    The article claims that **UK holidays are cheaper and provide similar benefits**. If you are not deterred by the threat of drizzle, perhaps that is true. To me, however, **it is worth spending a fraction more to avoid wasting your holidays sheltering from the British rain**.

Yours faithfully,
Ms Karen Samuels

You need to make your viewpoint on the statement clear.

Introducing a counter-argument, then contradicting it, can help to build up your argument.

Your answer would need to be longer than this in the exam, with a few more paragraphs that support your argument.

You need to write for your audience, but keep your writing high level...

You will need to pay attention to purpose and audience — make sure your letter completes the task in the question and is written in an appropriate style. Whoever your audience is, you always need to write well.

Worked Answer

Before you leave this section, have a look at this worked answer for Paper 2.

Q1

> "In order to prepare young adults for the challenges of raising a family, it should be made compulsory for them to spend time volunteering with young children."
>
> Write an article for a broadsheet newspaper in which you argue for or against this statement.

When you're planning, it might help to jot down all your ideas first, and then organise them afterwards.

PLAN

own experience at nursery in Y10 — negative — put off having children. Cover some counter-arguments. My arguments = time pressure on young people; not all want to become parents; natural anyway? Where do you find all the children/parental permission etc.

- Para 1: own experience at nursery in Y10

- Para 2: Counter-arguments: skills (selflessness, communication, imagination), responsibility, prep for parenthood

- Para 3: not all want to become parents (figure?); those who do will be fine (natural process)

- Para 4: time pressure on young people as it is — studying, home life, part-time job already perhaps, already pressured enough into thinking of future

- Para 5: logistical problems (finding the children; those children's parents' views on it; how/who/what)

- Para 6: conclusion — well done to those doing it, sure it's rewarding, but shouldn't be compulsory

Make sure you know what your overall opinion is before you start writing.

It's great to use interesting language techniques, like similes, to help your reader to empathise with you.

Your opinion on the statement needs to be clear — even if you don't state it explicitly like this.

DON'T PUSH TEENS INTO PARENTING PRACTICE

When I was fifteen, my school Careers Advisor decided that the best way to teach her Year Tens about the wonderful ways of life was to dump them into the world of work. And so, like a bemused traveller without a map, I found myself, dazed and confused, in my local preschool. I have nothing against this preschool in particular, but the week I spent there was one of the most unpleasant of my life. After the fourth day of being smeared with paint, wet sand and the bodily fluids of various toddlers, I swore I would never work with children again. Which is why I find it remarkable that there are proposals to make this experience compulsory.

It is true that there are several strong arguments in favour of making volunteering with young children compulsory for young adults. It would teach them the patience, selflessness and imaginative thinking necessary for raising a child — important lessons for future parenthood. Furthermore, after first-hand exposure to young

Using an anecdote provides an engaging opening.

The descriptive language in this sentence helps the reader to imagine the scene at the preschool.

Show that you're responding to the prompt in the question.

Worked Answer

The second paragraph is <u>slightly inappropriate</u> for the <u>form</u> — it's become a bit like an essay. It would be better if the <u>style</u> was <u>less formal</u>...

children, other young adults may decide that parenthood would not suit them at all, and be able to make more informed choices later in life.

However, I struggle to comprehend how any young adult could actually finish their compulsory volunteering thinking "yes please". The lessons I was taught at the preschool included "there is no such thing as a clean child" and "home time is the only time worth treasuring". <u>It's also worth remembering</u> that some young people already have no intention of becoming parents. In a recent survey, <u>10%</u> of them said they had no desire to have children. I would like to see how many of the other 90% flock to join them after an <u>enforced week of torture</u> such as mine.

...like this. This kind of <u>informal phrase</u> is better suited to a broadsheet newspaper article.

<u>Facts and figures</u> are <u>appropriate</u> for a broadsheet newspaper article.

<u>Hyperbole</u> can be used to add <u>humour</u>, making your answer <u>entertaining</u>.

This is before we even consider that many young people simply wouldn't have the time for volunteering. My own week of work experience meant losing a week of lessons while studying for my GCSEs. Plenty of young people are already ground to the bone, juggling <u>home life, academics and extra-curricular activities</u> in the hope of getting that important first job. <u>Surely this should take priority over spending stressful time with children?</u>

Rhetorical techniques (like <u>rhetorical questions</u> and <u>lists of three</u>) make your answer more <u>persuasive</u>.

Broadsheet newspaper articles should have a <u>personal tone</u>.

Where these children would come from is another mystery. <u>Personally</u>, I can't imagine my own parents willingly donating me for an unknown teenager to take care of. I also feel sorry for whichever local schools, preschools or councils would become responsible for dealing with the <u>mountains of paperwork</u> involved.

This <u>metaphor</u> adds <u>emphasis</u> to the point about logistical problems.

This conclusion refers back to the <u>statement</u> in the question, which links the answer together nicely, and shows good <u>organisation</u>.

In theory, bringing young people and young children together for voluntary work seems like a lovely idea. I'm sure there are plenty of young people who already volunteer with young children, and I'm sure they benefit from it. This does not mean that we should start forcing all of their peers into it too — a few hours with a messy, crying child isn't going to prepare you <u>for the challenges of raising a family</u>, because you're never going to want to have a family at all.

- This answer is mostly well-matched to its form (a broadsheet newspaper article), and shows a good awareness of purpose (to persuade and entertain) and audience (readers of a broadsheet newspaper).
- It also uses a variety of language techniques effectively (e.g. similes, hyperbole and rhetorical questions).
- The structure is good too. It's written in clear paragraphs, with an engaging introduction and conclusion.
- To get the very top marks, this answer could use some more ambitious vocabulary and punctuation. The second paragraph would also need to be better-matched to the form in the question.

Exam-Style Questions

These questions will help you to prepare for the non-fiction writing question in paper 2. Make sure you quickly plan your answers — in the real exam, there are marks for a well-organised response to this question.

Q1

"Active hobbies, such as sports, are falling by the wayside because of the popularity of tablets and smartphones. Being constantly glued to screens is bad for our nation's health."

Write an article for a broadsheet newspaper in which you argue for or against this statement.

Q2

One of your classmates has said: "I think going to bed early is a waste of time. All the good television programmes are on late at night."

Write a speech in which you try to persuade your class that it's important to get a full night's sleep.

Q3

"Young people should widen their horizons. It's important that they travel and experience new cultures before they start their adult life."

Write a leaflet persuading students to take a gap year before starting work or college.

Q4

"We should build more houses in rural areas. Having beautiful scenery is not as important as having a plentiful supply of housing for a growing population."

Write a letter to a local newspaper editor explaining your point of view on this statement.

Revision Summary

This is the final Revision Summary in this book (hurrah) so make sure you use it well.

- Try these questions and <u>tick off each one</u> when you <u>get it right</u>.
- When you've done <u>all the questions</u> under a heading and are <u>completely happy</u> with it, tick it off.

Writing with Purpose (p.70-77) ☑

1) What would be the purpose of an answer to this question?
   Write the opening of a short story about a lost pet. ☑

2) True or false?
   *You never have to work out the audience in a writing question
   — it will be stated for you explicitly every time.* ☑

3) Why might an advert for children's breakfast cereal have more than one audience? ☑

4) What three things do you always need to match to your purpose and audience? ☑

5) Give two ways in which you could start a story so that it's engaging for the reader. ☑

6) Rewrite this sentence so that it has a first-person narrative viewpoint.
   Frances skulked down the hallway, delaying her arrival at her Maths classroom. ☑

7) Give one effect of using a third-person narrative viewpoint. ☑

8) Which of these would be a good way to end a story?
   a) A question that creates a cliffhanger.
   b) An unexpected plot twist to shock the reader.
   c) And they all lived happily ever after. ☑

9) True or false? *You don't need to include as much plot or action when writing a description.* ☑

10) If you're asked to write a description of a character, you might describe their physical features.
    a) What's another thing you could describe about them?
    b) Write a brief description of a famous person. ☑

Writing in Different Styles (p.80-87) ☑

11) Give two layout features that you could include in a newspaper article. ☑

12) What is a broadsheet newspaper? ☑

13) Name two structural features that you could use to break up information in a leaflet. ☑

14) What would be the form and purpose, and who would be the audience, in an answer to this
    exam question?
    *"Holidays to Europe are overrated — today's European cities are busy, expensive and dull."
    Imagine you have just visited a city in Europe. Write an article for a travel magazine
    in which you explain your point of view on this statement.* ☑

15) Briefly explain the logical structure you should use when writing a report or an essay. ☑

16) What is the main difference between a report and an essay? ☑

17) How should your style of writing be different in a game review for a teen magazine,
    and an album review for a broadsheet newspaper? ☑

18) What is usually your main purpose when you're writing a speech? ☑

19) Write down an example opening and ending for:
    a) a letter to a local councillor, arguing in favour of building a new shopping centre near
       where you live
    b) a letter to a named teacher, asking for an extension on your homework deadline. ☑

Sample Exam — Paper 1

These two pages show you some example questions that are like the ones you'll see in paper 1 — the source to go with questions 1-4 is on p.94. First have a good read through the source and the questions, then have a look at the handy graded answer extracts we've provided on pages 95-103.

Question 1 asks you to Find some Information

0	1	Read again lines 12 to 19 of the source.

Read again lines 12 to 19 of the source.

List **four** things from this part of the text about the baby.

[4 marks]

Question 2 is about the writer's use of Language

0	2

Look in detail at lines 1 to 11 of the source.

How does the writer use language here to describe Mabel's life in Alaska?

You could include the writer's choice of:

*   words and phrases
*   language features and techniques
*   sentence forms.

[8 marks]

Question 3 is about the Structure of the Whole text

0	3

You now need to think about the **whole** of the **source**.

This text is from the opening of a novel.

How has the writer structured the text to interest you as a reader?

You could write about:

*   what the writer focuses your attention on at the beginning
*   how and why the writer changes this focus as the source develops
*   any other structural features that interest you.

[8 marks]

Sample Exam — Paper 1

Question 4 asks for a **Personal Response** to the text

| 0 | 4 | Focus this part of your answer on the last part of the source, **from line 20 to the end**. |

A student, having read this section of the text, said: "The writer makes it really clear how Mabel is feeling. It makes me feel the emotions she's feeling too."

To what extent do you agree?

In your response, you could:

- write about your own feelings on reading the passage
- evaluate how the writer created those feelings
- support your opinions with quotations from the text.

[20 marks]

You have to do some **Creative Writing** for **Question 5**

| 0 | 5 | You are going to enter a creative writing competition. |

Your entry will be judged by a panel of people of your own age.

Either:

Write a description suggested by this picture:

© wingmar/iStockphoto.com

Or:

Write the opening part of a story that is set in a cold place in winter.

(24 marks for content and organisation
16 marks for technical accuracy)

[40 marks]

The answers to these questions are in the rest of the section...

You don't have to answer these questions yourself. Instead, read on for some sample answers, which will give you an idea of what you need to write in your exam. You can refer back to these pages if you need to.

Exam Source

Here's the text to go with the questions on pages 92-93. It's an extract from the opening of *The Snow Child* by Eowyn Ivey, a novel which was published in 2012, but is set in 1920. In the novel, a woman named Mabel and her husband, Jack, have moved to the cold, remote Alaskan wilderness to start a new life.

Wolverine River, Alaska, 1920

Mabel had known there would be silence. That was the point, after all. No infants cooing or wailing. No neighbor children playfully hollering down the lane. No pad of small feet on wooden stairs worn smooth by generations, or clackety-clack of toys along the kitchen floor. All those sounds of her failure and regret would be left behind, and in their place there would be silence.

5   She had imagined that in the Alaska wilderness silence would be peaceful, like snow falling at night, air filled with promise but no sound, but that was not what she found. Instead, when she swept the plank floor, the broom bristles scritched like some sharp-toothed shrew nibbling at her heart. When she washed the dishes, plates and bowls clattered as if they were breaking to pieces. The only sound not of her making was a sudden 'caw, cawww' from outside. Mabel wrung dishwater from a rag and looked out the kitchen

10 window in time to see a raven flapping its way from one leafless birch tree to another. No children chasing each other through autumn leaves, calling each other's names. Not even a solitary child on a swing.

❄

There had been the one. A tiny thing, born still and silent. Ten years past, but even now she found herself returning to the birth to touch Jack's arm, stop him, reach out. She should have. She should have cupped the baby's head in the palm of her hand and snipped a few of its tiny hairs to keep in a locket at her throat.

15 She should have looked into its small face and known if it was a boy or a girl, and then stood beside Jack as he buried it in the Pennsylvania winter ground. She should have marked its grave. She should have allowed herself that grief.

     It was a child, after all, although it looked more like a fairy changeling. Pinched face, tiny jaw, ears that came to narrow points; that much she had seen and wept over because she knew she could have loved it still.

❄

20 Mabel was too long at the window. The raven had since flown away above the treetops. The sun had slipped behind a mountain, and the light had fallen flat. The branches were bare, the grass yellowed gray. Not a single snowflake. It was as if everything fine and glittering had been ground from the world and swept away as dust.

     November was here, and it frightened her because she knew what it brought — cold upon the valley

25 like a coming death, glacial wind through the cracks between the cabin logs. But most of all, darkness. Darkness so complete even the pale-lit hours would be choked.

     She entered last winter blind, not knowing what to expect in this new, hard land. Now she knew. By December, the sun would rise just before noon and skirt the mountaintops for a few hours of twilight before sinking again. Mabel would move in and out of sleep as she sat in a chair beside the woodstove. She

30 would not pick up any of her favorite books; the pages would be lifeless. She would not draw; what would there be to capture in her sketchbook? Dull skies, shadowy corners. It would become harder and harder to leave the warm bed each morning. She would stumble about in a walking sleep, scrape together meals and drape wet laundry around the cabin. Jack would struggle to keep the animals alive. The days would run together, winter's stranglehold tightening.

35   All her life she had believed in something more, in the mystery that shape-shifted at the edge of her senses. It was the flutter of moth wings on glass and the promise of river nymphs in the dappled creek beds. It was the smell of oak trees on the summer evening she fell in love, and the way dawn threw itself across the cow pond and turned the water to light.

     Mabel could not remember the last time she caught such a flicker.

Graded Answers — Question 1

There are four marks on offer in question 1. Re-read the question on page 92, then have a look at this page.

Include the right **Number** of **Facts**

1) <u>Question 1</u> asks for <u>four</u> things about the <u>baby</u>, and there are <u>four marks</u> available. That means you get one mark for <u>each</u> thing that you write down about the baby.

2) Careful though — all your facts need to come from <u>lines 12-19</u>.

3) It's also important to <u>check</u> every fact carefully — anything that's <u>inaccurate</u> or not directly about the <u>baby</u> won't get a mark.

4) There's no need to <u>analyse</u> your facts or add any extra information — you just need to show that you can <u>find</u> information from the text.

The facts you pick out can either be explicit or implicit (see p.20 for more on this).

Here's a **Grade 4-5** answer

A   It was "tiny".

B   It looked like "a fairy changeling".

C   It was the reason Mabel and Jack moved to Alaska.

D   Mabel kept some of its hair in a locket.

The first two answers are about the baby, and they're taken from the right part of the text, so they'd get a mark each.

This isn't mentioned in lines 12-19, so it wouldn't get a mark.

This isn't true — make sure you read the text carefully so your answers are accurate.

This is a **Grade 6-7** answer

A   It was "born still and silent".

B   It had "tiny hairs".

C   It had pointy ears.

D   Mabel is upset about the baby.

These two answers would get a mark each.

For question 1, it's fine to paraphrase instead of directly quoting — this answer would also get a mark.

This doesn't make a point about the baby — it's about Mabel's feelings, so it wouldn't get a mark.

And here's a **Grade 8-9** answer

A   It was born ten years ago.

B   It had a "small face".

C   It had a "tiny jaw".

D   The baby didn't have a marked grave.

All four answers would get a mark.

You can infer this from the text. Mabel says she "should have marked its grave", which implies that the baby's grave wasn't marked.

Graded Answers — Question 2

Question 2 (take a look back at p.92) is a bit more challenging than question 1.

Pick out key Language Features and explain their Effects

1) Question 2 tests how well you can explain the effects of the language used in the extract.

2) The sample question asks you specifically about the language used to describe Mabel's life — so you shouldn't write about the language used to describe anything else.

3) You need to use P.E.E.D. for this question — every point you make should be backed up with an example that's fully explained and developed (see p.10).

4) You also need to use a range of technical terms to describe the writer's techniques.

5) To get top marks, you need to write about all of the bullet points under the question:

- The effect of specific words and phrases, such as how specific verbs are used (see p.44-45).
- Language features and techniques, such as metaphors, similes and onomatopoeia (see p.48-51).
- The effect of different sentence forms, such as short or long sentences (see p.64-65).

Make sure you read each question carefully — this question is only asking about language, not structure.

Here's a Grade 4-5 answer extract

It's great to include quotes, but try to keep them short.

The writer says **"the broom bristles scritched like some sharp-toothed shrew nibbling at her heart"**. This shows that Alaska isn't as "peaceful" as Mabel expected. The shrew eating her heart makes it sound like she isn't enjoying her life in Alaska.

The first sentence in the second paragraph is very long, which shows how significant silence is to Mabel's life in Alaska. **The writer compares the silence to "snow" and "air", which makes it feel like her life is empty.**

This emptiness is different to the "clackety-clack" **(which is onomatopoeia)** and "hollering" of the first paragraph, which makes the silence seem even more like it's an important part of Mabel's life.

There is a raven "flapping its way from one leafless birch tree to another" too, which makes you feel like something bad is going to happen.

This starts to discuss the effect of the language on the reader.

It's important to mention techniques like this, but you need to write more about the effect they have, too.

This last paragraph doesn't seem relevant to the question — it needs to be clearly linked back to Mabel's life.

1) This answer makes some good points about how the writer uses language to describe Mabel's life.

2) It could be improved by explaining the effect of the language more fully, as it's not always clear how the examples are relevant to the question.

3) It could also do with using more technical terms — it only uses one, and it doesn't explain the effect it has very well.

Graded Answers — Question 2

Here's a **Grade 6-7** answer extract

Referring to the writer shows that you understand they chose to use this language for a reason.

The writer uses a short, direct first sentence to introduce the idea that the most prominent thing about Mabel's life in Alaska is how silent it is: "Mabel had known there would be silence."

The language used in this extract implies that Mabel finds this **"silence"** threatening and uncomfortable. The verb **"scritched"** sounds like a small animal clawing the "plank floor", which emphasises Mabel's uneasiness. The word is also onomatopoeic, so it interrupts the "silence", but in a way that's painful and upsetting. The writer is emphasising that the "promise" of peace Mabel hoped to find in Alaska has not been fulfilled; instead, she has been left unhappy.

The image of the solitary raven and the "leafless" trees links Mabel's surroundings with the idea of lifelessness. This increases the overall negative tone of the passage, **which leaves the reader with a strong impression that Mabel's life is unhappy.**

Good use of a brief quote to back up a point.

It's really good to focus on the effects of specific words.

It's important to keep linking the answer back to the question.

1) This answer makes some good points about the <u>effects</u> of the language the writer has chosen, which are <u>backed up</u> with appropriate quotations and <u>linked back</u> to the question.

2) It could be improved by mentioning even more <u>language features</u> or <u>techniques</u>.

This is a **Grade 8-9** answer extract

This extract uses sensory verbs to create images of childhood: verbs such as **"wailing"** and "hollering" suggest a loud, frenetic atmosphere. This is contrasted sharply with the **"silence"** of Alaska, which is mentioned twice, at the beginning and end of the first paragraph. **This contrast has a jarring effect on the reader, and suggests that Mabel's life in Alaska is characterised by a sense of emptiness and loss.**

The writer also uses onomatopoeic verbs such as "scritched" and "clattered" to suggest that the "silence" in Alaska makes any noise seem unnaturally loud and unpleasant, and to bring the reader into the uncomfortable life that Mabel leads. These verbs are used in combination with the vivid **simile** of a shrew "nibbling" at Mabel's heart, **which emphasises her discomfort and suggests that, instead of the peace she had hoped to find, Mabel's life is deeply unhappy.**

The writer uses direct speech only once in this extract, when there is "a sudden 'caw, cawww'" from a raven. The intrusiveness of this direct speech is emphasised because of the hard 'C' sound at the beginning of each word. Because the speech feels so out of place, the reader starts to empathise with the intrusion Mabel feels at the noise. **This further emphasises the discomfort of her life.**

This answer uses a good range of short quotes to back up the points it makes.

It's important to focus on the effect that the language has.

Uses a technical term for a language technique, then fully explains it.

This answer stays focused on the question throughout.

1) This is a <u>really good</u> answer. It makes several points about the writer's <u>choice</u> of language and the <u>effect</u> it has, and then <u>develops</u> each point fully.

2) It also uses complex <u>technical terms</u> correctly and supports each point with relevant <u>quotations</u>.

Graded Answers — Question 3

Question 3 is all about the structure of the text. These sample answers will show you what's required.

Think about how the text is **Put Together** and the **Effect** this has

1) Question 3 is about the <u>structure</u> of the text — you need to talk about <u>how</u> the writer has used structure to make the text more <u>interesting</u> to read.

2) This question covers the <u>whole text</u>, so make sure you talk about the <u>overall structure</u> of the extract as you're answering the question.

3) However, you should also comment on the position of specific <u>sentences</u> and the structure of <u>paragraphs</u> — aim to comment on a <u>range</u> of structural features.

4) To get top marks, you'll need to write about <u>everything</u> the bullet points mention:

> • You need to write about the <u>beginning</u> of the text, and why the writer chooses to start by focusing on Mabel's <u>present-day life</u>.
>
> • You need to comment on the <u>overall structure</u> of the text, by talking about how the writer <u>changes</u> what she's focusing on throughout, and the <u>effect</u> that this has on the reader.
>
> • Any <u>other</u> structural features that interest you — this could include <u>anything else</u> you spot, such as repeated <u>images</u> or places where the text focuses on something <u>specific</u>.

Don't forget to use P.E.E.D. (see p.10) — every point you make needs to be backed up, explained, and developed.

Here's a **Grade 4-5** answer extract

This answer references the question — it talks about why the text is interesting.

A better technical term could be used here, such as 'contrasts'.

In the first paragraph, the writer tells you that there is "failure and regret" in Mabel's past, but it doesn't tell you why straight away. **This keeps you interested to find out more.**
    The writer next writes about what Mabel thought Alaska would be like before she arrived there, then **compares** it to what it's actually like now that she lives there. This is interesting because it shows how it is different from how she thought it would be.
    It then talks about the past, ten years ago, when she had a baby "born still and silent". It makes you feel sorry for Mabel and **helps you understand why she wanted to move away from other people.**
    Next the writer writes about the future, as Mabel explains what her life will be like over the coming winter. **So it goes from present to past to future, which is an interesting structure.**

This would be better if it made it clear why she wanted to move away from other people.

This sums up the overall structure, but it needs developing further. It also might have been clearer to mention this at the beginning of the answer.

1) This answer describes some <u>structural features</u> of the text and starts to comment on the <u>effect</u> they have.

2) However, it doesn't go into enough <u>detail</u> about how the structure helps to grab the <u>reader's interest</u>, or <u>fully develop</u> why the writer's choice of structure is <u>effective</u>.

Graded Answers — Question 3

Here's a **Grade 6-7** answer extract

The writer moves from a description of Mabel's present life in Alaska to a recollection of the past, then finally to her fears about the future. This is an unusual structure that helps the reader to understand Mabel, and so engages their interest.

In the first and second paragraphs the focus is on the silence of the present, which emphasises Mabel's sense of "failure and regret". This grabs the reader's interest by making you wonder why Mabel has moved to such a bleak place and what has caused her "regret".

These questions are answered in the third paragraph, in which the writer describes Mabel's memory of having a stillborn baby "Ten years past". This focus on the past highlights all the reasons why Mabel feels "failure and regret". This increases the reader's sympathy and helps them to identify with Mabel.

In the last section of the extract the focus is shifted to the future as Mabel begins to think about the winter to come. This change in focus is emphasised by the writer's use of repetition; in lines 29-34, she repeats the verb "would" to continually focus the reader on what Mabel is sure will happen. By directing the reader's attention to the future and Mabel's certainty about what it will bring, the writer makes the reader want to continue reading to find out if she's right.

This is a strong opening that sums up the overall structure.

This explains an effect of the structure, but could go into more detail about why this would interest the reader.

Good focus on answering the question.

This comments on how the focus changes throughout the extract.

This answer could be developed more fully to explain how each element of structure holds the reader's interest.

This is a **Grade 8-9** answer extract

The passage has a complex non-chronological structure, which seems to follow Mabel's train of thought. This gives the reader an insight into Mabel's mind, which creates interest by building empathy for the character.

The overall structure shifts from present, to past, to future and back to present. However, within this structure the present intrudes time and time again, for example "Now she knew". This constantly brings the focus of the text back to Mabel's current situation, which serves both as a reminder of the monotony of her life, and as a means of highlighting her dread of the winter to come. In this way, the structure simultaneously holds Mabel (and the reader) frozen in time whilst propelling her relentlessly towards the future she fears, creating a narrative tension which interests and engages the reader.

This impression is furthered by the recurrent references to nature that punctuate the narrative. The weather outside is currently "flat" and still, but it promises cold "like a coming death" and "glacial wind". This hint of coming crisis builds the tension in the narrative, which keeps the reader gripped.

High-level vocabulary makes this answer stand out.

This makes an interesting point about the large-scale and smaller-scale structure of the passage...

... and then fully explains its effect.

This explains how the structure helps maintain the reader's interest.

This is a really good answer — it makes several original points about the structure and its effect. The points are fully developed to explain how the structure helps to hold the reader's interest.

Graded Answers — Question 4

Question 4 (see p.93) is worth 20 marks, so it's worth spending some time working out how to answer it.

Write about **Whether** you **Agree** with the **Statement** and **Why**

1) Question 4 is about evaluating how effective the text is.

2) The sample question gives you a statement, which has two parts to it — you need to give your opinion on how the writer shows Mabel's feelings, and how this makes you feel.

3) You also need to state how much you agree or disagree with the statement.

4) Use P.E.E.D. (see p.10) and make sure you include technical terms to get top marks.

5) The bullet points under the question give you guidance about what you need to include in your answer:

- You need to write about your own feelings as you read the text.

- You also need to talk about the techniques the writer uses to create these feelings, i.e. the language or structural devices they use.

- The question specifically mentions using quotes in your answer, so you need to include plenty of relevant evidence for every point you make.

Here's a **Grade 4-5** answer extract

> Overall, I agree with the student. I mostly feel the same emotions Mabel is feeling, and I think the writer makes it really obvious how she's feeling.
>
> Mabel feels frightened of the winter, and especially of the "darkness". The description of the "few hours of twilight" each day makes you imagine what it would be like not to see daylight for months, **so you can start to understand Mabel's feelings of fear and anxiety**.
>
> The writer also suggests that Mabel is unhappy. She does this by making the Alaskan winter seem very uncomfortable, **with the "glacial wind through the cracks" in the walls and "wet laundry" everywhere**.
>
> **Some of the words rhyme, which sounds really repetitive, so it makes it seem like Mabel's life is monotonous.** The way the words sound makes me feel bored and dull too.

This is good — it gives an opinion on the statement.

This starts to address how the text makes the reader feel.

This could be developed by writing about how these phrases help the reader feel what Mabel is feeling.

This is a good point about language and its effect, but it needs a clear example from the text and more explanation.

1) This answer starts to comment on how Mabel feels, and how the text makes the reader feel.

2) However, some of the points in this answer need to be developed further by explaining how the writer's choice of language and structure affects the reader.

3) Every point should also be backed up with a good example from the text.

Graded Answers — Question 4

Here's a **Grade 6-7** answer extract

I strongly agree with the student that the writer makes you feel how Mabel feels. She uses descriptive techniques to create a very strong sense of the atmosphere of Mabel's life and emotions.

Mabel is "frightened" by winter, and the writer uses vivid language to show and emphasise this feeling. For example, the writer compares the winter to **"a coming death"** to show the danger Mabel thinks she is facing, then reinforces this impression using violent words such as **"choked"** and **"stranglehold"**. This use of powerful descriptive vocabulary helps me to imagine myself in Mabel's position and feel her fear.

The writer also suggests that Mabel feels powerless in the face of her fears. The verbs "would stumble" and "would struggle" indicate her hopeless feelings regarding the winter to come. **This description of the winter months helps the reader to empathise with Mabel and the inevitable difficulties that her future will bring.**

This shows that you've thought about the extent to which you agree with the statement.

This paragraph picks out specific language features and comments on their impact.

This shows that you're thinking about the effect of the text on the reader.

1) This answer clearly focuses on how the writer uses language to create a <u>vivid impression</u> of how Mabel is feeling.

2) It uses a good range of relevant <u>quotes</u> as evidence, and <u>develops</u> the points by relating them to the effect on the <u>reader</u>.

This is a **Grade 8-9** answer extract

To an extent I agree with the student's statement. The focus of the passage shifts from the dismal external landscape to an oppressive interior of "shadowy corners" and "wet laundry". **This highlights to the reader how trapped Mabel feels by the "stranglehold" of the encroaching winter.** Her home, which should be a place of safety, has become a place of fear, surrounded by "darkness" and vulnerable to "glacial winds". **The writer describes common sensations like darkness and cold, which the reader can easily recognise. This makes Mabel's feelings seem very clear, and helps me to empathise with her plight.**

However, it also seems that this bleak depiction of winter is a result of Mabel's attitude, which **lessens the extent to which I empathise with her feelings**. The repetition of "would not" to describe her lack of activity hints at her negative mindset, which is reinforced by the short, blunt sentence on line 39. By contrasting Mabel's lack of hope with Jack's "struggle", the writer implies that there are more proactive responses to the hardships of winter, and suggests that Mabel's dread is at least partly irrational.

This shows an understanding of how the text's structure affects the reader's response.

This explains how the language used conveys Mabel's feeling and affects the reader.

Keep referring back to the statement to make sure your answer is focused.

The second paragraph makes a well-developed counter-argument.

1) This is a <u>top grade</u> answer — it gives an answer that clearly responds to the <u>statement</u> in an <u>original</u> way.

2) It has a clear <u>structure</u>, and its points are backed up with relevant <u>quotes</u> and <u>examples</u>.

Graded Answers — Question 5

You'll have a choice of two tasks for question 5, but you only need to do one. See p.93 for the full question.

Include lots of Description in your answer

1) To write a good answer to this question, you need to match your writing to the form, purpose, and audience in the question.

> • The form needs to be either a description or the beginning of a story. Think about the kind of language and writing structures that work well for these forms (see pages 74-77).
>
> • For both tasks, it's a piece of creative writing that's being judged, so the purpose is to entertain the judges. You need to use a range of sophisticated vocabulary and language techniques, and a structure that grabs and holds the judges' interest.
>
> • Your audience is mentioned explicitly in the question — it's a panel of judges who are the same age as you. You need to adapt your language, tone and style so that it's appealing to a teenage audience.

2) There are also loads of marks on offer for spelling, punctuation and grammar in this question, so it's really important to write accurately and clearly (see p.16-18).

Here's a Grade 4-5 answer extract

This sets the scene, but it could do with some more imaginative description.

The small house stood on its own, surrounded by fir trees and rocks. Snow had gathered against the walls in deep piles. It did not look very inviting, but to Anneka it was the most welcome sight in the world. She had got lost in the woods and she had been worried that she would have to spend the night outside in the forest, which was freezing cold and **as scary as a spider's nest.**

It's good to use descriptive techniques like similes, but this one isn't very original and it doesn't really create the right tone.

Anneka walked towards the door and knocked. To her surprise the door swung open and she could see inside the house. She saw a single room with a fire burning in the fireplace and a table set for two, with hot food piled high on the plates. There was only one thing missing from the scene, there were no people inside.

This is a good piece of descriptive vocabulary.

Anneka walked **tentatively** into the room and began to warm her hands in front of the fire, wondering where the people who lived in the house had gone. The room looked as if someone had just stepped out, but the only path Anneka had seen was the one she had come along, and she had not passed anyone else. **Surely they couldn't have just disappeared?**

The punctuation in this sentence isn't quite right — a colon would fit better.

This sets up a mystery, which makes the reader want to know what has happened.

1) This answer has a fairly clear structure and gets straight into the story.

2) However, it lacks description, and the vocabulary isn't very varied. It could also be made more exciting or complex for its teenage audience.

All these extracts are from answers to the second task in question 5 on page 93 — the opening of a story.

Graded Answers — Question 5

Here's a **Grade 6-7** answer extract

This uses the opening sentence of the story to set the scene nicely.

Robin lowered the axe he had been using to chop wood and peered towards the mountains, his eyes squinting in the sharp orange glow of the slowly setting Sun. He was sure he had seen a movement up there, **a flash of scarlet against the sparkling white of the snow-capped peaks**. But who would be mad enough to venture into the mountains at dusk, in winter, with snow and freezing temperatures forecast that night?

Robin sighed wearily, deciding that it must have been his imagination playing tricks on him, as it so often did out here in the mountains.

A low, ominous rumble echoed down the valley, interrupting his thoughts. Robin froze momentarily, listening intently, **then snapped into action**, frantically gathering his tools as the sound grew louder and closer.

The avalanche roared destructively and unstoppably towards his isolated home.

This answer uses interesting language to make the descriptions more vivid and to entertain the audience.

This uses the senses to help the reader to imagine the scene.

The change of pace creates excitement in this story.

1) This has a clear <u>structure</u>, uses good <u>descriptions</u> and builds <u>interest</u> for the reader.

2) It could be improved by using more <u>complex</u> sentence structures and a <u>wider range</u> of punctuation.

This is a **Grade 8-9** answer extract

I surfaced suddenly from a dreamless sleep, the skin on my forearms tingling with an instinctive awareness that something was wrong. There — that noise again! A skittering, scrabbling, scuffling noise in the far corner of the dimly lit room. **I sat up in bed, the quilt clutched to my chest** with stone-numb hands, my breath forming foggy billows in the chilly air.

The sun was just rising; its feeble light trickled through the window, fractured into myriad rainbows by the intricate whorls and fingers of ice on the frosty pane. As a brighter beam pierced the gloom, I gasped. There, huddled by the door, a young wolf cub gazed at me with sorrowful, strangely human eyes. His tawny fur was matted with blood, **as rich and red as the morning light that now illuminated it fully.**

I eased myself out of the wooden bunk, crouched down on the splintered floorboards and held out a trembling hand towards the cub. He gazed at me uncertainly, then slowly, slowly, he stretched forward and snuffled at my fingers, his breath **as warm and ticklish as a damp feather duster.**

This beginning immediately sets the tone and atmosphere by creating tension.

This uses a first-person narrator to establish a strong connection with the reader.

Vivid description and interesting vocabulary help to set the scene.

Unusual imagery helps to set this answer apart.

1) This has a structure that <u>interests</u> the reader by <u>slowly revealing</u> what's going on.

2) It's also packed with interesting <u>imagery</u> and unusual <u>vocabulary</u> to make it more <u>entertaining</u> to read, which helps it to fit the <u>purpose</u> and <u>audience</u> of the question.

Sample Exam — Paper 2

These two pages show you some example questions that are like the ones you'll see in paper 2 — the sources to go with questions 1-4 are on pages 106-107. First have a read through the sources and the questions, then have a look at the graded answer extracts we've provided on pages 108-117.

Question 1 asks you to identify if statements are True or False

| 0 | 1 | Read the first part of **source A**, from lines 1 to 17. |

Choose **four** statements below which are **TRUE**.
- Shade the boxes of the ones that you think are true
- Choose a maximum of four statements.

A	Lisa made her first batches of soup with her parents.	☐
B	Lisa wasn't initially excited about making and selling soup.	☐
C	Lisa's parents liked the first sample of soup she made them try.	☐
D	Lisa's aunt didn't like throwing food away.	☐
E	Lisa's parents thought the business was a great idea from the start.	☐
F	People were surprised by Lisa working at such a young age.	☐
G	Lisa's dad wasn't very good at negotiating with farmers.	☐
H	Lisa chose working on her business over spending time with friends.	☐

[4 marks]

Question 2 is about Summarising information

| 0 | 2 | You need to refer to **source A** and the **whole of source B** for this question: |

Use details from **both** sources. Write a summary of the differences between Lisa Goodwin's parents and the parents of the Victorian street sellers.

[8 marks]

Sample Exam — Paper 2

Question 3 is about the writer's choice of Language

| 0 | 3 | You now need to refer **only** to **source B**, the interview with the flower seller. |

How does the flower seller use language to appeal to the reader's emotions?

[12 marks]

Question 4 asks you to Compare writers' Viewpoints

| 0 | 4 | For this question, you need to refer to the **whole of source A** together with **source B**, the interview with the nut seller. |

Compare how Lisa Goodwin and the nut seller convey their different attitudes to work and childhood.

In your answer, you should:
- compare their different attitudes
- compare the methods they use to convey their attitudes
- support your ideas with quotations from both texts.

[16 marks]

You have to Explain your Viewpoint in Question 5

| 0 | 5 | "More children should get a job before the age of sixteen. Part-time work would teach children valuable skills that they don't learn in school." |

Write an article for a broadsheet newspaper in which you explain your point of view on this statement.

(24 marks for content and organisation
16 marks for technical accuracy)
[40 marks]

You don't have to actually answer these questions...

On the next two pages, you'll find source texts A and B — make sure you read them carefully. Then use the sample answers on pages 108-117 to build your understanding of how to write great paper 2 answers.

Exam Source A

Here is exam source A, to go with the questions on pages 104-105. It's an autobiographical article written by a young entrepreneur (a person who starts up a business) for a newspaper in the 1990s.

Setting up SouperStar — From Soup Pan to Soup Stand

Lisa Goodwin recalls how she set up her first business at the age of eight.

When I first told my parents that I wanted to sell soup, I must have been about eight years old — like most sensible parents, they thought I was joking. That weekend, I'd been at my aunt's house helping her harvest vegetables from her garden. It had been a bumper year, and we'd been staggering back and forth, shifting armfuls of all sorts of things into the house. With my aunt, not a single thing could
5 go to waste, so we set about making soup. Gallons of the stuff. We were surrounded by steaming and bubbling pots and pans, and the air was thick with scents of leek and potato, carrot and coriander and spicy butternut squash. Anyway, when my parents didn't take me seriously, I went straight to the fridge to dig out one of the soups my aunt and I had made — it was cream of mushroom, I think — and they absolutely lapped it up. "See!" I said, smiling. So it was then that SouperStar was born.

10 From day one I couldn't wait to get stuck in. My parents would dutifully help me select produce, whizz up batches of soup and drive me here, there and everywhere so that I could set up shop. I would go to school fairs, farmers' markets — anywhere that would have me. Dad was my champion haggler. He'd barter with local farmers to get crates of carrots or potatoes at rock-bottom prices. If he could get anything for free, well, that was even better! I think a lot of people were bemused by the sight of this
15 young kid, buying produce and selling soup, and my parents put up with it because they thought that I would grow out of it at some stage. While other kids my age were glued to the TV or playing in the park, I was peeling vegetables and frying croutons.

I begged and pleaded with my parents to let me be home-schooled, as I wanted to dedicate more time to the business, but they insisted I should have a "normal" childhood, and fill my head with "necessary" stuff
20 like formulae and equations. A few years later, and I was sitting my O levels* — but instead of panicking over revision, I was, of course, dreaming up new recipes. With all my exams passed and done with, I wanted to press on and really dedicate myself to SouperStar. I think at this point my parents genuinely realised how determined I was, and they began to take it a lot more seriously too.

I struck upon the idea of selling soup at our local train station during the winter months — there was a
25 constant stream of customers all in desperate need of something that would warm up their hands and fill their bellies. Before long, I was hiring extra staff in order to open up soup stands in other nearby train stations and Mum was coming up with advertising slogans and snazzy package designs (her years of marketing experience came in pretty handy here). As the business grew and grew, Mum and Dad couldn't keep up with all the support I needed, so it made sense for them to get even more involved.
30 Mum reduced her hours at work and Dad quit his job entirely. Fast-forward to today, and I'm the managing director of one the most successful food companies in the area.

Of course, financially, it's worked out well for us (thanks must go to my parents for the initial investment, not to mention being old enough to buy the wine for my French onion soup!), but for me it was never the dream of becoming a millionaire that got me started or even kept me going. It was the passion for
35 building a great business based on great food — and that remains at the heart of SouperStar today.

Glossary

* O levels — the qualifications that preceded GCSEs, with examinations taken at the age of 16.

Exam Source B

This is exam source B, which consists of two interviews from the 1840s conducted with children who work as street sellers. These articles, alongside many others like them, were published in a newspaper to highlight the plight of the poor in London.

The first interview is with a young girl who sells flowers, and is an orphan.

"Mother has been dead just a year this month; she took cold at the washing and it went to her chest; she was only bad a fortnight; she suffered great pain, and, poor thing, she used to fret dreadful, as she lay ill, about me, for she knew she was going to leave me. She used to plan how I was to do when she was gone. She made me promise to try to get a place and keep from the streets if I could, for she seemed
5   to dread them so much. When she was gone I was left in the world without a friend. I am quite alone, I have no relation at all, not a soul belonging to me. For three months I went about looking for a place, as long as my money lasted, for mother told me to sell our furniture to keep me and get me clothes. I could have got a place, but nobody would have me without a character*, and I knew nobody to give me one. I tried very hard to get one, indeed I did; for I thought of all mother had said to me about going into the
10 streets. At last, when my money was just gone, I met a young woman in the street, and I asked her to tell me where I could get a lodging. She told me to come with her, she would show me a respectable lodging-house for women and girls. I went, and I have been there ever since. The women in the house advised me to take to flower-selling, as I could get nothing else to do. One of the young women took me to market with her, and showed me how to bargain with the salesman for my flowers. At first, when I went out to
15 sell, I felt so ashamed I could not ask anybody to buy of me; and many times went back at night with all my stock, without selling one bunch. The woman at the lodging house is very good to me; when I have a bad day she will let my lodging go until I can pay her. She is very kind, indeed, for she knows I am alone. What I shall do in the winter I don't know. In the cold weather last year, when I could get no flowers, I was forced to live on my clothes, I have none left now but what I have on. What I shall do I don't know — I
20 can't bear to think on it."

The second interview is with a young girl who sells nuts.

"It's in the winter, sir, when things are far worst with us. Father can make very little then — but I don't know what he earns exactly at any time — and though mother has more work then, there's fire and candle to pay for. We were very badly off last winter, and worse, I think, the winter before. Father sometimes came home and had made nothing, and if mother had no work in hand we went to bed to save fire and
25 candle, if it was ever so soon. Father would die afore he would let mother take as much as a loaf from the parish. I was sent out to sell nuts first: 'If it's only 1d.** you make,' mother said, 'it's a good piece of bread.' I didn't mind being sent out. I knew children that sold things in the streets. Perhaps I liked it better than staying at home without a fire and with nothing to do, and if I went out I saw other children busy. No, I wasn't a bit frightened when I first started, not a bit. Some children — but they was such little
30 things — said: 'O, Liz, I wish I was you.' I had twelve ha'porths*** and sold them all. I don't know what it made; 2d. most likely. I didn't crack a single nut myself. I was fond of them then, but I don't care for them now. I could do better if I went into public-houses, but I'm only let go to Mr. Smith's, because he knows father, and Mrs. Smith and him recommends me. I have sold nuts and oranges to soldiers. I was once in a great crowd, and was getting crushed, and there was a very tall soldier close by me, and he lifted me,
35 basket and all, right up to his shoulder, and carried me clean out of the crowd. He had stripes on his arm. 'I shouldn't like you to be in such a trade,' says he, 'if you was my child.' He didn't say why he wouldn't like it. Perhaps because it was beginning to rain. Yes, we are far better off now. Father makes money. I don't go out in bad weather in the summer; in the winter, though, I must. I don't know what I shall be when I grow up. I can read a little. I've been to church five or six times in my life. I should go oftener and
40 so would mother, if we had clothes."

Glossary

* a character — a reference
** d. — pence
*** ha'porths — half-pennys' worth

Graded Answers — Question 1

You don't have to write anything for question 1 — instead you have to shade in some boxes.
Remind yourself of the question on p.104, then read through these sample answers.

You need to pick out the True Statements

1) Question 1 gives you <u>eight</u> statements about a part of one of
   the sources — you have to pick out which statements are <u>true</u>.

2) Only <u>four</u> of the statements are true, and there are <u>four marks</u>
   available — so you need to shade in <u>four boxes</u>.

3) Always make sure you've shaded in <u>exactly</u> four boxes. If you've shaded in the statements that you're
   <u>sure</u> about and you still haven't shaded in four, have a <u>guess</u> at the others — you might get them right.

4) This sample question is about <u>lines 1-17</u> of <u>source A</u>, so you
   only need to look at that part of the text to find the answers.

5) Read the statements <u>carefully</u> as they might be about something that is <u>implicit</u>
   — something that isn't stated outright, but is <u>implied</u> by what the text says.

Here's a **Grade 4-5** answer

This answer has spotted <u>two</u> of
the true statements — <u>D</u> and <u>F</u>.

This is false — the text
says "From day one I
couldn't wait to get stuck
in", so she was excited
from the very beginning.

A	Lisa made her first batches of soup with her parents.	☐
B	Lisa wasn't initially excited about making and selling soup.	▩
C	Lisa's parents liked the first sample of soup she made them try.	☐
D	Lisa's aunt didn't like throwing food away.	▩
E	Lisa's parents thought the business was a great idea from the start.	☐
F	People were surprised by Lisa working at such a young age.	▩
G	Lisa's dad wasn't very good at negotiating with farmers.	▩
H	Lisa chose working on her business over spending time with friends.	☐

This is true — the text says
Lisa's aunt believed that
"not a single thing could
go to waste". This implies
that she wouldn't want to
throw any food away.

This is true — the text says
"people were bemused" at
her working because she was
a "young kid". The word
"bemused" shows that they
were confused and surprised.

This is false — the text says Lisa's dad
was her "champion haggler". This implies
he was good at negotiating with farmers.

Graded Answers — Question 1

This is a **Grade 6-7** answer

This answer has spotted <u>three</u> of the true statements — <u>D</u>, <u>F</u> and <u>H</u>.

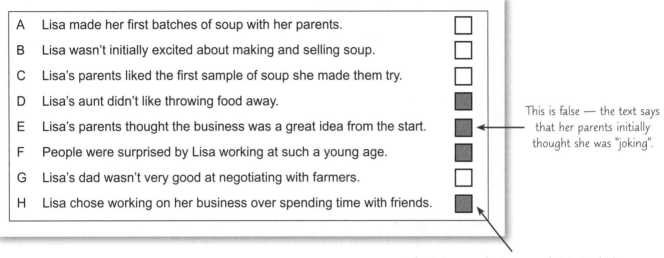

A	Lisa made her first batches of soup with her parents.	☐
B	Lisa wasn't initially excited about making and selling soup.	☐
C	Lisa's parents liked the first sample of soup she made them try.	☐
D	Lisa's aunt didn't like throwing food away.	■
E	Lisa's parents thought the business was a great idea from the start.	■
F	People were surprised by Lisa working at such a young age.	■
G	Lisa's dad wasn't very good at negotiating with farmers.	☐
H	Lisa chose working on her business over spending time with friends.	■

This is false — the text says that her parents initially thought she was "joking".

This is true — the text says that instead of "playing in the park" as other children did, Lisa was "peeling vegetables". This shows that she was making soup instead of playing with other children.

And here's a **Grade 8-9** answer

This answer has spotted all <u>four</u> of the true statements — <u>C</u>, <u>D</u>, <u>F</u> and <u>H</u>.

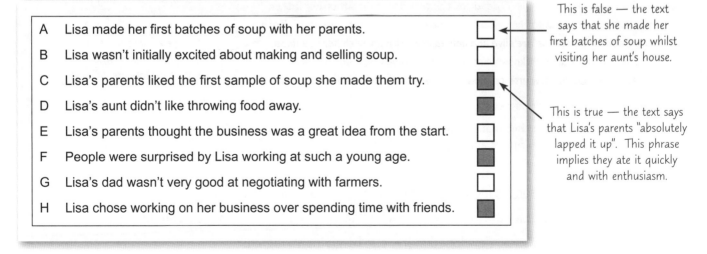

A	Lisa made her first batches of soup with her parents.	☐
B	Lisa wasn't initially excited about making and selling soup.	☐
C	Lisa's parents liked the first sample of soup she made them try.	■
D	Lisa's aunt didn't like throwing food away.	■
E	Lisa's parents thought the business was a great idea from the start.	☐
F	People were surprised by Lisa working at such a young age.	■
G	Lisa's dad wasn't very good at negotiating with farmers.	☐
H	Lisa chose working on her business over spending time with friends.	■

This is false — the text says that she made her first batches of soup whilst visiting her aunt's house.

This is true — the text says that Lisa's parents "absolutely lapped it up". This phrase implies they ate it quickly and with enthusiasm.

Graded Answers — Question 2

It's time for question 2 (take a look back at p.104 for the full question).

Pick out information from **Both** sources

1) Question 2 is testing your ability to pick out information from <u>both</u> sources, then <u>summarise</u> it to show the <u>differences</u> between them.

2) The sample question asks you to pick out information about the <u>parents</u> that feature in the sources — make sure your points focus on the parents, and not <u>anything else</u>.

3) You need to <u>summarise</u> the <u>differences</u> between the parents. This involves making a <u>point</u> about each of the parents, backing it up with good quotations as <u>evidence</u>, then clearly <u>explaining</u> how this shows a difference between them.

4) You could then <u>develop</u> your points, e.g. by linking different points together or offering insights into <u>why</u> the parents are different.

> Use <u>P.E.E.D.</u> (see p.10) and make sure you include <u>technical terms</u> to get top marks.

5) To get top marks, you need to <u>interpret</u> information from the texts — this means picking out the things that <u>aren't immediately obvious</u> about the parents.

Here's a **Grade 4-5** answer extract

> This is a good use of a short quotation to back up the point.

> This needs a quote or an example to back up the point.

> This is good — it shows that a comparison is being made.

> There needs to be an explanation here of how the sets of parents are different.

The nut seller's parents are poor as they are described as **"badly off"** and sometimes they have to go to bed early to save money. **Lisa Goodwin's parents seem to be well off.** This difference means that the nut seller's parents expect their daughter to go out to work rather than go to school. **On the other hand,** Lisa Goodwin's parents don't expect Lisa to go out to work and even "insisted" that she stay in school.

The flower seller's mother is dead and the text doesn't mention her father. Her mother worried about her a lot as it says she used to "fret dreadful". **Both Lisa Goodwin's parents are alive and helped her out a lot with her business.**

The nut seller doesn't know what she wants to be when she grows up, whereas Lisa Goodwin wants to "dedicate" herself to her business.

> This final sentence isn't related to the question, so it wouldn't get any marks.

1) This answer gives <u>some differences</u> between the parents in the two sources.

2) It would be better if <u>all</u> the points were backed up with <u>quotes</u> or <u>examples</u> from the text.

3) The points could also be <u>developed more</u>, e.g. by giving thoughtful insights into the reasons <u>why</u> the parents are different.

Graded Answers — Question 2

Here's a **Grade 6-7** answer extract

The nut seller's parents are a working-class couple living in 19th-century London, who have been **"badly off"**, though the child feels they are **"better off now"**. However, the child is expected to contribute to the household income, even **"if it's only 1d."**. The nut seller says she was **"sent out"**, which suggests her parents forced her to work.

This contrasts with Lisa Goodwin's parents, who do not seem to have any financial worries as they were able to provide Lisa with "the initial investment" for her business. Unlike the nut seller's parents, **Lisa's parents didn't expect their daughter to work at a young age; in fact they thought she was "joking" when she suggested starting her own business.**

Before she died, the flower seller's mother was worried about her daughter being on "the streets", which shows she was concerned for her safety. Lisa Goodwin's parents just wanted her to have a "normal childhood" and go to school. **This shows the differences between the time periods the two sets of parents were living in, and their levels of wealth.**

Good use of short, relevant quotes to support the points.

This answer makes inferences about the parents — it comments on the thoughts and actions of the parents that aren't directly stated.

This is good — it explains the differences by showing awareness of the context in which the texts were written.

This answer makes several <u>good points</u>, and uses <u>relevant quotes</u> to back <u>everything</u> up.

Here's a **Grade 8-9** answer extract

The parents of the nut seller and the parents of Lisa Goodwin have very different attitudes to their own needs and their child's employment. The nut seller's parents are a poor, working-class couple living in 19th-century London. The child recounts how they were "very badly off" in recent winters, but that they are "far better off now". Despite this apparent improvement in their income, the child is still "sent out" to work to contribute to the household income. Lisa Goodwin's parents, by contrast, need no extra support. They dutifully sacrificed their own careers in order to support their daughter's ambitions. **Lisa's parents prioritise her ambitions over their own, whereas the nutseller's parents prioritise the need to survive over their child's future prospects. This could be because the concerns of a more affluent family in the 20th century were often different to those of a less wealthy family in the 19th century.**

The mother of the flower seller **demonstrates a very different attitude** to the parents of Lisa Goodwin. She expresses deep concern for her child's safety through her plea that she should "keep from the streets". Lisa Goodwin's parents, however, are concerned at her desire to work so young and perceive her greatest need is to have a "normal childhood". **Once again, this demonstrates the very different situations of the sets of parents: the flower seller's mother is destitute and dying, and thinks only of her child's safety.** Lisa Goodwin's parents have the luxury of being able to be concerned about the extent of their child's education.

This is great — a point is made straight away.

This is an interesting interpretation of the differences between the parents.

This clearly compares the parents in each source.

Higher level vocabulary and sentence structures help to make this a top level answer.

This answer makes <u>well-developed</u> points, backs them up with <u>good evidence</u> and makes an interesting link to the <u>social</u> and <u>historical context</u> of the texts in order to explore the differences between the parents.

Graded Answers — Question 3

Question 3 is all about analysing how language is used for effect. Have a look back at page 105 to remind yourself of the question, and then have a read through these sample answers.

Think about the writer's **Choice** of **Words**

1) Question 3 is about how the writer has used language to affect the reader.

2) Make sure you read the question carefully — in this example, you're only supposed to write about the flower seller interview from source B.

3) The sample question is about how the writer uses language to appeal to the reader's emotions — so think about how the language used would make readers feel, and how they might react.

4) To analyse language for this question, you should comment on things like:

> • The effect of specific words and phrases, such as how certain verbs are used (see p.44-45).
>
> • Language features and techniques, such as rhetorical devices (see p.48-54).
>
> • The effect of different sentence forms, such as short or long sentences (see p.64-65).

See section three for more detail on the use of language and its effects.

5) Make sure you use a range of technical terms to describe the writer's techniques, and keep your vocabulary varied and interesting.

Here's a **Grade 4-5** answer extract

Try to avoid repeating yourself in your answer — even if you want to make a similar point, try to phrase it differently.

The flower seller describes all the terrible things that have happened to her in the first person. This helps the reader understand how the girl must be feeling because it is told directly from her point of view.
The flower seller uses strong, emotional language to describe the death of her mother, for example she says that her mother "suffered great pain". This makes you feel sorry for the mother, as she was in pain, but also for the flower seller as it makes you think about how you would feel in her place.
The flower seller shows how lonely she feels when she says "I was left in the world without a friend." **This is a really effective way of making you feel sorry for her and the situation she's in.**

This paragraph makes a good point, closely related to the question, backed up with an example and with an explanation.

This needs to explain how the language affects the reader.

1) This clearly answers the question — all the points are about how the language might appeal to the reader's emotions.

2) There's room for improvement though — some of the points could do with more examples, and the answer could explain how the language appeals to the reader's emotions more clearly.

Graded Answers — Question 3

Here's a **Grade 6-7** answer extract

This is really focused on how the language is used.

The language the flower seller uses shows that she had to be the one looking after her mother, rather than the other way round. **Phrases such as "poor thing" and "fret dreadful" sound more like a mother talking about a child who is ill.** This creates sympathy for the flower seller, as readers would feel that she has been denied her childhood.

This is good — a language technique has been spotted, then the effect of it has been explained and developed.

The **repetition** in the flower seller's story emphasises how isolated she feels after her mother's death. She uses several similar phrases, such as "left in the world without a friend", "I am quite alone" and "not a soul belonging to me", **to reinforce how desolate she is. This makes the reader feel sorry for her, because after the tragedy of her mother's death, the girl has no one to turn to.**

The flower seller doesn't say how old she is, but the concern her mother feels for leaving her daughter alone — she "seemed to dread" the thought of her daughter on the streets — **suggests that she is too young to look after herself.** This makes the flower seller's story seem even more sorrowful.

Making inferences is great — this demonstrates to the examiner that you've read the text carefully and have really thought about its meaning.

This answer makes some <u>interesting inferences</u> about the <u>effects</u> of the language on the reader, but it could be improved by using more <u>technical terms</u> and higher-level <u>vocabulary</u>.

This is a **Grade 8-9** answer extract

The interview with the flower seller was one of a number of articles published to **highlight the plight of London's poor**. As such, the articles chosen would have been those that would **have the biggest emotional impact on the reader.**

The first-person narrative makes the reader feel they are actually being spoken to by the child, which increases the emotional appeal of her story. The use of her own words allows readers to see the **nuances** of her feelings; when she repeats how "alone" she is, without "a soul" and "no relation" to help her, the list form of the sentence makes her sorrow clear. This humanises her story, so it **resonates** more with the readership.

In line 15, the flower seller confesses she was initially too **"ashamed"** to sell any flowers. This word highlights how young she is, as it emphasises her naivety and inexperience. This makes the readers feel **sympathy** for the flower seller: she has been put in a position which is beyond her ability to cope with, but she has to in order to survive.

With her final words, the flower seller admits that she "can't bear" to think about the future: she has sold all her possessions and has no one to turn to. This uncertain and desperate ending leaves the reader feeling **despondent and helpless**, and would perhaps make them feel **guilty** enough to spur them into helping the poor themselves.

This answer makes an interesting point by looking at how the context of the article relates to the purpose of the text.

Sophisticated vocabulary makes this answer perceptive and detailed.

It's really good to focus on specific words and the effect they have.

This answer comments on the different emotions the text evokes — sympathy, helplessness, guilt. This is much better than repeating the same effect over and over.

This answer makes some interesting and <u>original points</u> about the <u>purpose</u> of the article. Including details like this will really <u>impress</u> the examiner — just make sure that they are <u>relevant</u> to the question.

Graded Answers — Question 4

Question 4 is worth 16 marks. Take a look back at page 105, then have a read through these answers.

Compare the writers' different Points of View

1) Question 4 is about what the writers think about work and childhood, as well as how they show what they're thinking.

2) There are some handy bullet points to guide you — make sure you read them carefully and cover what they ask for in your answer.

- You need to identify what the writers' attitudes to work and childhood are, and clearly compare them.

- You also need to compare how the writers have shown their attitudes to work and childhood, i.e. the words, phrases and language techniques they've used.

- You should back up every point you make with relevant evidence from the text — using short quotations is a great way to do this.

3) Make sure you focus on their attitudes to work and childhood, not anything else.

4) The question is also asking you to compare, so make sure you link the two writers' attitudes together using words and phrases such as 'however', 'in contrast' and 'whereas'.

Here's a Grade 4-5 answer extract

A better, more technical term to write about informal, conversational language would be "colloquial".

Lisa wanted to work during her childhood, as she says that she "couldn't wait to get stuck in." On the other hand, the nut seller doesn't seem bothered about working and says that "Perhaps" it's "better than staying at home".

Lisa uses **chatty** language to talk about her childhood and the work she did, for example she calls herself **"this young kid". This shows that she was keen to work when she was young, but she thought it was unusual**. The nut seller is different. She "didn't mind" working, and she thinks it's normal for children to be working as she says that she "knew children that sold things in the streets."

The nut seller does what she's told to do by her parents when it comes to work. She was "sent out to sell nuts". Lisa Goodwin does the opposite. She tries to tell them what to do as **she wanted to stop going to school and start work instead**.

This paragraph makes a good, simple comparison, backed up with quotes as evidence.

The example doesn't clearly show what the explanation is saying.

This isn't true — she wanted to be home-schooled. Read the text carefully to make sure you understand what it's saying.

1) This answer mentions some different attitudes and starts to comment on how language is used to show the attitudes.

2) However, it could go into more detail by using more examples, and explaining them more clearly and accurately.

Graded Answers — Question 4

Here's a **Grade 6-7** answer extract

Using technical terms correctly will get you marks.

Lisa's enthusiasm for work comes out through her strongly positive, upbeat tone and **colloquial language**: she describes how even as a child she would work "anywhere that would have" her, and the slang word "whizz" indicates how much she enjoyed making the soup. The attitude she demonstrates to her childhood is that she just wanted to work, rather than have the "normal childhood" that her parents wanted for her. The quotation marks she uses when she talks about "necessary" education show that she is being **ironic** and doesn't think the education is necessary at all.

The answer makes clear comparisons.

The nut seller, **however**, works because she has to rather than through a personal desire to work, and she seems **unenthusiastic about her employment**. This is shown by her **less positive tone and more reserved style**. She says that she **"didn't mind"** selling nuts and that it is simply "better than staying at home". She shows that, to her, a normal childhood is spent working in the streets like the other children she knew who were all "busy" working.

This paragraph consistently covers all the bullet points — what the writers' attitudes are, how they're conveyed and good quotes are used to back up the point.

This answer is good, but to really wow the examiner, try to include some <u>innovative</u> points...

This is a **Grade 8-9** answer extract

This answer picks out some of the more subtle attitudes to work and childhood shown by the writers.

Lisa's passion and positivity about her work are conveyed through her informal style, and colloquialisms such as "whizz up" and "snazzy". This conversational language portrays Lisa as someone who has a **confident and easy-going attitude to work**. She also uses humour to engage the reader, ending the piece with a joke about needing her parents to "buy the wine". This humour gives the text warmth, and demonstrates Lisa's zeal for work.

Lisa also shows a **proud and arrogant attitude** to her work and childhood. The bemusement she describes causing as a "young kid" working shows her pride in having worked amongst adults, and her disdain for "necessary" education shows her arrogance. She seems to believe that a "normal childhood" was not right for her, and that her parents insistence upon it was tiresome.

This develops the point by going into more depth about her attitude to work.

In sharp contrast to Lisa Goodwin, the nut seller "must" work. Her unenthusiastic attitude regarding work itself comes out through her more resigned tone: she says that it "is better than staying at home". **However, she does seem to be motivated by a desire to make more money. Her tone becomes more animated when describing her ideas about how she "could do better".**

The nut seller shows her naive attitude to working as a child through the device of a story: she recalls her encounter with a soldier who wouldn't like his own child "to be in such a trade", but she thinks that is because it was "beginning to rain". **It seems clear that the soldier is concerned for her safety, and that the nut seller doesn't comprehend the danger** she is in because of her youth and innocence.

This is a perceptive point — it makes an inference about the situation instead of just taking the writer's words literally.

Graded Answers — Question 5

Make sure you leave plenty of time to write your answer for question 5 — it's worth 40 marks.
Look back at the question on page 105, then read through these graded pieces of non-fiction writing.

Adapt your Writing Style to the Question

1) For question 5 you need to <u>respond</u> to the statement, by giving your <u>own perspective</u> on the value of part-time work for children under 16.

2) You need to match your writing to the <u>form</u>, <u>purpose</u> and <u>audience</u> you've been given in the question.

> • The <u>form</u> is a broadsheet newspaper article — so you could write in the style of an <u>opinion piece</u> and include <u>layout features</u> such as a <u>headline</u>.
>
> • The <u>purpose</u> is to <u>explain</u> your point of view, but as you're responding to a statement you could do this by making an <u>argument</u> for your viewpoint.
>
> • The <u>audience</u> isn't mentioned specifically, but you can <u>work it out</u>. It's a broadsheet newspaper article about work for teenagers, so it's likely to be read by <u>adults</u> with children who are under 16.

It doesn't matter whether you agree or disagree with the statement as long as your answer is engaging and well-structured.

3) It's also important to think about the <u>structure</u> of your writing, especially the <u>opening</u> and <u>ending</u>. You need to <u>link</u> your paragraphs together clearly, too.

4) Don't forget there are 16 marks on offer for <u>spelling</u>, <u>punctuation</u> and <u>grammar</u> for this question — it's really important to write <u>accurately</u> and <u>clearly</u> with a good range of <u>vocabulary</u> (see p.16-18).

Here's a Grade 4-5 answer extract

This answer uses a counter argument to strengthen the point it's making.

This opening sentence isn't really appropriate for a broadsheet newspaper.

NO PART-TIME JOBS FOR UNDER-SIXTEENS

I think that children under the age of 16 shouldn't get a part-time job. Although some people might argue that having a job teaches children about the value of money, time management and working as a team, I don't think that this is the case.

Firstly, most children have good time management skills without ever having a part-time job. Schools start at 9 am, and some even earlier than this, so arriving on time to lessons is already second nature to most children. **Why should children have a part-time job when they already know how to manage their time? Secondly,** most children have been working as a team since primary school. From sports teams in P.E., to group projects in Science, school teaches children how to work together from a very young age. **Why should children give up their weekends for a badly paid job when they already have great teamwork skills?**

A new paragraph should start here.

The repetition of rhetorical questions is a nice language feature — it makes the point of view come across more forcefully.

1) This answer makes some <u>good points</u> that are focused on the <u>question</u>.

2) It could be better matched to the <u>form</u> that the question asks for, though — the <u>tone</u> and <u>style</u> aren't really appropriate for a <u>broadsheet newspaper</u>.

3) The language could also be more varied and interesting — including a bit of <u>humour</u> or using more <u>creative vocabulary</u> would gain more marks.

Graded Answers — Question 5

The answer uses more sophisticated punctuation confidently and correctly.

The tone of this answer is suitable for the form and purpose. It's a bit more chatty than the previous answer, but it still uses good vocabulary.

SAVE THE LEARNING FOR THE CLASSROOM

Lots of young people have a part-time job, and I am sure that employment teaches them a whole host of valuable skills: communication, time management and independence to name but a few. However, these skills aren't just learnt in the workplace: many young people develop and refine these skills in the classroom. **Take, for instance, communication.** Every day in school, pupils communicate with a wide range of people for a wide range of purposes. Pupils learn to talk respectfully to teachers and other members of staff; they learn how to make engaging conversation with their friends; and they learn how to communicate their ideas effectively to their peers during group work. **School doesn't just allow pupils to practise their verbal communication — it allows them to develop their written communication too.** Essays teach students how to summarise their thoughts, argue effectively and present their opinions. What part-time job could develop communication more effectively than this?

The ideas are linked together fluently.

1) This answer uses language techniques, a <u>clear structure</u> and <u>creative vocabulary</u> to get its point across.

2) There's still room for improvement though. Making the author's <u>personality</u> come across more strongly would make the answer even more <u>compelling</u> and <u>closely matched</u> to the form.

Really interesting and varied vocabulary makes this answer high level.

The writer shows a clear awareness of their audience.

Lots of rhetorical techniques are used in this paragraph to make the writer's point of view clear and their argument compelling.

A sarcastic tone makes the argument convincingly, but also gives a sense of the writer's personality.

MINIMUM WAGE, MINIMUM GAIN

Part-time jobs have little value for teenagers under sixteen, argues Charlie Lin.

If someone were to ask me whether I thought under-sixteens should get part-time jobs, my answer, **unequivocally**, would be "no". **As I write this, I can imagine the shocked looks on my readers' faces** and the **disdainful** cries of "but employment teaches valuable life skills!" To these critics, I say this: there's nothing a part-time job can teach children that they can't learn from other, more rewarding options, such as getting involved with extra-curricular activities.

If you don't believe me, then think about the jobs that are actually available to under-sixteens. Paper rounds, waiting tables, shop assistant — essentially an assortment of mundane, badly-paid Saturday jobs. And what 'valuable life skills' might they learn while toiling away for less than minimum wage? "Teamwork!" you might cry triumphantly, "working in a cafe would teach a young person how to work as part of a team." **This may certainly be true if you believe being belittled by the chef and bossed around by the manager counts as 'teamwork'.** I, however, do not. If that same child was part of a football team, working alongside their peers, practising hard to achieve a common goal (annihilating the rival team), now that would be teamwork.

1) The writer's <u>opinion</u> and <u>personality</u> is clear in this answer, and it's <u>fluently written</u>.

2) The tone is humorous and chatty, but also subtle, which makes the answer <u>engaging</u> and <u>readable</u>.

As final preparation, here are some <u>practice papers</u> to test how well-prepared you are for the real thing.

- There are <u>two</u> practice papers:
  Paper 1: Explorations in Creative Reading and Writing   (pages 118-121)
  Paper 2: Writers' Viewpoints and Perspectives   (pages 122-126)

- Before you start each paper, read through all the <u>instructions</u>, <u>information</u> and <u>advice</u> on the front.

- You'll need some paper to write your answers on.

- When you've finished, have a look at the answers starting on page 127 — they'll give you some ideas of the kind of things you should have included in your answers.

- <u>Don't</u> try to do both of the papers in one sitting.

CGP   Practice Exam Paper
GCSE English Language

General Certificate of Secondary Education

GCSE
English Language

Paper 1 Explorations in Creative Reading and Writing

Time allowed: 1 hour 45 minutes

Centre name				
Centre number				
Candidate number				

Surname
Other names
Candidate signature

Instructions to candidates
- Answer **all** the questions.
- Write your answers in **black** ink or ball-point pen.
- Write your name and other details in the boxes above.
- Cross out any rough work that you do not want to be marked.
- You should **not** use a dictionary.

Information for candidates
- The marks available are given in brackets at the end of each question.
- There are 80 marks available for this exam paper.
- You must use good English and clear presentation in your answers.

Advice for candidates
- You should spend about 15 minutes reading through the source and all five questions.

This extract is the opening of a short story set in New Zealand, written in 1922 by Katherine Mansfield.

At the Bay

Very early morning. The sun was not yet risen, and the whole of Crescent Bay was hidden under a white sea-mist. The big bush-covered hills at the back were smothered. You could not see where they ended and the paddocks and bungalows began. The sandy road was gone and the paddocks and bungalows the other side of it; there were no white dunes covered with reddish grass beyond them; there was nothing to mark which was beach and where was the sea. A heavy dew had fallen. The grass was blue. Big drops hung on the bushes and just did not fall; the silvery, fluffy toi-toi* was limp on its long stalks, and all the marigolds and the pinks in the bungalow gardens were bowed to the earth with wetness. Drenched were the cold fuchsias, round pearls of dew lay on the flat nasturtium leaves. It looked as though the sea had beaten up softly in the darkness, as though one immense wave had come rippling, rippling — how far? Perhaps if you had waked up in the middle of the night you might have seen a big fish flicking in at the window and gone again...

Ah-Aah! sounded the sleepy sea. And from the bush there came the sound of little streams flowing, quickly, lightly, slipping between the smooth stones, gushing into ferny basins and out again; and there was the splashing of big drops on large leaves, and something else — what was it? — a faint stirring and shaking, the snapping of a twig and then such silence that it seemed some one was listening.

Round the corner of Crescent Bay, between the piled-up masses of broken rock, a flock of sheep came pattering. They were huddled together, a small, tossing, woolly mass, and their thin, stick-like legs trotted along quickly as if the cold and the quiet had frightened them. Behind them an old sheep-dog, his soaking paws covered with sand, ran along with his nose to the ground, but carelessly, as if thinking of something else. And then in the rocky gateway the shepherd himself appeared. He was a lean, upright old man, in a frieze* coat that was covered with a web of tiny drops, velvet trousers tied under the knee, and a wide-awake* with a folded blue handkerchief round the brim.

One hand was crammed into his belt, the other grasped a beautifully smooth yellow stick. And as he walked, taking his time, he kept up a very soft light whistling, an airy, far-away fluting that sounded mournful and tender. The old dog cut an ancient caper or two and then drew up sharp, ashamed of his levity, and walked a few dignified paces by his master's side. The sheep ran forward in little pattering rushes; they began to bleat, and ghostly flocks and herds answered them from under the sea. "Baa! Baaa!" For a time they seemed to be always on the same piece of ground. There ahead was stretched the sandy road with shallow puddles; the same soaking bushes showed on either side and the same shadowy palings*. Then something immense came into view; an enormous shock-haired giant with his arms stretched out. It was the big gum-tree outside Mrs. Stubbs' shop, and as they passed by there was a strong whiff of eucalyptus. And now big spots of light gleamed in the mist. The shepherd stopped whistling; he rubbed his red nose and wet beard on his wet sleeve and, screwing up his eyes, glanced in the direction of the sea. The sun was rising. It was marvellous how quickly the mist thinned, sped away, dissolved from the shallow plain, rolled up from the bush and was gone as if in a hurry to escape; big twists and curls jostled and shouldered each other as the silvery beams broadened. The far-away sky — a bright, pure blue — was reflected in the puddles, and the drops, swimming along the telegraph poles, flashed into points of light. Now the leaping, glittering sea was so bright it made one's eyes ache to look at it. The shepherd drew a pipe, the bowl as small as an acorn, out of his breast pocket, fumbled for a chunk of speckled tobacco, pared off a few shavings and stuffed the bowl. He was a grave, fine-looking old man. As he lit up and the blue smoke wreathed his head, the dog, watching, looked proud of him.

Glossary
*toi-toi — a type of tall grass
*frieze — coarse woollen cloth
*wide-awake — a type of wide-brimmed hat
*palings — pointed fence-posts

Section A: Reading

*You should spend about 45 minutes answering **all** the questions in this section.*

1   Read again the first part of the source, **lines 1 to 11**.

   List **four** things from this part of the text that show what Crescent Bay looks like beneath the mist.

   (4 marks)

2   Look in detail at **lines 16 to 22** of the source.

   How does the writer use language here to describe the shepherd and his animals?

   You could include the writer's choice of:
   *   words and phrases
   *   language features and techniques
   *   sentence forms.

   (8 marks)

3   You now need to think about the **whole** of the **source**.

   This text is from the opening of a short story.

   How has the writer structured the text to interest you as a reader?

   You could write about:
   *   what the writer focuses your attention on at the beginning
   *   how and why the writer changes this focus as the extract develops
   *   any other structural features that interest you.

   (8 marks)

4   Focus this part of your answer on the second half of the source, from **line 23 to the end**.

   A student, having read this section of the text said "The writer is successful in creating a detailed and interesting scene for the reader. It is like watching a film of what is happening."

   To what extent do you agree?

   In your response, you could:
   *   write about your own impressions of the scene
   *   evaluate how the writer has created these impressions
   *   support your opinions with quotations from the text.

   (20 marks)

Section B: Writing

You should spend about 45 minutes answering the question in this section.
You are advised to plan your answer.

5   A publisher is running a creative writing competition for school children,
    which you have decided to enter.

    Your entry will be judged by a panel of published authors.

Either:

Write a description suggested by this picture:

Or:

Write the opening part of a story that takes place in a misty setting.

(24 marks for content and organisation
16 marks for technical accuracy)

(40 marks)

General Certificate of Secondary Education

GCSE
English Language

Paper 2 Writers' Viewpoints and Perspectives

Time allowed: 1 hour 45 minutes

Centre name					
Centre number					
Candidate number					

Surname
Other names
Candidate signature

Instructions to candidates
- Answer **all** the questions.
- Write your answers in **black** ink or ball-point pen.
- Write your name and other details in the boxes above.
- Cross out any rough work that you do not want to be marked.
- You should **not** use a dictionary.

Information for candidates
- The marks available are given in brackets at the end of each question.
- There are 80 marks available for this exam paper.
- You must use good English and clear presentation in your answers.

Advice for candidates
- You should spend about 15 minutes reading through the sources and all five questions.

Source A

The following text is an extract from an article written by a nanny, Monica Albelli.
It was published in a broadsheet newspaper in 2013.

Confessions of a Nanny

Being a nanny — whether you're a Mary Poppins, a Nanny McPhee or a Mrs Doubtfire — is
a very tricky job. You have to be liked by two opposing "teams" to which a "perfect" nanny means
completely different things. "You must be kind, you must be witty, very sweet and fairly pretty...
If you don't scold and dominate us, we will never give you cause to hate us" — this is how the
5   children in Mary Poppins, Michael and Jane, want the newspaper ad for their nanny to read. Their
father, Mr Banks, is keener on discipline. Mrs Banks seems to believe perfection lies somewhere in
between that and the children's ideal.

I have always loved children and had a natural ability to connect with them with ease, no
matter their gender, nationality or character. But when you're a nanny, kids come with parents.
10   And parents come with problems, opinions and expectations of their own, often in conflict between
themselves.

Lesley, a successful publisher, and Brian, a dentist, were Scots in their mid-40s. They
worked long hours but seemed to love Therese, seven, Tom, nine, and William, 11. Their approach
when it came to the kids' upbringing though was completely different from each other. Confident
15   and motivated, Lesley believed her children's time should be spent doing homework, reading
books or playing educational games. Brian, cheerful and laid back, wanted us to "just have fun".
He asked me not to be strict with the kids, while Lesley kept pressuring me to turn them into
responsible and hard-working individuals. I would arrive at their house to find a note from Brian,
asking me to take them to the park, and then receive a text from Lesley with a to-do list.
20   Lesley would often come home late to find the kids already asleep. "I'm not a good mum,"
she once confessed. "I'm actually a bit jealous. I think they are starting to like you more than they
like me."

I reassured her that this was not true and that she was doing her best.

The kids and I had bonded. Once, as I was getting ready to leave, Tom curled around my
25   leg, while Lesley tried to persuade him he had to let me go. They liked having me around so much
that they started asking Brian if I could sleep over. Had we bonded too much?

Then things changed. Lesley seemed upset about something, and Brian was more and more
absent. One day they told me they wouldn't be needing me any more as they had decided to get
an au pair, who could also help with the house. I knew that wasn't the real reason. They had, I
30   realised, been asking me to become everything they weren't and, as soon as I started to achieve
that, they felt threatened.

I tried to see it from their point of view. Being a nanny is difficult, but being a parent is even
harder. Having a nanny is also hard.

I remembered what a friend used to say whenever I shared my frustrations with her: "You
35   care too much. It's just a job."

Should a nanny be indifferent, see herself as a doctor and treat all family members as her
patients, being impartial and never getting emotionally involved? How can Mary Poppins be
indifferent? She is cool and funny, strict at times, but always caring — the perfect nanny. But she is
a fictional character, and so are Mr and Mrs Banks, and Michael and Jane.
40   Many dysfunctional families later, I have learned to care at the same time as keeping a
distance, and that there is no such thing as the perfect family — or the perfect nanny.

Source B

The following text was written by Charlotte Brontë, a famous 19th-century author. Charlotte was working as a governess — a woman employed to teach and care for the children in a household. This is an extract from a letter written to her sister in 1839.

Dearest Lavinia,*

     I am most exceedingly obliged to you for the trouble you have taken in seeking up my things and sending them all right. The box and its contents were most acceptable.

     I have striven hard to be pleased with my new situation. The country, the house, and the
5 grounds are, as I have said, divine. But, alack-a-day! there is such a thing as seeing all beautiful around you — pleasant woods, winding white paths, green lawns, and blue sunshiny sky — and not having a free moment or a free thought left to enjoy them in. The children are constantly with me, and more riotous, perverse, unmanageable cubs never grew. As for correcting them, I soon quickly found that was entirely out of the question: they are to do as they like. A complaint to Mrs. Sidgwick
10 brings only black looks upon oneself, and unjust, partial excuses to screen the children. I have tried that plan once. It succeeded so notably that I shall try it no more. I said in my last letter that Mrs. Sidgwick did not know me. I now begin to find that she does not intend to know me, that she cares nothing in the world about me except to contrive how the greatest possible quantity of labour may be squeezed out of me, and to that end she overwhelms me with oceans of needlework, yards of cambric
15 to hem, muslin night-caps to make, and, above all things, dolls to dress. I do not think she likes me at all, because I can't help being shy in such an entirely novel scene, surrounded as I have hitherto been by strange and constantly changing faces. I see now more clearly than I have ever done before that a private governess has no existence, is not considered as a living and rational being except as connected with the wearisome duties she has to fulfil. While she is teaching the children, working for
20 them, amusing them, it is all right. If she steals a moment for herself she is a nuisance. Nevertheless, Mrs. Sidgwick is universally considered an amiable woman. Her manners are fussily affable. She talks a great deal, but as it seems to me not much to the purpose. Perhaps I may like her better after a while. At present I have no call to her. Mr. Sidgwick is in my opinion a hundred times better — less profession, less bustling condescension, but a far kinder heart.

25   As to Mrs. Collins' report that Mrs. Sidgwick intended to keep me permanently, I do not think that such was ever her design. Moreover, I would not stay without some alterations. For instance, this burden of sewing would have to be removed. It is too bad for anything. I never in my whole life had my time so fully taken up.

     Don't show this letter to papa or aunt, only to Branwell.* They will think I am never satisfied
30 wherever I am. I complain to you because it is a relief, and really I have had some unexpected mortifications to put up with. However, things may mend, but Mrs. Sidgwick expects me to do things that I cannot do — to love her children and be entirely devoted to them. I am really very well. I am so sleepy that I can write no more. I must leave off. Love to all. — Good-bye.

C. BRONTË.

Glossary
* A nickname for Charlotte's sister, Emily.
* Branwell — their brother.

Section A: Reading

*You should spend about 45 minutes answering **all** the questions in this section.*

1   Read again **source A**, from lines 1 to 19.

Choose **four** statements below which are TRUE.

- Shade the boxes of the ones that you think are true
- Choose a maximum of four statements.

A   Monica Albelli thinks being a nanny is a difficult job. ☐

B   Parents and children usually look for the same things in a nanny. ☐

C   Parents almost always agree on the duties of a nanny. ☐

D   Lesley and Brian are both professionals of a similar age. ☐

E   Lesley and Brian are affectionate parents. ☐

F   Brian likes his children to play educational games. ☐

G   Both parents think discipline is important. ☐

H   Lesley and Brian sometimes gave Monica conflicting instructions. ☐

(4 marks)

2   You need to refer to **source A** and **source B** for this question.

Use details from **both** sources. Write a summary of the differences between Lesley and Mrs Sidgwick.

(8 marks)

3   You now need to refer **only** to **source B**.

How does Charlotte Brontë use language to try to influence her sister?

(12 marks)

4   For this question you need to refer to the **whole of source A** together with **source B**.

Compare how the two writers convey their different attitudes to looking after other people's children.

In your answer, you should:
- compare their different attitudes
- compare the methods they use to convey their attitudes
- support your ideas with quotations from both texts.

(16 marks)

Section B: Writing

You should spend about 45 minutes answering the question in this section.
You are advised to plan your answer.

5   "Parents are often too strict with their children. They expect them to work far too hard, at school and at home. Young people should be allowed to have fun while they still can."

Write an article for a broadsheet newspaper in which you
explain your point of view on this statement.

(24 marks for content and organisation
16 marks for technical accuracy)

(40 marks)

Answers

Page 30 — Warm-Up Questions

1) a) True
   b) False

2) a) Rita
   b) Rita
   c) Rakesh
   d) E.g. "bad enough that we have to go to this reunion at all"
      E.g. "Rita glared pointedly at her watch"
      E.g. "admiring his reflection"

3) a) To advise. E.g. 'because the writer uses simple language that the reader will understand to suggest what the reader should do'.
   b) To entertain. E.g. 'because the writer uses descriptive verbs such as "crawling" and "gallop" to engage the reader'.
   c) To persuade. E.g. 'because the writer uses a rhetorical question to encourage the reader to agree with their argument'.

4) E.g. 'Writer A dislikes mixed schools, and believes that all schools should be single-sex. In contrast, Writer B likes mixed schools. Writer B also differs from Writer A because Writer B thinks that parents should be the ones to choose.'

Pages 31-32 — Exam-Style Questions

1) Any four correct facts about George, either paraphrased or directly quoted from the text. For example:
   • George has a nasal voice.
   • George is wearing a "garish purple suit".
   • George has an "elaborate hairstyle".
   • George brings a bottle of wine to the party.
   • George has "greasy" hands.
   • George is wearing several rings.
   • George likes whisky.

2) Answers should analyse both texts, using relevant quotes from both texts to summarise several differences between the writers. Here are some things you could mention:
• The writer in Source B believes that men and women have equal importance in a marriage ("a partnership of equals"), whereas the writer in Source A prioritises the man ("amenable to the needs of the husband").
• The writer in Source A says that women belong at home ("The home is her sphere"), but the writer in Source B does not ("most women today would spurn the idea that they should... take sole care of a home").
• The writer in Source A believes that a perfect home is one where the husband does no housework ("need not lift a finger"), but the writer in Source B thinks that a perfect home involves sharing it equally ("it is essential for domestic responsibilities to be shared evenly").

3) The following four statements should be ticked:
   • On the second day, the writer got up early.
   • The writer enjoyed the pony trek.
   • You can abseil at Lowbridge Park.
   • The writer liked the archery instructor.

4) All your points should use relevant examples and terminology, and comment on the effects of the language used. Here are some things you could mention:
• Opening rhetorical question ("But Who Do I Vote For?") suggests that the writer is on the reader's side.
• Casual style to make the reader comfortable, e.g. "Unless you've been living under a rock for the past month".
• Use of the imperative form ("don't panic", "have a look") to give clear guidance to the reader.

• Minimal technical language to avoid intimidating or confusing the reader.
• Introductory/concluding paragraphs create a clear structure and summarise the information to make it easier for the reader to understand.

Page 40 — Exam-Style Questions

1) Answers should clearly compare the different ideas and techniques in each text, using quotations to support points. Here are some things you could mention:
• In Source A, the writer illustrates their dislike of a new art style using hyperbole ("nothing short of an abomination"). In Source B, the writer expresses their admiration for a new art style, also using hyperbole ("They're revolutionaries").
• Both sources use formal language, e.g. "I read with concern" in Source A, "progression in the medium" in Source B. This makes their opinion seem more important / authoritative.
• Source B makes the restrictions of traditional art seem negative using a metaphor, "the iron shackles of 'traditional art'", whereas Source A thinks that the rules of traditional art are good: new artists should have "learnt from" older examples.

2) Your answer should offer an opinion on the statement. It should comment on the techniques used to describe both characters, using relevant examples and terminology to support each point. Here are some things you could mention:
• I agree that you can identify with both characters, because dialogue is used to give an insight into each character's mindset, such as Annie: "Don't be ridiculous." and Lucas: "They'll kill me." This indicates that Annie is calmer and less prone to being overdramatic in comparison to Lucas.
• The cumulative use of short sentences in Lucas's speech also emphasises his stress and helps the reader to identify with his panic, e.g. "I've looked everywhere. It's lost. They'll kill me."
• The contrast between the two characters makes each character's personality stand out more and their individual perspective seem clearer. E.g. the adjectives used to describe Lucas's actions ("frantic", "manic") contrast with the adverbs used to describe Annie's actions, which are carried out "cautiously" or "calmly".

Page 46 — Warm-Up Questions

1) a) Detached
   b) Upbeat
   c) Sentimental

2) Sentence a)

3) E.g. 'The tone is conversational. The writer uses slang phrases such as "cheesed off", and contractions like "it's", as well as humour when describing the trip to "River C and Swamp D".'

4) a) E.g. 'Customers are advised that we do not accept credit cards.'
   b) E.g. 'It is essential to ensure you have the correct tools before proceeding.'

5) Noun: Bella   Verb: approached   Adverb: excitedly

6) E.g. 'The word "whispered" suggests that the speaker and listener are working together, whilst "spat" suggests that the speaker doesn't like the listener.'

7) a) ii) money
   b) E.g. 'It suggests that the narrator is very motivated by money. They see their sibling's theatre show as an opportunity to "cash in" and talk about time as something you can "buy".'

8) E.g. 'The verbs are very violent, which creates the impression that the wind is powerful and destructive.'

Page 47 — Exam-Style Questions

1) All your points should use relevant examples and terminology, and comment on the effects of the language used. Here are some things you could mention:
   - An informal style that uses phrases like "up to your neck" and "bag loads of new skills", which encourage a young audience to connect with the writer and the holidays they're offering.
   - The inclusion of the sentence "There's nothing wrong with wanting a break." to show that the writer understands the mindset of young people, so that they are more inclined to trust the writer's claims.
   - The short, punchy sentences that make up the last paragraph create an excited tone, which engages the reader's interest.
   - Descriptive but simple adjectives ("incredible", "fantastic") emphasise how fun the activities are.

2) All your points should use relevant examples and terminology, and comment on the effects of the language used. Here are some things you could mention:
   - Words and phrases associated with cold to emphasise the woman's detached personality ("icily", "stone cold").
   - The adverb in the phrase "breath caught painfully" suggests that the man's fear is physically painful.
   - The simile "like a condemned man", which emphasises that the man feels resigned to his fate, and indicates that the woman is in a position of great power.

Page 57 — Warm-Up Questions

1) E.g. 'It suggests that the lake is something to be wary of.'

2) E.g. 'The second text compares the water to something that the reader is familiar with, to make it easier to visualise.'

3) a) Personification. E.g. 'It makes the computer seem like it's mocking the writer, which conveys the writer's frustration.'
   b) Onomatopoeia. E.g. 'It helps the reader to imagine the noise created by the students.'
   c) Alliteration. E.g. 'It makes the text more memorable.'

4) E.g. 'Sarcasm is nastier than irony, because it has a mocking tone that's often meant to insult someone.'

5) Yes. E.g. 'The text is sarcastic because the positive phrase "Ivan is a brilliant secretary" contrasts with the negative context "he keeps forgetting to bring a pen".'

6) a) Antithesis. E.g. 'It highlights the contrast between the writer's expectations and reality, which makes the reality seem more disappointing.'
   b) Parenthesis. E.g. 'It creates familiarity between the writer and the readers, so they are more likely to be persuaded.'
   c) Hyperbole. E.g. 'It emphasises how terrible the writer feels the rain would be.'

7) E.g. 'It gives the writer's opinion as fact ("By far the best hobby") and makes generalisations, such as claiming that all young people "adore" playing cribbage.'

8) E.g. 'The descriptive adjectives "blistering" and "prickly" suggest that the weather is physically uncomfortable. The imagery "as if I were underwater" helps the reader to imagine the physical strain on the narrator, which is furthered by the descriptive verb "trudged".'

Pages 58-59 — Exam-Style Questions

1) All your points should use relevant examples and terminology, and comment on the effects of the language used. Here are some things you could mention:
   - The use of animal similes and metaphors to indicate how vulnerable the workers are — "like mice in a cage", "lambs" — in contrast to the soldiers, who are "wolves".
   - The use of a simile to suggest the officer speaks in a forceful way — "fired his orders like cannon balls."
   - The use of the descriptive verbs "huddled" and "shivered" to suggest the workers' weakness. This contrasts with the verbs "trampled" and "marched", which are used to suggest that the soldiers are powerful and authoritative.

2) All your points should use relevant examples and terminology, and comment on the effects of the language used. Here are some things you could mention:
   - Alliterative phrases such as "labyrinth of lost lanes" to emphasise how confusing the writer finds Kuala Lumpur.
   - Personification of vehicles that "rumble past impatiently" which conveys the idea that everything in the city is animated and full of life.
   - Onomatopoeic verbs such as "whine" and "buzz" help the reader to understand the writer's attitude to Kuala Lumpur as a loud and confusing place.

3) Answers should clearly compare the different ideas and techniques in each text, using quotations to support points. Here are some things you could mention:
   - The writer of Source A has a fairly balanced viewpoint: they acknowledge positive aspects, like the room's size, as well as negative aspects, such as the "limited refreshment". This makes the writer seem more reasonable.
   - The writer of Source B has a more negative viewpoint than the writer of Source A — they instantly "doubted" that the bedding was clean, which, combined with a complete absence of positive points about the room, shows that the writer is quite biased.
   - Hyperbole is used in Source B to emphasise the writer's dislike of the hotel room — "hadn't been opened for about a century". The writer of Source A, however, uses discourse markers such as "Nevertheless" and "but" to show their more balanced viewpoint.

4) Your answer should offer an opinion on the statement. It should comment on the techniques used to describe the party, using relevant examples and terminology to support each point. Here are some things you could mention:
   - The cumulative effect of using several descriptive verbs together in "joking, laughing, making introductions", to convey a sense of action and excitement to the reader.
   - Onomatopoeic verbs such as "thumping" and "clinking" to help the reader to imagine what the party sounds like.
   - The focus on describing colours in the third paragraph, which appeals to the senses to help the reader to visualise the upbeat mood of the party.

Page 68 — Exam-Style Questions

1) All your points should use relevant examples and terminology, and comment on the effects of the structural features used. Here are some things you could mention:
   - The shift in time that the extract uses — it starts in the present day, goes back to the past, then returns to the present. This allows the reader to become emotionally invested in Joan, so the ending has a greater impact.
   - The progression from "she had already been looking forward to the next visit", to "there wouldn't be a next visit", which emphasises the sadness of the fact that Joan's life is drawing to a close.

- The motif of Joan looking at the sea, which is revisited in the first and last paragraph, and is contrasted by the way she "raced into the sea" in the second paragraph. This structure adds interest to the end of the story.

2) All your points should use relevant examples and terminology, and comment on the effects of the structural features used. Here are some things you could mention:
- The perspective shift from the people in the stalls to their focus on the drapes of the stage. This allows the reader to first view the excitement of the audience and then share their anticipation of what's to come.
- The change of focus onto the character of Mikhail backstage in the second paragraph. This gives the reader information about what is going on behind the scenes, building on the tension introduced in the first paragraph by showing Mikhail's nerves. By adding a personal element to the text, the writer encourages the reader to become more engaged in the story.
- The switch from Mikhail's thoughts to the stage manager's dialogue in the third paragraph, interrupting Mikhail's thought process from the previous paragraph. This increases the tension again by reminding the reader that time is still passing and that Mikhail's performance is rapidly approaching. This makes the reader feel nervous for him and want to read on to find out how his performance goes.

Page 78 — Warm-Up Questions

1) b) rhetorical questions and d) emotive language

2) E.g. 'Hiding away in the sleepy village of Lyttlewich, Howtonshire, is a true gem of English architecture that you can't afford to miss. Thousands of visitors flock to the ancient Lyttlewich Church every year to marvel at its truly stunning artwork. Isn't it about time you joined the crowd?'

3) a) E.g. 'Fertilisers provide things that plants need to grow.'
   b) E.g. 'The ear bones are some of the smallest in the body.'
   c) E.g. 'Roman soldiers used weapons to defeat their enemies.'

4) a) E.g. 'Money can be tricky to get your head around, so why aren't schools teaching us how to deal with it?'
   b) E.g. 'Before you start making your yummy cake, ask an adult to help you get everything you'll need.'

5) a) E.g. 'I took a deep breath and stepped onto the alien spaceship, ready for my next adventure.'
   b) E.g. 'The familiar sounds of the river rushing outside my window were all I needed to hear; I was finally home.'

6) a) E.g. 'First person, to give an insight into the character's thoughts and feelings.'
   b) E.g. '"Eerie", to make the forest seem scary and sinister. "Timid", to make the character seem afraid.'
   c) E.g. 'The moon was shining as brightly as a new penny.'

7) a) E.g. 'From the diving board, the swimmers below look like a shoal of brightly coloured fish.'
   b) E.g. 'The noises in the pool echo like whalesong.'
   c) E.g. 'I feel the roughness of the tiles under my bare feet.'
   d) E.g. 'The bitter chlorine catches in the back of my throat.'

8) Answers should include ideas for descriptive techniques and devices that could be used to describe a family member.

Page 79 — Exam-Style Questions

1) Answers need to be entertaining for an audience of adult regular readers. They need to use interesting language techniques to create a suitable tone and style. Writing needs to be structured and clear. Here are some techniques you could include:
- The five senses: The air smelt of damp vegetation.
- Personification: The leaves whispered in the night.
- A first-person narrator: I shivered with cold as a brisk winter breeze crept into our tent.

2) Answers need to be entertaining for an audience of adults. They need to use interesting language techniques to create a suitable tone and style. Writing needs to be structured and clear. Here are some techniques you could include:
- Personification: The flowers in the fields blinked owlishly in the moon's light.
- An unusual character: The town's oldest resident, Agatha Hart, was a tiny lady who wore layers of colourful, clashing clothing, which made her look at least twice her diminutive size.
- Direct address: Perhaps you might think that nothing exciting could ever happen in a sleepy town like Drizzleford. You'd be wrong.

3) Answers need to be entertaining for an adult. They need to use interesting language techniques to create a suitable tone and style. Writing should be structured and clear. Here are some techniques you could include:
- The five senses: The sun felt warm on Gráinne's face.
- Metaphors: The rock was a formidable enemy, and Gráinne had conquered it.
- Alliteration: The solid slate surface sat sturdily under her shoes.

Page 90 — Exam-Style Questions

1) Answers need to create an appropriate tone and style using suitable vocabulary and language techniques. They need to include a headline and may include other layout features, such as a strapline or subheadings. Writing needs to be well-organised, clear and technically accurate. Here are some techniques you could include:
- Onomatopoeia: Their only memory of childhood will be the dull buzz of yet another message notification.
- Complex sentences: As time goes on, we will witness our children becoming steadily more housebound; this cannot be allowed to happen.
- Antithesis: As smartphones get smarter, our children are becoming dimmer.

2) Answers need to reflect purpose and audience using suitable vocabulary and language techniques. They should include an opening and closing address to the audience. Writing needs to be well-organised, clear and technically accurate. Here are some techniques you could include:
- Rhetorical questions: Do you really care about TV more than your health and wellbeing?
- Lists of three: The more sleep you get, the happier, healthier and brainier you'll be.
- Emotive language: It's absolutely vital that you get enough sleep: your health and happiness depend on it.

3) Answers need to create an appropriate tone and style using suitable vocabulary and language techniques. They should have a title, and should be broken into clear sections using e.g. subheadings or boxes. Writing needs to be well-organised, clear and technically accurate. Here are some techniques you could include:
- Direct address: You should leap at the chance to swap humdrum, drizzly British life for something new.
- Lists of three and alliteration: Travel will give you the confidence, compassion and courage you'll need in your adult life.
- Analogy: Trying to understand different cultures without going out and experiencing them is like trying to bake a cake without flour: dense and disappointing.

130

4) Answers need to create an appropriate tone and style using suitable vocabulary and language techniques. They should include an address and date, address the recipient directly and use a formal sign-off. Writing needs to be well-organised, clear and technically accurate. Here are some techniques you could include:
- Formal language: Dear madam, I write to express my concern over the state of the nation's housing supply.
- Anecdotal evidence: I have witnessed dozens of young people struggle to find appropriate, affordable housing.
- Linking phrases: Moreover, as a country, our population is crammed disproportionately into cities and towns.

Pages 120-121 — Practice Paper 1

1) 1 mark for each valid response given, up to a maximum of four marks. Answers might include:
- There are big bush-covered hills at the back
- There are paddocks
- There are bungalows
- There's a sandy road
- There are white dunes covered in reddish grass
- There are fuchsias / nasturtiums / toi-toi grass
- The bungalows have gardens with colourful plants

2) All your points should use relevant examples and terminology, and comment on the effects of the language used. Here are some things you could mention:
- Descriptive verbs such as "huddled" are used to suggest that the sheep are fearful. This is reinforced by the words used to describe their movements: the sheep "trotted along quickly" as if in fear.
- In contrast, the writer presents the dog as unafraid and even nonchalant. It runs along "carelessly" suggesting that it is "thinking of something else". This makes the roles of the animals clear: the dog is a working pet, whilst the sheep are animals in captivity.
- The writer uses imagery to give really fine details of how the shepherd looks: his coat is "covered with a web of tiny drops". This detail helps to give the reader a clear picture of the shepherd, but also to help them feel the cold, wet conditions.
The entrance of the shepherd is described using a shorter, less detailed sentence than the ones that surround it ("And then in the rocky gateway the shepherd himself appeared."). This helps to make his entrance seem dramatic, which emphasises his character's importance.

3) All your points should use relevant examples and terminology, and comment on the effects of the structural features used. Here are some things you could mention:
- The writer starts the text using short statements to give the reader the broadest facts about the scene, it is "Very early morning" and "The sun was not yet risen". This then progresses to much longer sentences to build the fine details of what the bay looks like. However, these are still broken up by a further short statement, "A heavy dew had fallen". In this way the writer manages to build detail, whilst emphasising the most important points so the reader feels how chilly, early and damp it is.

- The focus then moves from the bay, "Round the corner" and begins to describe the animals and the shepherd. The descriptions given at this point are short, giving small insights: the sheep-dog is "old" and the shepherd is "a lean, upright old man". They act as introductions to the characters, drawing the reader further in to the scene.
- In the long, final paragraph, the writer brings together the misty scene she has described with the characters she has introduced. The reader is taken on a short journey along the "sandy road" which continues to emphasise the "shadowy" early morning.
- The paragraph ends with the revelation of the mist rapidly rolling away, revealing everything that was hidden in the first paragraph. This makes it feel to the reader as if the day has begun, and the opening of the story is now over.

4) Your answer should offer an opinion on the statement. It should comment on the techniques the writer uses to make the text detailed and interesting, using relevant examples and terminology to support each point. Here are some things you could mention:
- I agree in some ways that it is like watching a film. Phrases such as "came into view" and "in the direction of the sea" create a cinematic effect for the reader, directing the reader's focus in the way that a camera might. In this section of the text it is effective as it allows the reader to see what the shepherd is seeing, drawing them into the scene with him.
- However, the writer adds more detail than you would normally be able to experience in a film. She appeals to the senses as she describes the "whiff of eucalyptus" and the shepherd's "wet beard", which adds to the richness of the description and allows the reader to feel even more like they are inside the scene.

5) Answers to either question need to use an appropriate tone, style and register to match the purpose, form and audience. Writing needs to be well-organised, clear and technically accurate. Here are some techniques you could include:
In a description:
- Figurative language: A faint curtain of mist rose off the lake, swathing everything in a sheet of fine white cloud.
- Similes: Just past the end of the jetty, waiting like a promise, was the little red boat.
- Descriptive words and phrases: Tendrils of gelatinous pond weed emerged from the water's edge.
In the opening of a story:
- An interesting, dramatic opening sentence: The mist appeared too suddenly for them to avoid it.
- An opening that directly addresses the reader: If you'd seen what I saw on that misty October evening, you'd have done the same thing.
- A descriptive opening that sets the scene: The mist had emerged a few hours ago, curling slyly around the trunks of the gnarled old oaks in the wood.

Answers

Pages 125-126 — Practice Paper 2

1) 1 mark for shading each of the following statements:
   A Monica Albelli thinks being a nanny is a difficult job.
   D Lesley and Brian are both professionals of a similar age.
   E Lesley and Brian are affectionate parents.
   H Lesley and Brian sometimes gave Monica conflicting instructions.

2) Answers should use relevant quotes from both texts to summarise several differences between the two people. Here are some things you could mention:
   - Mrs Sidgwick and Lesley are very different people, particularly in their attitude towards the people they employ. Mrs Sidgwick does not treat her governess as if she's a person; it is thanks to Mrs Sidgwick that Charlotte feels as if she is "not considered as a living and rational being". In contrast, Monica hints that, to an extent, Lesley treated her as a friend: for example, she "confessed" to Monica about her insecurities regarding her children.
   - Lesley seems to care more about other people's feelings than Mrs Sidgwick. Lesley doesn't tell Monica the "real reason" that she was fired, suggesting that she might be trying to save Monica's feelings. In contrast, Charlotte writes as if Mrs Sidgwick does not consider Charlotte's wellbeing; Charlotte has "never" been so "fully" occupied before, which makes her so tired that she "can write no more".
   - Mrs Sidgwick does not seem to take an interest in her children's education. Charlotte maintains that Mrs Sidgwick "does not intend to know me", even though the children are with her "constantly". This implies that she is distanced from her children and their well-being. Lesley, however, has strong views concerning Albelli's role, wanting her to create "responsible and hard-working individuals". Although Lesley also becomes distanced from her children, she views this development negatively; she feels "jealous" and "threatened" by Albelli, and replaces her.

3) All your points should use relevant examples and terminology, and comment on the effects of the language used, focusing on how it is used to influence her sister. Here are some things you could mention:
   - Brontë uses a combination of formal and informal language in order to influence her sister. She uses polite, formal language in places, such as the phrase "I am most exceedingly obliged". This is a courtesy that would make her sister feel pleased. This formal language is then combined with familiar terms like "papa" and informal phrases, such as "Love to all" to appeal to the relationship between Brontë and her sister, making Brontë more likeable. This in turn would make her sister more inclined to agree with Brontë's viewpoint.
   - Brontë also uses persuasive language to express her viewpoint. For example, she uses a list of three, describing the children she takes care of as "riotous, perverse, unmanageable". The cumulative effect of these negative adjectives helps to emphasise Brontë's displeasure with her current situation, which encourages her sister to sympathise with her difficulties.
   - Brontë employs metaphors to stress the extent of the hardships she is facing, for example, "she overwhelms me with oceans of needlework". The word "oceans" implies that she feels her work is vast and never-ending, and "overwhelms" makes Brontë seem vulnerable. This helps to encourage feelings of tenderness and sympathy in her sister.

4) Answers should clearly compare the different attitudes and techniques in each text, using quotations to support points. Here are some things you could mention:
   - Brontë's letter suggests that she feels limited and confined by the duties involved in looking after other people's children. She refers to her wards as being "constantly" with her. Brontë's choice of adverb suggests that she gets no respite from the children; it also indicates that she resents this constant imposition.
   - Albelli indicates a similarly close proximity to her wards: the image of the young boy "curled" around her leg is a symbol of the closeness between them. However, she uses rhetorical questions to suggest that this closeness is desirable, which challenges negative attitudes such as Brontë's. She questions "How can Mary Poppins be indifferent?", to suggest that nannies should aim to be close to children in their care, even whilst maintaining some degree of professional detachment.
   - Brontë suggests that the expectations of her role as a nanny are unattainable. She states that she cannot do what Mrs Sidgwick demands; "to love her children and be entirely devoted to them". Emotive language used throughout the extract supports this, with verbs such as "overwhelms" and "squeezed" implying that she is over-exerted. In contrast, Albelli highlights the danger of nannies surpassing expectations and fulfilling the role of a mother, as Lesley feels "threatened" by her success with the children. This implies that Albelli feels the problems faced by parents over childcare are greater than the problems experienced by nannies.

5) Answers need to use an appropriate tone, style and register to match the purpose, form and audience. They need to include a headline and may include other layout features, such as a strapline or subheadings. Writing needs to be well-organised, clear and technically accurate. Here are some techniques you could include:
   - Direct address: Our parents are trying their best to help us succeed, but they need to understand that putting us under so much pressure will ultimately be counterproductive.
   - Repetition: Working hard isn't always a negative thing: it creates a sense of achievement, a sense of ambition and a vital sense of purpose.
   - Facts and statistics: Some of the most academically successful education systems have the highest rate of student dissatisfaction.
   - Satirical language: Draining the joy from a young person's life with constant chores and homework is, of course, one of the hallmarks of good parenting.
   - Rhetorical questions: Should children look back on their childhood and struggle to remember anything but homework and chores?

Glossary

adjective	A word that <u>describes</u> a noun or a pronoun, e.g. heavy, kind, unusual.
adverb	A word that gives <u>extra information</u> about a <u>verb</u>, e.g. carefully, rarely, tightly.
alliteration	When words that are <u>close together</u> start with the <u>same sound</u>. E.g. "the <u>b</u>eat of the <u>b</u>and".
analogy	A <u>comparison</u> to show how one thing is <u>similar</u> to another, making it easier to <u>understand</u> or more <u>memorable</u>. E.g. "watching cricket is about as much fun as watching paint dry."
antithesis	A <u>rhetorical technique</u> where <u>opposing</u> words or ideas are presented <u>together</u> to show a contrast.
audience	The <u>person</u> or <u>group of people</u> that read or listen to a text.
biased writing	Gives <u>more support</u> to one point of view than to another, due to the writer's own <u>opinions</u> affecting the way they write.
broadsheet	A more <u>formal</u> type of newspaper, which often focuses on more <u>serious</u> topics. E.g. *The Guardian* or *The Telegraph*.
chronological writing	Presented in <u>time order</u>, from earliest to latest.
cinematic writing	Writing that makes the reader feel like they're watching a <u>film</u>.
clause	Part of a sentence that has a <u>subject</u> and a <u>verb</u>. <u>Main clauses</u> make sense on their own.
colloquial language	<u>Informal</u> language that sounds like ordinary <u>speech</u>.
command	A sentence that <u>tells</u> the reader to do something.
commentary (newspaper article)	A type of newspaper article that expresses the <u>opinions</u> of the writer on a theme or news event. Also called a <u>column</u> or <u>opinion piece</u>.
complex sentence	A sentence that links together <u>two or more clauses</u>.
compound sentence	Two <u>main clauses</u> joined to make one sentence using a <u>conjunction</u> such as 'or', 'but' or 'and'. E.g. "The cat came in, <u>and</u> the dog left the room."
connotations	The <u>suggestions</u> that words can make <u>beyond</u> their obvious meaning. E.g. 'stroll' means 'walk', but it has connotations of moving slowly.
context	The <u>background</u> to something, or the situation <u>surrounding</u> it, which affects the way it's understood. E.g. the context of a text from 1915 would include the First World War.
counter-argument	The <u>opposite</u> point of view to the writer's own view. This is useful when writing to argue or persuade — first give the counter-argument, then explain why you <u>disagree</u> with it.
determiner	A word that goes before a <u>noun</u> to show possession or quantity (e.g. 'his', 'two').
direct address	When a writer talks <u>straight to the reader</u>, e.g. "you might recall..."
double negative	A sentence construction that <u>incorrectly</u> expresses a <u>negative idea</u> by using <u>two</u> negative words or phrases, e.g. "I <u>don't</u> want <u>no</u> trouble."
emotive language	Language that has an <u>emotional</u> effect on the reader.
empathy	The ability to <u>imagine</u> and <u>understand</u> someone else's <u>feelings</u> or <u>experiences</u>.
exclamation	A sentence that conveys strong <u>emotions</u>, usually ending with an <u>exclamation mark</u>.
explicit information	Information that's <u>directly stated</u> in a text.
figurative language	Language that is used in a <u>non-literal</u> way to create an effect, e.g. personification.

Glossary

first person	A <u>narrative viewpoint</u> where the narrator is one of the <u>characters</u>, written using words like 'I', 'me', 'we' and 'our'.
flashback	A writing technique where the scene shifts from the <u>present</u> to an event in the <u>past</u>.
form	The <u>type</u> of text, e.g. a letter, a speech or a newspaper article.
frame narrative	A narrative in which one story is presented <u>within</u> another.
generalisation	A statement that gives an <u>overall impression</u> (sometimes a misleading one), without going into details. E.g. "children today eat too much junk food."
hyperbole	When <u>exaggeration</u> is used to have an <u>effect</u> on the reader.
imagery	A type of <u>figurative language</u> that creates a <u>picture in your mind</u>, e.g. metaphors and similes.
imperative verb	A verb that gives orders or directions, e.g. "<u>run</u> away" or "<u>stop</u> that".
impersonal tone	A tone of writing that <u>doesn't</u> try to directly <u>engage</u> with the reader.
implicit information	Information that's hinted at <u>without</u> being said outright.
inference	A <u>conclusion</u> reached about something, based on <u>evidence</u>. E.g. from the sentence "Yasmin wrinkled her nose at the lasagne", you could <u>infer</u> that Yasmin doesn't like lasagne.
intensifier	A word that is used <u>alongside</u> an adjective to provide <u>emphasis</u>, e.g. "<u>very</u> friendly".
inversion	Altering the <u>normal word order</u> for <u>emphasis</u>, e.g. "On the table sat a hedgehog."
irony	Saying one thing but <u>meaning the opposite</u>. E.g. "What a great idea of mine to go for a nice long walk on the rainiest day of the year."
language	The <u>choice of words</u> and <u>phrases</u> used.
limited narrator	A narrator who only has <u>partial knowledge</u> about the events or characters in a story.
linear structure	A type of narrative structure that tells the events of a story in <u>chronological</u> order.
linguistic devices	<u>Language techniques</u> that are used to have an <u>effect</u> on an audience, e.g. onomatopoeia.
list of three	Using <u>three</u> words (often adjectives) or phrases together to create <u>emphasis</u>.
metaphor	A way of <u>describing</u> something by saying that it <u>is</u> something else, to create a vivid image. E.g. "His eyes were deep blue pools."
motif	A <u>recurring</u> image or idea in a text.
narrative	Writing that tells a <u>story</u> or describes an <u>experience</u>.
narrative viewpoint	The <u>perspective</u> that a text is written from, e.g. <u>first-person</u> point of view.
narrator	The <u>voice</u> or <u>character</u> speaking the words of the narrative.
non-linear structure	A type of narrative structure that tells the events of a story in a <u>non-chronological</u> order.
noun	A <u>naming</u> word that refers to a <u>person</u>, <u>thing</u>, <u>place</u> or <u>idea</u>, e.g. Alex, soup, Germany, love.
objective writing	A <u>neutral</u>, <u>unbiased</u> style of writing which contains <u>facts</u> rather than opinions.
omniscient narrator	A narrator who <u>knows</u> the thoughts and feelings of all the characters in a narrative.
onomatopoeia	A word that <u>imitates</u> the sound it describes as you say it, e.g. 'whisper'.

Glossary

pace	The <u>speed</u> at which the writer takes the reader through the events in a story.
paraphrase	Describing or rephrasing something in a text <u>without</u> including a direct quote.
parenthesis	A <u>rhetorical technique</u> where an <u>extra</u> clause or phrase is <u>inserted</u> into a complete sentence.
personification	Describing a non-living thing as if it's a <u>person</u>. E.g. "The sea growled hungrily."
possessive determiner	A <u>determiner</u> such as 'your' or 'my' that tells you who something <u>belongs</u> to.
possessive pronoun	A <u>pronoun</u> such as 'yours' or 'mine' that tells you who something <u>belongs</u> to.
pronoun	A word that can <u>take the place</u> of a noun in a sentence, e.g. 'he', 'she', 'it'.
purpose	The <u>reason</u> someone writes a text. E.g. to persuade, to argue, to advise, to inform.
register	The specific <u>language</u> used to <u>match</u> writing to the <u>social situation</u> that it's for.
repetition	The technique of <u>repeating</u> words for effect.
rhetoric	Using <u>language</u> techniques (e.g. repetition or hyperbole) to achieve a persuasive <u>effect</u>.
rhetorical question	A question that <u>doesn't need an answer</u>. E.g. "Why do we do this to ourselves?"
sarcasm	Language that has a scornful or mocking tone, often using <u>irony</u>.
satire	A style of text that <u>makes fun</u> out of people or situations, often by <u>imitating</u> them and <u>exaggerating</u> their flaws.
second person	A <u>narrative viewpoint</u> that is written as if the <u>reader</u> is one of the <u>characters</u>.
sensory language	Language that appeals to the <u>five senses</u>.
simile	A way of describing something by <u>comparing</u> it to something else, usually by using the words 'like' or 'as'. E.g. "He was as pale as the moon."
simple sentence	A sentence that is only made up of a <u>single main clause</u>.
slang	Words or phrases that are <u>informal</u>, and often specific to one <u>age</u> group or <u>social</u> group.
Standard English	English that is considered to be <u>correct</u> because it uses formal, standardised features of <u>spelling</u> and <u>grammar</u>.
statement	A type of sentence that is used to deliver <u>information</u>.
structure	The <u>order</u> and <u>arrangement</u> of ideas in a text. E.g. how the text begins, develops and ends.
style	The <u>way</u> that a text is <u>written</u>, e.g. the type of language, sentence forms and structure used.
subject	The person or thing that performs the action described by the verb. E.g. in "<u>Billy</u> ate a sandwich", Billy is the subject.
tabloid	A <u>less formal</u> type of newspaper, which often focuses on more <u>sensational</u> topics.
third person	A <u>narrative viewpoint</u> where the narrator remains <u>outside</u> the events of the story, written using words like 'he' and 'she'.
tone	The <u>mood</u> or <u>feeling</u> of a piece of writing, e.g. happy, sad, serious, light-hearted.
verb	A <u>doing</u> or <u>being</u> word, e.g. dig, breathe, are, is.
viewpoint	The <u>attitude</u> and <u>beliefs</u> that a writer is trying to convey.

Index

Index

ENAS42